Introduction to English Civil Law

for German-Speaking Lawyers and Law Students

Vol. 2

2005

Prof. Dr. iur. utr. Rainer Wörlen
Fachbereich Wirtschaftsrecht
Fachhochschule Schmalkalden

ALPMANN UND SCHMIDT Juristische Lehrgänge Verlagsges. mbH & Co. KG
48149 Münster, Annette-Allee 35, 48001 Postfach 1169, Telefon (0251) 98109-33/28
AS-Online: www.alpmann-schmidt.de

Prof. Dr. iur. utr. Wörlen, Rainer

Introduction to English Civil Law, Vol. 2
for German-Speaking Lawyers and Law Students
3. Auflage 2005
ISBN 3-89476-802-9

©Verlag: Alpmann und Schmidt Juristische Lehrgänge
Verlagsgesellschaft mbH & Co. KG, Münster

Vorwort

Die Zielsetzung der beiden Bände, „Introduction to English Civil Law – for German-Speaking Lawyers and Law Students, Vol. 1 + 2" ist jeweils im nachfolgenden Vorwort *(preface)* zu den Erstauflagen 1999 und 2000 eingehend beschrieben. Die Lektüre dieses Vorworts wird denen, die mit diesen Büchern gewinnbringend studieren möchten, dringend ans Herz gelegt: Zumindest den Abschnitt **„IV. Zur Arbeitsweise mit diesem Buch"** sollten sie (Sie) nicht auslassen!

Mit der „Introduction" wurde Neuland in der deutschen juristischen Ausbildungsliteratur betreten.
Der Mut der Verleger (vgl. S. V, „Acknowledgements"), dieses „exotische" Werk zu publizieren, wurde belohnt: Der Absatz blieb zwar durchaus etwas hinter „Harry Potter und der Stein der Weisen" zurück, aber er fiel nicht in die „Kammer des Schreckens". Auch in Österreich und der Schweiz wurde das Werk gut angenommen, sodass eine dritte Auflage erforderlich wurde.

Da das englische Recht bisher von einer „Schuldrechtsreform" verschont blieb, hielten sich inhaltliche Veränderungen gegenüber den Vorauflagen in Grenzen.

Auf die bereits im Vorwort zur zweiten Auflage 2002 erwähnten „Woolf Reforms 1998"[1], die zu den (am 26.04.1999 in Kraft getretenen) „Civil Procedure Rules 1999" mit einer nicht unerheblichen Modernisierung des englischen Zivilprozessrechts führten, wird nicht näher eingegangen: Die vorliegende „Introduction" soll nur einen ersten Einblick in das *materielle* englische „Civil Law" geben.

Dennoch ein kurzer Hinweis: Im Zuge der Reform des englischen Zivilprozessrechts hat sich einiges in der juristischen Terminologie geändert. Zum Beispiel wurde aus dem „plaintiff" (Kläger) der – zuvor in Schottland schon so bezeichnete – „claimant". Doch da alle von mir zitierten *cases* (Fälle) vor 1999 entschieden und niedergeschrieben wurden, habe ich die neue Terminologie nicht übernommen.

Deutsche „Lawyers and Law Students", die sich künftig auf dem Parkett des englischen Rechts im „United Kingdom" bewegen, sollten sich aber an die neuen Begriffe gewöhnen. Zur ersten Information habe ich daher im Anschluss an den Index einige der wichtigsten Ausdrücke in einem kurzen Glossar („Old Terms – New Terms – German Terms") aufgeführt.

Inhaltliche Veränderungen ergaben sich vor allem durch einige in den Vorauflagen noch nicht berücksichtigte *statutes* (Gesetze/Verordnungen), die mir zum Teil entgangen waren, oder nach Redaktionsschluss in Kraft getreten sind. Dies sind insbesondere: *„Sale and Supply of Goods Act 1994", „Employment Rights Act 1996", „Contracts (Rights of Third Parties) Act 1999", „Limited Liability Partnerships Act 2000", „Enterprise Act 2002", „Courts Act 2003",* sowie *„Maximum Number of Judges Order 2003".*

---

[1] Benannt nach ihrem Schöpfer Lord Woolf, seinerzeit „Master of the Rolls", heute „Lord Chief Justice of England and Wales" (vgl. Vol. 1, S. 42).

Verbessert wurde wiederum eine erkleckliche Anzahl von Druckfehlern, auf die mich dankenswerterweise meine inzwischen zum Teil diplomierten Studierenden in Schmalkalden (namentlich die Dipl. Wirtschaftsjuristinnen *Sebnem Keskin* und *Tina Kleinspehn*, einige deutsche anglophile Kollegen (Rechtsanwalt und Solicitor *Thomas Blaser*, Überlingen, und Prof. Dr. *Jörg Peter*, Fachhochschule Wildau) sowie meine englischen Juristenfreunde (above all William Herbert and his wife Lindsey, both solicitors, Birmingham) hingewiesen haben.

Ein ganz besonderer Dank anderer Art gilt meinem Freund *His Honour Judge Dr. Peter Jackson* (The Crown Court of Southwark, London), „Master of the Bench" (vgl. Vol. 1, chapter three, II und IV) of „The Honourable Society of the Middle Temple", London. Ihm verdanke ich die selten gebotene Möglichkeit, im September 2004 wieder eine Woche lang die ehrwürdige „Middle Temple Library" (and other facilities of the „Middle Temple") zur Aktualisierung der Neuauflagen nutzen zu dürfen.

Schließlich gilt mein großer Dank, last but not least, auch stud. iur. Karen Fairweather (Birmingham/Bayreuth), die mit größter Sorgfalt und Gewissenhaftigkeit die mühevolle Korrektur der beiden Manuskripte für die 3. Auflage erfreulich unbarmherzig durchgeführt hat.

Hinweise und Anregungen richten Sie bitte an meine folgende Anschrift:

Hauptstr. 472, Residenz 46; 53639 Königswinter; Fax: 02223/900170;
E-Mail: r.woerlen@fh-sm.de
Internet: www.r-woerlen.de

London/Königswinter/Schmalkalden, Ende September 2004

Rainer Wörlen

Preface

(Vorwort – zur ersten Auflage)

– zugleich (unter IV) eine Arbeitsanleitung –

I. Wenn man als Deutscher ein englischsprachiges Buch über englisches Zivilrecht schreibt, hat das ganz besondere – persönliche und sachliche – Gründe. *„Persönlich"* habe ich in zahlreichen Aufenthalten im "United Kingdom" und auf Malta (dessen Amtssprache, bei allerdings unterschiedlichem Rechtssystem, Englisch ist) eine besondere Affinität zu den Bewohnern „dieser Inseln", zu ihrer Landschaft sowie zu ihrer Sprache und dem englischen Recht entwickelt. Die Faszination, die das englische Rechtssystem auf einen ausländischen Juristen ausüben kann, ist schwer in Worte zu fassen, man kann sie nur „fühlen", muss sie „erlebt" haben. Z.B.: Wenn man Sitzungen des "High Court"[1] in den "Royal Courts" am "Strand"[1] im Herzen von London oder des "House of Lords"[1] im Parlamentsgebäude "live" verfolgt, bei *Clive Max Schmitthoff* weiland eine vierwöchige Vorlesung "Introduction to modern English law" gehört, einige der ehrwürdigen "Inns of Court"[1] besucht hat und anlässlich eines Empfangs in der "Law Society"[1] dem schon zu Lebzeiten legendären *Lord Denning* (der am 05.03.1999 im Alter von 100 Jahren starb) die Hand reichen durfte.

II. Eine *sachliche* und zutreffende Begründung gibt *Graf von Bernstorff*[2] in *seinem* Vorwort:

»Das englische Recht ist für international tätige Unternehmen und Juristen sowie für rechtsvergleichend arbeitende Studenten von großer Bedeutung. Die wichtigsten Finanzplätze der Welt finden sich in Staaten, die „englischem" Recht folgen. Die Staaten des *Commonwealth* folgen bis heute den Grundprinzipien englischen Rechts, sodass die in diesem Buch niedergelegten Ausführungen in vielerlei Hinsicht auch in anderen Ländern der Welt nutzbar sind. Internationale Verträge unterliegen häufig englischem Recht. Die Außenhandelspraxis arbeitet überwiegend auf der Basis englischen Rechts. Kurzum: die Praxis hat sich mit dem englischen Recht immer wieder auseinanderzusetzen.«

---

[1] Was sich hinter diesen Namen verbirgt, könnten Sie nach der Lektüre von Vol. 1 dieses Werks wissen.

[2] Vgl. "Bibliography" (= Literaturverzeichnis).

Außerdem: »Da der Commonwealth heute über 1,5 Milliarden Menschen umfasst, unterliegt jeder vierte Mensch dem englischen Recht, das...die wohl wichtigste Rechtsordnung der Welt darstellt« .[1]

Für Juristen, die sich auf internationalem Parkett bewegen wollen, sind gute Kenntnisse der englischen Sprache und Grundkenntnisse des englischen Rechts unerlässlich. Dieser Erkenntnis haben eine Vielzahl deutscher Universitäten und Fachhochschulen Rechnung getragen: an manchen rechtswissenschaftlichen Fakultäten und Fachbereichen wurden Lehrstühle für „angelsächsisches" oder „anglo-amerikanisches" Recht errichtet, und vielerorts werden Kurse von Muttersprachlern ("native speakers") in englischer Rechtssprache sowie Vorlesungen über englisches Recht gehalten.

III.   Das vorliegende Werk entspricht weitgehend meiner im *Fachbereich Wirtschaftsrecht* der Fachhochschule Schmalkalden gehaltenen Vorlesung "Introduction to English civil law", die sich mit zwei Semesterwochenstunden auf drei Semester erstreckt. Als Zivilrechtler habe ich mich auf das englische *"civil law"* beschränkt, da ich vom öffentlichen Recht, inklusive Strafrecht, nichts (mehr) verstehe...

Es gibt bereits einige Lehrbücher und Grundrisse zum englischen und anglo-amerikanischen Recht, die von deutschen Autoren in deutscher Sprache geschrieben wurden (vgl. "Bibliography"→ *Bernstorff, Blumenwitz, Henrich, Reimann*). So qualitätsvoll (wie insbesondere das – auf das US-amerikanische Privatrecht beschränkte – Buch von *Reimann*) diese Bücher auch sind, sie sind nicht in der Lage, *Recht und Sprache gleichermaßen zu vermitteln.* Die englischen Rechtsbegriffe werden überwiegend als bekannt vorausgesetzt und selten erklärt, sodass man diese Bücher obwohl auf Deutsch geschrieben - ohne englisch-rechtliche Vorbildung und ohne ein spezielles englisch-deutsches Rechtswörterbuch zu benutzen, kaum verstehen kann.

Es gibt bereits auch eine Reihe von Lehrbüchern über „anglo-amerikanische Rechts*sprache*" (vgl. "Bibliography" → *Byrd, Heidinger/Hubalek, Riley*), die als Sprachlehrbücher von hoher Qualität sind. Sie sind – da sie nur Fragmente aus englischer Rechtsliteratur und Rechtsprechung wiedergeben können – naturgemäß nicht geeignet, *ein Rechtsgebiet geschlossen darzustellen.*

---

[1] *Bernstorff, S.1.*

II

Dieses Buch ist eine **Kombination aus einem englischsprachigen Lehrbuch über englisches Zivilrecht und einer Einführung in die englische Rechtssprache**. Es ist damit, insbesondere auch durch die Präsentation von deutschen Übersetzungen neben dem englischen Text, ein Novum.[2]

IV. **Zur Arbeitsweise mit diesem Buch:**

Der vorliegende Band II (= Vol. 2) ist die Fortsetzung von „Introduction to English Civil Law, Vol. 1" mit den Kapiteln „Classification and sources of English Law, The administration of law, The legal profession, How to find the law, Persons in law, The law of contract". Die in Vol. 1 vermittelten Kenntnisse sind in diesem Vol. 2 nicht zwingend, aber dringend erforderlich.

Alle Worte, die <u>im Text unterstrichen</u> sind, erscheinen in deutscher Übersetzung auf dem rechten Rand jeder Seite. Dabei wurde nicht immer die „wörtliche", sondern die jeweils am geeignetsten erscheinende „freie" Übersetzung gewählt. Es wurden nicht nur spezifische Rechtsbegriffe übersetzt, sondern auch eine Vielzahl von Wörtern der Umgangssprache, von denen ich glaube, dass sie nicht unbedingt zum Wortschatz eines Lesers gehören, dessen Schulenglisch nicht besser als „befriedigend" war. (Als solcher sollte man allerdings wissen, dass z.B. das Verb *"to seek"* heißt, wenn *"sought"* am Rand mit „suchen" übersetzt wird). Wiederholungen sind dabei bewusst vorgenommen. Sehr treffend weist *Black* in der Einführung zu seinem „Legal Reader" auf die Binsenwahrheit (= *truism*) hin: *„Repetitio mater studiorum est"* (= *„repetition is the mother of learning"* – „Wiederholung ist die Mutter des Lernens"). *Black's* moderner Abwandlung dieser Binsenwahrheit schließe ich mich gerne an: *„Understanding is the key of learning"*! Wiederholung wiederum fördert das Verständnis! Aus diesem Grund wird am Ende von Teilabschnitten deren

---

[2] *Ähnlich:* Der kurze und sehr gute „Legal Reader" von *Donald R.Black* (vgl."Bibliography"), der auf insgesamt 133 Seiten eine kurze Einführung in das anglo-amerikanische Rechts(system) gibt, die Vokabeln dabei aber in gesonderten Listen ausweist.

Inhalt jeweils anhand von grafischen Übersichten zusammengefasst, sodass Sie sich die wichtigsten Begriffe und Rechtsinstitute sowie ihre Bedeutung nochmals einprägen können, bevor Sie mit dem Lesen und Lernen (= Studieren) fortfahren. Nehmen Sie sich dabei nicht zuviel vor,
sondern arbeiten Sie langsam und gründlich! Da man eine *Sprache* inten-
siver lernt, wenn man sie nicht nur liest und spricht, sondern auch
schreibt, empfehle ich Ihnen, sich – wie zu Schulzeiten – ein *Vokabelheft*
anzulegen, in dem Sie nach der Lektüre von Teilabschnitten (spätestens
am Ende jeden Kapitels) alle Ihnen unbekannt gewesenen Vokabeln no-
tieren und abschnittsweise *auswendig lernen*!

Von einem (ursprünglich beabsichtigten) alphabetisch geordneten englisch-
deutschen Vokabelverzeichnis am Ende des Buchs habe ich abgesehen:
Das lästige Nachschlagen soll ja gerade auf ein Minimum reduziert werden.
Sollten Ihnen an der einen oder anderen Stelle meine *rechtlichen* Ausführungen nicht ausreichen, empfehle ich, das jeweils angesprochene Thema
in einer der im Literaturverzeichnis erscheinenden Gesamtdarstellungen
zum Englischen Recht oder gar in einem der großen englischsprachigen
Standardwerke zu dem jeweiligen speziellen Rechtsgebiet nachzuarbei-
ten. Die wichtigsten dieser Werke sollten in Ihrer Hochschul- oder Semi-
narbibliothek vorhanden sein. Um Ihnen die Auswahl zu erleichtern, wird
am Ende jeden Kapitels unter "Further reading" Literatur zur Vertiefung
zitiert, die ich bei der Anfertigung dieses Kapitels benutzt habe.

Da es sich bei diesem Werk um eine Einführung in das *englische* Zivilrecht und *nicht* um ein *rechtsvergleichendes* (vgl. hierzu das vorzügliche
Standardwerk von → *Zweigert/Kötz*) Werk handelt, habe ich Hinweise
auf Ähnlichkeiten mit und Unterschiede zu dem deutschen Bürgerlichen
Recht *kursiv* nur spärlich, zumeist auf Fußnoten verteilt.

Für Hinweise und Anregungen aus dem Leserkreis bin ich stets dankbar.

Schmalkalden, im Januar 2000   *Rainer Wörlen*

Acknowledgements

(Danksagungen/Anerkennungen)
– zu den Vorauflagen –

Mein Dank gilt an erster Stelle den Herren Rechtsanwälten *Josef Alpmann* und *Josef A. Alpmann* für ihre mutige Entscheidung, dieses Werk in ihrem Hause zu verlegen.

Viele kluge Köpfe und fleißige Hände haben zu seiner Entstehung beigetragen:

Für die Korrektur meines handschriftlichen Manuskripts habe ich zunächst meiner (englischen) Sprachlehrerin *Rosemary d'Emanuele* und vor allem ihrer (maltesischen) Kollegin *Romina Fennech*, LLD, sehr herzlich zu danken. Beide gehörten zum Kollegium des "Institute of English Language Studies" (IELS) in Sliema/Malta, wo das Manuskript entstanden ist.

Für die mühevolle Anfertigung des Typoskriptes danke ich meinen studentischen Hilfskräften *Kathrin Stenzel*, *Sandra Külbel*, *Yvonne Gallina* und *Daniela Brussock* vom Fachbereich Wirtschaftsrecht der Fachhochschule Schmalkalden, denen ich in der PC-Anwendung hoffnungslos unterlegen bin.

Für die Korrektur der Druckfahnen konnte ich dank der tatkräftigen Werbung durch meinen Kollegen *Nigel Foster* von der *Cardiff University Wales* einige hochqualifizierte britische Juristinnen und Juristen gewinnen: *Carsten Zatschler* (The Honourable Society of the Inner Temple, London), *Ruth Dukes* (University of Edinburgh), *Mark J. Vermes* (University of Warwick), *Michael Poole* (University of East Anglia, Norwich), *Jonathan Welsh* (Cardiff University) und *Rachael L. Brumfitt* (University of Exeter). Auch ihnen gebührt ein herzliches "Thank you"!
Last but not least habe ich auch den Solicitors *Lindsey* und *William Herbert* (Birmingham) zu danken, die mir wertvolle Hinweise zur Verbesserung gegeben haben.

Contents

Chapter Seven

Chapter Eight

Chapter Nine

The law of trusts..110

Chapter Ten

Chapter Eleven

Table of cases

Table of statutes

Table of diagrams

Abbreviations

CD	Civil Defence
cf.	confer („vgl.")
CJ	Chief Justice
Co.	Company
dies.	dieselben
E.C.T.	electro-convulsive-therapy
e.g.	exempli gratia (for example)
ed./Ed.	edition („Aufl.")/Editor (Hrsg.)
f.	following
GCSE	General Certificate of Secondary Education
Hrsg.	Herausgeber
i.e.	id est
IELS	Institute of English Language Studies
J.	Justice
L.J.	Lord Justice
LLD	Doctor of Laws
Ltd.	Limited
M.R.	Master of the Rolls
p.	page
pty.	party/proprietary
R.	Regina (Rex)
Re	In that matter
s.	see/section
s.a.	see above
s.o.	siehe oben
ss.	sections
St.	Saint
T.	Treuhandverhältnis
UK	United Kingdom
v	versus
vgl.	vergleiche
Vol.	volume

Bibliography

I. English (and Anglo-American) law in English

Adams	Law for Business Students, 3rd ed., London ... 2003
Baker	An Introduction to English Legal History, 4th ed., London ... 2002
Barker & Padfield	Law, 11th ed., London ... 2002
Bell	Real Property (Cracknell's Law Students' Companion), 4th ed., London 2004
Bermingham	Nutcases: Tort, 3rd ed., London-Hong Kong-Dublin 2002
Black	Black's Legal Reader – An Introduction to the Anglo-American Law and Legal System, 1. Aufl., Hannover 1998/99
Borkowski	Textbook on succession, 2nd ed., Oxford 2002
Boucher & Corns	GCSE Law – Casebook, 3rd ed., London 1995
Brown	GCSE Law, 8th ed., London 2002
Chang & Welden	Nut cases: Equity and Trust, 3rd ed., London ... 2003; Nut cases: Land Law, 2nd ed., London ... 2000
Cheshire and Burn's	Modern Law of Real Property, 16th ed. (by *Burn*), London-Edinburgh-Dublin 2000
Cooke	Law of Tort, 6th ed., Harlow (Essex) 2003
Cracknell	Torts (Cracknells Law Students' Companion), 9th ed., Horsmonden 2000; Equity and Trusts (Cracknell's Law Students' Companion), 4th ed., London 1995
Cretney and Masson	Principles of Family Law, 7th ed., London 2003
Denham	Law – a modern introduction, 4th ed., London 1999

Doods	Family Law (Cracknell's law Students' Companion), 4th ed., London 1997
Edwards and Stockwell	Trusts and Equity, 6th ed., Harlow (Essex) 2003
Geldart	Introduction to English Law, 11th ed. (by *Yardley*), London 1995
Giliker & Beckwith	Tort, 2nd ed., London 2004
Harpwood	Principles of Tort Law, 4th ed., London 2000
Harris	An Introduction to Law, 6th ed., London-Edinburgh-Dublin 2002
Harvey & Marston	Cases & Commentary on Tort, 5th ed., Harlow (Essex) 2004
Hedley	Tort, 4th ed., London-Edinburgh-Dublin 2004
Hepple, Howarth & Matthews	Tort, Cases & Materials, 5th ed., London-Edinburgh-Dublin 2000
Heuston & Buckley	(Salmond & Heuston) on the Law of Torts, 21th ed., London 1996
Hudson	Equity & Trusts, 3rd ed., London-Sydney 2003
Jones	Textbook on Torts, 8th ed., London 2002
Keenan	Smith & Keenan's English Law, 14th ed., London ... 2004
Kidner	Casebook on Torts, 8th ed., Oxford 2004
Lawsen & Kudden	The Law of Property, 3rd ed., Oxford 2002
Lowe & Douglas	(Bromley's) Family Law, 10th ed., London-Edinburgh-Dublin 2005
Lunney/Oliphant	Tort Law – Text and Materials, Oxford 2000
Lyall	An Introduction to British Law, 2. Aufl., Baden-Baden 2002
Markesinis/Deakin	Tort Law, 5th ed., Oxford 2003
Megarry & Wade	The Law of Real Property, 7th ed., London 2005 (by *Ch. Harpum*)

Parker and Mellows	The Modern Law of Trusts, 8th ed., London 2003
Parry & Clark	The Law of Succession, 11th ed., London 2002
Pearce and Stevens	The Law of Trusts and Equitable Obligations, 3rd ed., London–Dublin–Edinburgh 2002
Pettit	Equity and the Law of Trusts, 9th ed., London 2001
Riddall	The Law of Trusts, 6th ed., London, Dublin & Edinburgh 2002
Rose	Blackstone's Statutes on Contract, Tort & Restitution, 12th ed., London 2004/05
Scamell (Ed.)	Butterworths Property Law Handbook, 5th ed., London-Edinburgh-Dublin 2002
Shears & Stevenson	(James') Introduction to English Law, 13th ed., London-Dublin-Edinburgh 1996 (cited as "*James*' Introduction ... ")
Stapleton	Product Liability, London ... 1994
Stevens & Pearce	Land Law, 3rd ed., London 2005
Sydenham	Nutshells: Equity & Trust, 6th ed., London ... 2004
Tayfoor	Law Cartoons: Tort, London 1995
Templeman & Bell	Land: The Law of Real Property – Casebook, 2nd ed., London 1999, Revision Work Book, 3rd ed., London 2004, Textbook, 4th ed., London 2004
Templeman & Burr	Conveyancing – Casebook, 2nd ed., London 2004, Revision Work Book, 1st ed., London 1997;Textbook, 4th ed., London 2003
Templeman & Cutler	Equity and Trusts: Casebook, 3rd ed., London 2003
Templeman & Dodds	Family Law: - Casebook, 3rd ed., London 2004; Revision Work Book, 4th ed., London 2004, Textbook, 4th ed., London 2003
Templeman & Doherty	Equity and Trusts: Revision Work Book, 4th ed., London 2004
Templeman & Halliwell	Equity and Trusts: Textbook, 4th ed., London 2003

Templeman & Pitchfork	Obligations: The Law of Tort – Casebook, 3rd ed., London 2004; Revision Work Book, 3rd ed., London 2004; Textbook, 4th ed., London 2003
Templeman & Spedding	Succession: Casebook, 2nd ed., London 2000; Revision Work Book, 3rd ed., London 2003; Textbook, 3rd ed., London 2001
Tiernan	Nutshells: Torts, 6th ed., London ... 2003
van Gerven/Lever/Larouche	Cases, Materials and Text on National, Supranational and International Tort Law, Oxford and Portland (Oregon), 2000 ["Ius Commune Casebook for the Common Law of Europe"]
Ware	Succession (Cracknell's Law Students' Companion), 2nd ed., London 1995
Weir	A Casebook on Tort, 10th ed., London 2004
Winfield & Jolowicz	On Tort, 16th ed., London 2002
Wragg	Nutshells: Family Law, 6th ed., London ... 2004

II. English (and Anglo-American) law in German

Bernstorff, Graf von	Einführung in das englische Recht, 2. Aufl., München 2000
Blumenwitz	Einführung in das anglo-amerikanische Recht, 7. Aufl., München 2003
David/Grasmann	Einführung in die großen Rechtssysteme der Gegenwart, 2. Aufl., München 1988 (auf der Grundlage von *David/Spinosi*, Les grands systèmes de droit contemporains", 8. Aufl., Paris 1982)
Henrich/Huber	Einführung in das englische Privatrecht, 3. Aufl., Darmstadt 2003
Reimann	Einführung in das US-amerikanische Privatrecht, 2. Aufl., München 2004
Zweigert/Kötz	Einführung in die Rechtsvergleichung, 3. Aufl., Tübingen 1996

III. English legal terminology   Rechtssprache

Byrd	Einführung in die anglo-amerikanische Rechtssprache, 2. Aufl., München-Wien-Bern 2001
Chartrand, Millar & Wilshire	English for Contract and Company Law, London 1997
Gibbons	Language and the Law, London-New York 1994
Heidinger/ Hubalek	Anglo-Amerikanische Rechtssprache – Praxishandbuch für Rechtsanwälte, Wirtschaftsjuristen und Wirtschaftstreuhänder –, 3. Aufl., Wien 2004

IV. Dictionary of legal (and commercial) terms

Dietl/ Lorenz	Wörterbuch für Recht, Wirtschaft und Politik mit erläuternden und rechtsvergleichenden Kommentaren, Teil I: Englisch-Deutsch, 6. Aufl., München 2000; Teil II: Deutsch-Englisch, 5. Aufl., München 2005
dies.	CD-Wörterbuch für Recht, Wirtschaft und Politik, Teil I und Teil II: Englisch-Deutsch/Deutsch-Englisch. Rund 160.000 Fachbegriffe übersetzt und teilweise erläutert. 2. Aufl. München 2005
Epstein (General Editor)	Law and Commercial Dictionary in Five Languages – English to German, Spanish, French, Italian – , Bd. I: A-J, Bd. II: K-Z, München-Paris-Minnesota 1985
Flory /Froschauer	Grundwortschatz der Rechtssprache Deutsch-Englisch/ Englisch-Deutsch, 3. Aufl., Neuwied 2005
Köbler	Rechtsenglisch – Deutsch-englisches und englisch-deutsches Rechtswörterbuch für jedermann, 6. Aufl., München 2005
Lindbergh	Internationales Rechtswörterbuch, Deutsch-Englisch-Französisch, Neuwied 1995
Romain: *Romain/Bader/Byrd* *Romain/Byrd/Thielecke*	Wörterbuch der Rechts- und Wirtschaftssprache Teil I: Englisch-Deutsch, 5. Aufl., München 2000; Teil II: Deutsch-Englisch, 4. Aufl., München 2002

Chapter Seven

The law of tort

Recht der unerlaubten Handlung/Deliktsrecht

I. Introduction:
The meaning of the <u>term</u> "tort"

Begriff

Using an English-German <u>dictionary of legal terms</u> one will find that the English word "tort" means *„unerlaubte Handlung, (zivilrechtliches) Delikt, Schädigung"*. The adjective "tortious" is translated as *„deliktisch, unerlaubte Handlungen betreffend"*. A "tortious act" is also an *„unerlaubte Handlung (im Sinne des Zivilrechts)"*. And you will find the <u>term</u> *„unerlaubte Handlung"* also as a translation for "trespass" (which, moreover, means: *„Besitzstörung, widerrechtliches Betreten, Vergehen"*, even: *„Schadensersatzklage wegen unerlaubter Handlung"*!).

Rechtswörterbuch

Begriff

This reveals that the "torts" and "trespasses" of English civil law are only, <u>in part</u>, <u>congruent</u> with the German *„unerlaubte Handlung"*. According to German civil law, an *„unerlaubte Handlung"* means an <u>unlawful</u>, <u>culpable</u> act, which <u>injures</u> the <u>rights</u> of another person who thereby <u>suffers damage</u>.

teilweise – deckungsgleich

widerrechtlich – schuldhaft

verletzen – Rechte (und Rechtsgüter!) – Schaden erleiden

The meaning of "torts" is wider. "Torts" include <u>facts and situations</u> which in, *German* law, do not only <u>entitle</u> to a <u>tortious action</u>, but also give rise to other <u>claims</u>, as, for example, the <u>right to possession</u>, the <u>right to a forbearance</u> or the <u>right for disturbance of possession</u>. Therefore actions in tort do not always <u>claim</u> damages.

Tatbestände

berechtigen

deliktische Schadensersatzklage – Ansprüche – Herausgabeanspruch –Unterlassungsanspruch – Besitzstörungsanspruch – beanspruchen

The different torts are not <u>systemised</u>, which is a result of their historical evolutions over a long period of time.
The oldest torts [e.g. detinue – cf. vol. 1, p. 28 "*writ of detinue*" – which was abolished by the *Torts (Interference with Goods) Act 1977*, s. 2(1) or e.g. trespass] <u>derive</u> from <u>medieval</u> common law.

in ein System bringen

Konflikt/Einwirkung/Eingriff – herrühren/entstammen mittelalterlich

1

The <u>archaic</u> common law with its few remedies was, in many cases, not able to give <u>satisfaction</u> to the injured party (i.e. plaintiff). This led to a jurisdiction "in equity" being developed by the Lord Chancellor (cf. vol. 1, p. 30). Do you remember the <u>deficiency</u> of the old common law: "No writ, no remedy"? (If not, cf. vol. 1, p. 27).

archaisch
Genugtuung

Defizit/Schwäche

The most important <u>all-purpose</u> writ which covered the common civil <u>wrongs</u> in medieval law was *trespass*! This was available for all *direct* injuries to persons, goods, or land. Thus, personal injury of another, e.g. <u>assault</u> and <u>battery</u>, damage to personal goods, to <u>gates</u>, <u>hedges</u>, lands, or <u>mere</u> entry upon lands or <u>cattle trespass</u>, fell within the <u>ambit</u> of "trespass".

„Allheilmittel"
Rechtsverletzung

gewaltsame Drohung/Gewalt-anwendung – Körperverletzung – Tor /Zugang – Hecken – bloß – Viehdurchgang – Geltungsbereich

The word "tort", derives from the Latin *tortus*, meaning <u>crooked</u> or <u>twisted</u>, and the French *tort*, meaning wrong! In English law, as you should have understood by now, the word "tort" is used to <u>denote</u> civil wrongs, as distinct from <u>criminal wrongs</u>.

korrupt/betrügerisch/unehrlich – verdreht/entstellt

bezeichnen
Straftaten

And, as this short introduction should indicate to you: the "law of torts" could also be a "law of trespasses". So how can we give a definition of "tort"?

Let us consult two of the leading textbooks on the law of torts: *Salmond & Heuston* and *Winfield & Jolowicz*.
According to *Salmond*, a tort is "*a civil wrong for which the remedy is a common law action for <u>unqualified damages</u>, and which is not exclusively the breach of a contract or the breach of trust or other merely equitable obligation.*"

unbeschränkter Schadensersatz

Winfield <u>asserts</u> that "*tortious liability arises from the breach of a duty <u>primarily</u> fixed by law; such duty is <u>towards</u> persons generally, and its breach is <u>redressable</u> by an action for unqualified damages*".

behaupten/feststellen
in erster Linie – gegenüber
wiedergutmachungsfähig

According to *Lord Denning* "*the <u>province</u> of a tort is to <u>allocate</u> <u>responsibility</u> for <u>injurious conduct</u>.*"

Aufgabenbereich
zuweisen – Verantwortlichkeit – schädigendes Verhalten

Having said (and hopefully understood) all that, we can now proceed.

II. Trespass

There are three types of trespass:

- trespass to the person
- trespass to goods and
- trespass to land.

1. Trespass to the person

This tort <u>comprises</u> three forms, which are <u>assault</u>, <u>battery</u> and <u>false imprisonment</u>.

umfassen – Drohung mit Gewaltanwendung – Körperverletzung – Freiheitsberaubung

a) Assault

Contrary to <u>common belief</u>, to <u>assault</u> someone is to cause him to fear <u>physical violence</u>. If you touch a person, it is battery.

allgemeine Auffassung – mit Gewalt drohen – körperliche Gewaltanwendung

One legal definition of assault is that it is "*an act of the defendant which causes the plaintiff reasonable <u>apprehension</u> of the <u>infliction</u> of a battery on him by the defendant*" (*Winfield & Jolowicz*).

Befürchtung – Zufügung

There are several ways in which you can <u>assault</u> someone, even without touching him, for example by <u>threatening</u> words ("Your money, or your life"), by <u>shaking your fist in a threatening manner</u> (like a boxer) or by <u>pointing</u> a <u>weapon</u> at him.

angreifen/tätlich bedrohen

drohend(en)

mit der Faust drohen

richten auf – Waffe

It is also possible to assault someone with a harmless object, since the essential element in assault is <u>fear</u>.

Angst

When, for example, A points a <u>firearm</u> at B, which A knows to be unloaded, though B does not, and it is so near that it might <u>produce</u> injury if it were loaded and <u>went off</u>, this <u>constitutes</u> an assault. In *The Times* of 21 January 1991, you could even have read that a man was <u>jailed</u> for six years for attempting to rob a bank ... with a banana! The robbery was <u>committed</u> on the day he finished a <u>prison sentence</u> for the same <u>offence</u>.

Schusswaffe

bewirken – losgehen – darstellen

einsperren

begehen

Gefängnisaufenthalt Vergehen/ Verbrechen

b) Battery

Battery is the direct and intentional application of physical force to another person without lawful justification.

Any physical contact may equally be "force". So a possible battery may be: to spit at someone, to pour water over someone, to snatch a chair away as someone sits down or to throw a stone at someone.

However, a certain amount of contact in everyday life would not constitute a battery. For instance: jostling in a queue or stepping on someone's foot in a crowd.

On the other hand, it should be noted that mere unauthorised touching is actionable, regardless of the motive: a kiss given with love and affection constitutes an assault or a battery, if the receiver does not authorise the act. It is intentional bodily contact and thus, a person may claim damages if he (or she) did not voluntarily accept the kiss.

c) False imprisonment

False imprisonment consists of the infliction of bodily restraint on another without lawful justification. This may happen in any place where a person is wrongfully deprived of his liberty to go where he pleases. Thus, there need be no imprisonment such as incarceration in a prison cell. The mere holding of the arm of another against his will is sufficient. The imprisonment, however, must be for an unreasonable length of time and must be total. Thus, to restrain a person from going in three directions but, at the same time, leaving him free to go in a fourth is not false imprisonment.

Example – Bird v Jones (1845) –:
A bridge company lawfully stopped a public footpath on Hammersmith Bridge. A spectator insisted on using the footpath, but was stopped by two policemen who barred his entry. The plaintiff was told he might proceed to

---

Glossary (margin):

absichtlich/vorsätzlich – Anwendung – körperliche Gewalt – Rechtfertigungsgrund gleichermaßen

spucken – gießen

wegziehen

werfen

hier: Umfang

drängeln/drücken – Warteschlange von Menschen – darauftreten – Menge

unerlaubte Berührung – belangbar/(ein)klagbar – unabhängig von Leidenschaft/Zuneigung

körperlich

Einschränkung der Bewegungsfreiheit

widerrechtlich – berauben
gefallen/möchten – nötig sein
Einschließung – Gefängniszelle

freistellen

hier: stilllegen

anhalten – versperren

---

another point around the <u>obstruction</u> but that he could not go forward. He <u>declined</u> and remained for about half an hour and then sued for false imprisonment. *Held*: that there was no false imprisonment since the plaintiff was free to go another way.	Hindernis ablehnen/sich weigern

It is possible that the person imprisoned might even be unaware of it at the time. So a person can be imprisoned <u>whilst</u> asleep, whilst in a state of drunkenness and whilst he is a <u>lunatic</u>.

während
Geistesgestörter

Example – Meering v *Grahame-White Aviation Co. Ltd. (1919) –:*	
The plaintiff, being suspected of stealing a <u>keg</u> of <u>varnish</u> from the defendants, his employers, was asked by two works' security officers to accompany them to the work office to answer questions. The plaintiff, not realising that he was <u>suspected</u>, <u>assented</u> to the <u>suggestion</u> and even suggested a <u>short cut</u>. He remained in the office for some time during which the works' security officers stayed outside the room without his knowledge. The plaintiff later sued for false imprisonment and the question arose as to whether the plaintiff must know that the defendant is restraining his freedom. *Held*: that the plaintiff was imprisoned and his knowledge was irrelevant, though knowledge of imprisonment might increase the damages.	Fässchen – Lack verdächtigt – zustimmen – Vorschlag – Abkürzung

All forms of trespass to the person, assault, battery and false imprisonment, are actionable *per se*, which means that there is no need to prove damage. The plaintiff, however, must prove intent or negligence on the part of the defendant.

Example – Fowler v *Lanning (1959) –:*
By a writ, the plaintiff claimed damages for trespass to the person. In his statement of claim, he alleged that on

19th November 1957, at Vineyard Farm, Corfe Castle, in the County of Dorset, the defendant shot the plaintiff. By reason of the premises, the plaintiff sustained personal injuries and suffered loss and damage; particulars of the plaintiff's injuries were then set out. The defendant denied the allegations of facts and objected that the statement of claim disclosed no cause of action because the plaintiff had not alleged that the shooting was either intentional or negligent.

Held: that in an action for trespass to the person, the onus of proof in respect of the defendant's intent or negligence lay with the plaintiff and the plaintiff must prove that the shooting was intentional or that the defendant was negligent, stating the facts alleged to constitute the negligence. The plaintiff's statement of claim, therefore, disclosed no cause of action.

aufgrund der gegebenen Umstände – aushalten

Einzelheiten/Besonderheiten darstellen
Tatsachenbehauptungen – einwenden
offenbaren – Klagegrund

Last (Beweislast)

d) Defences

Einwendungen/Rechtfertigungsgründe

There are three possible defences available in an action for trespass to the person:

- consent,

- lawful arrest,

- self-defence.

Einwilligung

gesetzliche Haft/vorläufige Festnahme – Notwehr

It goes without saying that a person who has voluntarily consented to the commission of a tort may not sue on it. Of course, self-defence must be proportional to the attack, which means that no more force may be used in defence than is reasonably necessary. What is reasonable is a matter for decision by the court on the particular facts of each case.
An arrest of a person will not be lawful if an offence has not been committed by him. However, according to the *Police and Criminal Evidence Act 1984* [s. 24(4)], a person may, where an arrestable offence has been committed, without

freiwillig
Begehung
verhältnismäßig

Einzelfallumstände

Strafprozessordnung

6

warrant arrest any person who is or whom he suspects with reasonable cause to be guilty of the offence, in the act of committing an arrestable offence [s24(5)].

Haftbefehl – verdächtigen
schuldig
haftbegründend

2. Trespass to goods

Wrongful interference through trespass to goods is a tort against the possession of goods. Possession under English law is a difficult topic, which is considered more fully in the next chapter. For the moment, it will be sufficient to say that a person possesses goods when he has some form of control over them and has the intention to exclude others from possession.

widerrechtlicher Eingriff – Besitz
Thema/Gegenstand – ausführlicher – ausreichend

ausschließen

Example – The Tubantia (1924) –:

The plaintiff, a marine salvage company, was trying to salvage the cargo of the SS Tubantia which had been sunk in the North Sea. He had discovered the wreck and marked it with a marker buoy, and his divers were already working in the hold, when the defendant, a rival salvage company, appeared on the scene and started to send divers down to salvage the cargo from the wreck.

Held: that irrespective of whoever was the owner of the property salvaged, the plaintiff was sufficiently in possession of the wreck to found an action in trespass.

Schiffsbergungsgesellschaft
bergen
Wrack
Markierungsboje – Taucher
hier: Rumpf/Lagerraum – Rivale/ Konkurrent

The wrongful interference by trespass to goods must be direct and effected by force.

The trespass to goods is essentially a tort against possession, which means that it is not necessary that the possessor also be the owner.

As examples of trespass to goods, it may be noted that it is a trespass to snatch someone's hat, to kick someone's dog, to erase a tape-recording, to throw another's book out of the window or to scratch the panel of a car.

gewaltsam

Besitzer
Eigentümer

schnappen – treten
löschen – Tonbandaufnahme
kratzen – Blech

Most actions under the tort "trespass to goods" are <u>brought</u> as a result of intentional <u>dispossession</u>, which can be either *conversion* or *detention*.

Conversion <u>arises</u> when the defendant intentionally interferes with goods in a way that may be regarded as denying the plaintiff's <u>rights of possession or use</u>. If, for example, a car <u>subject to</u> a <u>hire-purchase</u> agreement is sold to a private person, the seller would, in such a case, have given the buyer a good <u>title</u> and at the same time denied the hire-purchase company the right of <u>ownership</u> of the car. In that case, the hire-purchase company can sue the seller for conversion. Detention of goods is now governed by the *Torts (Interference with Goods) Act 1977*, which <u>abolished</u> [s2(1)] the old tort of detinue (as mentioned above, p. 1).

Under s2(2) of this Act, the tort of wrongful interference by conversion has <u>replaced</u> the old action of detinue.

Thus, mere detention can now amount to conversion. In other words, detinue and conversion have <u>merged</u>.

S. 1 of the Act defines "wrongful interference with goods" as

- conversion of goods

- trespass to goods, and

- negligence and other torts in so far as they result in damage to goods or <u>interests</u> in goods.

Example – Parker v British Airways Board (1982) –:
The plaintiff was in B.A. first class lounge at Heathrow waiting for a flight. He found a gold <u>bracelet</u> on the floor and gave it to an employee of B.A. together with his name and address, asking that it should be returned to him if not claimed. It was not claimed, but B.A. sold it. The plaintiff sued in <u>conversion</u>.
Held (by the Court of Appeal)*:*that the plaintiff was entitled to the <u>proceeds</u> of sale.

Glossary (right column):

einreichen/vortragen
widerrechtliche Besitzentziehung – unrechtmäßiger Gebrauch fremden Eigentums – Vorenthaltung – entstehen/ vorliegen

Besitz- oder Nutzungsrechte Gegenstand von –Abzahlungskauf

hier: Besitzanspruch
Eigentum(srecht)

abschaffen

ersetzen

verschmelzen

hier: dingliches Recht (Besitzrecht)

Armband

Veruntreuung

Erlös

8

Example – Jarvis v Williams (1955) –:

Jarvis agreed to sell some bathroom fittings to Peterson and at Peterson's request delivered them to Williams. Peterson refused to pay the price and Jarvis agreed to take them back if Peterson would pay for <u>collection</u>. Peterson accepted this offer and Jarvis sent his <u>lorryman</u>, with a letter of authority, to collect the fittings but he was told that he could not take them, so he returned <u>empty-handed</u>. Jarvis claimed against Williams in conversion for the return of the goods.

Held: that on the delivery to Williams, the property in the goods passed to Peterson, and the arrangement for re-collection did not <u>revest</u> the property in Jarvis. It follows that, at the time of collection, Jarvis had no right of property in the goods to sustain an action in conversion.

> Abholung
> Lastwagenfahrer
>
> mit leeren Händen
>
> zurückerwerben

---

3. Trespass to land

a) Definition and examples

Trespass to land is the unlawful <u>entry</u> of a person or thing <u>into</u> land or into buildings in the possession of another. *Salmond & Heuston* define trespass to land as: *"Entering upon land in the possession of the plaintiff or remaining upon such land or placing any object upon it, in each case without lawful justification".*

> Eindringen
> auf

Examples of trespass to land are: leaving <u>parcels</u> on the wrong person's <u>doorstep</u>, <u>leaning</u> a <u>ladder</u> against the wall of the neighbour's house, throwing something into or entering oneself into another's <u>forecourt</u> and <u>removing</u> a <u>dustbin</u>. To trespass on land, one does not even need to <u>step</u> on the land. Putting one's hand through a window would be enough. Every <u>invasion</u> of property, <u>however small</u>, is a trespass to land. If the trespass is done voluntarily, mistake is no excuse. So, for example, if you <u>mow</u> grass thinking it is yours when, in fact, it

> Pakete
> Türschwelle – anlehnen – Leiter
> Vorhof/Vorgarten – entfernen – Mülleimer – betreten
>
> Eindringen – wie gering auch immer
>
> mähen

9

belongs to your neighbour, you would be committing a trespass to land. Trespass can even be committed without physically touching the land. Moreover, one should also note that, as concerns the ownership of land, the air above it also belongs to it to such height as is necessary for the ordinary enjoyment of the land. Thus, it constitutes an actionable wrong to <u>fly a kite</u>, or send a message by <u>carrier pigeon</u>, or <u>ascend</u> in an aeroplane, or <u>fire a bullet</u> over it, as in the "Tasmanian cat case" *Davies* v *Bennison* (1927), where the defendant shot a cat on the plaintiff's <u>roof</u>. The plaintiff was entitled to damages for trespass to land as well as for the value of the cat.

Drachen steigen lassen –
Brieftaube – aufsteigen
eine Kugel abfeuern

Dach

Example – *Southport Corporation* v *Esso Petroleum Co.* (1957) –:

The Esso company's tanker became stranded in the <u>estuary</u> of the river Ribble. The master of the tanker <u>discharged</u> oil in order <u>to refloat</u> the ship. The action of the wind and <u>tide</u> took the oil onto the Corporation's <u>foreshore</u> and caused damage. The Corporation sued in trespass and negligence. *Devlin*, J., at first instance, thought that trespass would <u>lie</u>, but on appeal to the Court of Appeal, *Denning*, L.J. <u>contended</u> that there could be no trespass because the injury was not direct, but was caused by the tides and <u>prevailing</u> winds; in trespass, the injury must be direct and not <u>consequential</u>.
Held (by the House of Lords, <u>agreeing</u> with *Denning*, L.J.): that the appeal was based on negligence and that the defendants were not liable for negligence.

Mündung
entladen
wieder flottmachen – Flut
Vorküste

zulässig sein

geltend machen
üblich/vorherrschend

nachfolgend
übereinstimmen

Example – *Kelson* v *Imperial Tobacco Co.* (1957) –:

The plaintiff was the <u>lessee</u> of a <u>one-storey</u> tobacconist's shop and brought an action against the defendants, seeking an injunction requiring them to remove from the wall above the shop a large cigarette advertising sign displaying the words 'Players Please'. The sign <u>projected</u> into the <u>airspace</u> above the plaintiff's shop to the extent of some

Pächter/Mieter – einstöckig

hier: hereinragen
Luftraum

eight <u>inches</u>. The plaintiff claimed that the defendants, by fixing the sign in that position, had trespassed on his airspace.

Held: that the invasion of an airspace by a sign of this nature constituted a trespass and, although the plaintiff's injury was small, it was an appropriate case in which to grant an injunction for the <u>removal</u> of the sign.

1 inch = 2,54 cm

Entfernung

Example – Woolerton and Wilson v Richard Costain (Midlands) Ltd. (1969) –:

In this case, the first instance court granted the owners of a factory and warehouse in Leicester an injunction restraining the defendants from trespassing on and <u>invading</u> airspace over their premises by means of a <u>swinging crane</u>.

Held (on appeal by the defendants): that the injunction was <u>suspended</u> for twelve months to enable the defendants to finish their work, the defendants having offered to pay for the right to continue to trespass and to provide insurance cover for neighbouring properties. It was also held that it was no answer to a claim for an injunction for trespass that the trespass did no harm to the plaintiff.

eindringen
schwingender Kran

aufschieben

b) <u>Defences</u>

Verteidigungsmittel/
Einwendungen/Rechtferti-
gungsgründe

Entries onto land do not constitute the tort of "trespass to land" if they are <u>justifiable</u>.

A trespass to land maybe justifiable for the following reasons: When the entry was made

    (1) by authority of law

        (such as a policeman or a <u>bailiff</u>),

    (2) by <u>leave</u> or <u>licence</u> granted by the <u>occupier</u>,

    (3) <u>involuntarily</u> (such as landing with a <u>parachute</u>),

    (4) where the highway was <u>impassable</u>, and

    (5) to <u>retake</u> or <u>retain</u> possession of one's own property.

rechtmäßig/nicht widerrechtlich

Gerichtsvollzieher

Gestattung – Erlaubnis –
Besitzer – unfreiwillig – Fall-
schirm
unpassierbar
zurücknehmen – behalten

c) Remedies

The following remedies are available to a plaintiff:

aa) Damages

This is, in general, the amount by which the value of the land is <u>diminished</u> as a result of the trespass, but not the cost of <u>reinstatement</u>.

vermindert
Wiederinstandsetzung

bb) Injunction

This may be used to stop the defendant from <u>continuing</u> or <u>repeating</u> the trespass.
The plaintiff may <u>apply</u> to the court for both damages and an injunction.

fortsetzen
wiederholen
ersuchen

cc) <u>Forcible ejection</u>

Zwangsräumung/gewaltsame Besitzentziehung

The occupier of the land may <u>eject</u> a <u>trespasser</u> after first <u>requesting</u> him to leave and giving him reasonable time to do so. No more force may be used than is reasonable in the circumstances. Otherwise, the occupier himself may be sued for assault and/or battery.

hinauswerfen – Besitzstörer
auffordern

Diagram 38

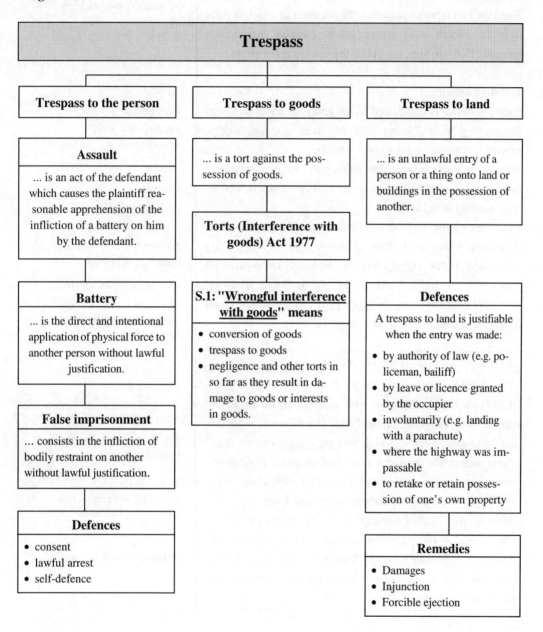

Trespass

Trespass to the person

Assault

... is an act of the defendant which causes the plaintiff reasonable apprehension of the infliction of a battery on him by the defendant.

Battery

... is the direct and intentional application of physical force to another person without lawful justification.

False imprisonment

... consists in the infliction of bodily restraint on another without lawful justification.

Defences

- consent
- lawful arrest
- self-defence

Trespass to goods

... is a tort against the possession of goods.

Torts (Interference with goods) Act 1977

S.1: "Wrongful interference with goods" means

- conversion of goods
- trespass to goods
- negligence and other torts in so far as they result in damage to goods or interests in goods.

Trespass to land

... is an unlawful entry of a person or a thing onto land or buildings in the possession of another.

Defences

A trespass to land is justifiable when the entry was made:

- by authority of law (e.g. policeman, bailiff)
- by leave or licence granted by the occupier
- involuntarily (e.g. landing with a parachute)
- where the highway was impassable
- to retake or retain possession of one's own property

Remedies

- Damages
- Injunction
- Forcible ejection

III. Nuisance

There are two types of nuisance (the meaning of which derives from the French word *nuire*): public nuisance and private nuisance. Both are torts, but public nuisance is also a crime.

	Belästigung/Beeinträchtigung/ Störung/Polizeiwidrigkeit
	schaden

1. Public nuisance

Public nuisance is constituted by an unlawful act or omission endangering or interfering with the lives, comfort, safety, property, or common rights of the public.

Whereas private nuisance can affect only one person, public nuisance is something which requires that a class of people be materially affected.

Examples of the tort (and crime) of public nuisance are: organising a pop music festival which generates largescale noise and traffic, obstructing a highway or making it dangerous for traffic, selling unhygienic food, throwing fireworks into the street or erecting a factory which emits excessive smoke.

	Unterlassung
	gefährden – stören – Wohlbefinden – Sicherheit
	Gruppe
	im Wesentlichen
	erzeugen – sehr umfangreich – behindern/sperren
	unhygienisch/verdorben
	errichten – Fabrik – erzeugen/ auswerfen/emittieren – übermäßig

> **Example – R.[1] v Shorrock (1993) –:**
>
> The defendant let a field on his farm for a weekend for £2000. He did not know for what purpose the field was let and he went away for the weekend. The field was used for an "acid house party" which was attended by more than 3000 people and created a great deal of noise. The police received nearly 300 complaints. The defendant was convicted of causing a public nuisance and fined.
>
> *Held* (by the Court of Appeal): that it was not necessary for the Crown[1] to prove that he had actual knowledge of the nuisance, as he ought to have known that there was a real risk that the consequences of letting the field would be to create this sort of nuisance.

	vermieten
	[cf. footnote 2] – aufsuchen/ besuchen
	Beschwerden
	verurteilt – verursachen – mit Geldstrafe belegen
	er hätte wissen müssen

---

[1] Remember that R. means Regina. The Crown, represented by the Director of Public Prosecutions (cf. vol. 1, p. 71), is the prosecutor, because public nuisance is a crime.

[2] **Acid** = Säure, umgangssprachlich für die Droge LSD; **acid house** = von schnellen (computererzeugten) Rhythmen geprägter Tanz- und Musikstil, der die Tanzenden in einen rauschartigen Zustand versetzen soll.

	Ankläger

Example – Attorney-General v *Gastonia Coaches (1976) –:*

G, who were coach operators, owned 22 coaches, of which 16 were parked in residential roads adjoining the Gastonia offices. No matter how carefully these coaches were parked, they inevitably interfered with the free passage of other traffic.

Held (in a related action by the Attorney-General): that Gastonia were guilty of a public nuisance. They were restrained from parking the vehicles on the highway. Damages were also awarded to private litigants who had suffered from the emissions of exhaust gases, excessive noise and obstruction of drives.

Busunternehmer
Wohnstraßen – angrenzen

behindern

Nebenklage

Prozesspartei
Auspuffgase
Behinderung der Zufahrt

As mentioned in the footnote above, public nuisance as a crime is usually prosecuted in the name of the Attorney-General.

verfolgen/anklagen

A private person who has suffered damage may bring an action in tort to the court if he can prove a particular harm, which is different from that of the general public.

Schaden/Beeinträchtigung
Allgemeinheit/Öffentlichkeit

Example – Castle v *S. Augustine Links Ltd. and Another (1922) –:*

On 18th August 1919, the plaintiff was driving a taxicab from Deal to Ramsgate when a ball played by the second defendant, a Mr Chapman, from the thirteenth tee on the golf course, which ran parallel with the Sandwich Road, struck the windscreen of the taxicab. In consequence, a piece of glass from the screen injured the plaintiff's eye and a few days later he had to have his eye removed. He then brought this action.

Held: that the plaintiff succeeded. Judgment of £450 damages was given by *Sankey*, J. The proximity of the hole to the road constituted a public nuisance.

Abschlag

aufschlagen

entfernen lassen

öffentliche Gefahrenquelle

2. Private nuisance

The tort of private nuisance consists of unlawful interference with the plaintiff's use or enjoyment of his land and injuries to <u>servitudes</u>. *"The very essence of private nuisance is the unreasonable use by a man of his land, to the <u>detriment</u> of his neighbour"*, as *Lord Denning* stated in *Miller* v *Jackson* (1977).

What is reasonable <u>is based on</u> the conduct of the <u>ordinary man</u> and will <u>depend</u> on such factors as time, place, presence or absence of <u>malice</u> and whether the effects are <u>temporary</u> or permanent.

Dienstbarkeiten (z.B. Wegerecht) – Nachteil/Schaden

richten nach/basieren auf – „normaler Mensch" – abhängen von

böse Absicht/Böswilligkeit/ Vorsatz – vorübergehend

There are many ways of interfering with the plaintiff's enjoyment of land which may <u>amount</u> to nuisance: excessive noise, <u>offensive smells</u>, factory <u>pollution</u> leaving dirty <u>marks</u> on <u>washing</u> or allowing <u>sewage</u> <u>to collect</u> on land.

In contrast to trespass, nuisance is not actionable *per se*. Some damage must have occurred to enable the plaintiff to sue.

The basic rule is that you should use your property without causing harm to any other person (as a German law student, in this context, you should remember *§ 903 BGB*, which contains the same maxim). More simply, one should *"give and take, or live and let live"* [this is how it was expressed in *Kennaway* v *Thompson* (1980) with which we shall deal very shortly] and be reasonable in the way you behave towards your neighbours.

hier: sich erweisen als/ausreichen für
belästigende Gerüche – Verschmutzung – Flecken – Wäsche – Abwasser – ansammeln

In considering whether an act or omission is a nuisance, the following points are relevant:

a) <u>Health and comfort</u>

Gesundheit und Wohlbefinden

There need be no direct injury to health. It is sufficient that a person has been prevented, to an <u>appreciable</u> extent, from enjoying the ordinary comforts of life.

spürbar/merklich

16

b) **Standard** of comfort

The standard of comfort must be expected to vary with the district. Thus, for example, in London there is a difference between *Belgrave Square* (where the German embassy is situated) and *Stepney*. One area may be quiet and peaceful, the other bustling and noisy. An exception, however, is light: light to a building will be dealt with equally wherever it occurs, for one requires as much light in *Belgravia*[1] as in *Whitechapel*[1].

Maßstab

erwarten
Wohnbezirk

geschäftig/belebt – Licht
wird gleich behandelt
denn – brauchen

c) **Sensitivity**

A person cannot take advantage of his peculiar sensitivity to noise and smells. An act which would not disturb an ordinary man will not be a nuisance just because the plaintiff or his property is unduly sensitive.

Empfindlichkeit

nur, weil
unangemessen

Example – Robinson v Kilvert (1889) –:

The defendant manufactured paper boxes in a cellar of a house and leased the floor above to the plaintiff. The defendant heated the cellar with hot dry air. This raised the temperature of the plaintiff's premises, above which were used for storing brown paper which (because of its special characteristics) lost its value. The plaintiff sued in nuisance. *Held:* that defendant was not liable. His heating of the premises would not have damaged ordinary brown paper, though it did damage the plaintiff's particularly sensitive paper.

Stockwerk

---

d) **Utility** of the nuisance

The utility of the alleged nuisance has no bearing. Pig sties, breweries, tanneries, fish and chip shops, quarries are perhaps

Nützlichkeit

behaupten – Bedeutung
Schweinestall – Brauerei –
Gerberei – Fischbraterei –
Steinbruch

---

[1] Districts of London.

Stadtteile

useful and necessary for the <u>community</u> but if their <u>operation</u> causes <u>discomfort</u> to the plaintiff, they are a nuisance. The fact that the <u>trade or industry</u> is of <u>public</u> <u>benefit</u> is not a defence in law. Moreover, the defendant cannot allege that the plaintiff came to the area knowing that the nuisance was in existence.

Gemeinschaft/Gesellschaft – Betrieb – Unbehagen/ Unwohlsein – Gewerbe – Nutzen für die Allgemeinheit

---

Example – Adams v *Ursell (1913) –:*

A fish and chip shop was alleged to be a nuisance as it caused the plaintiff's house to be <u>permeated</u> with the <u>odour</u> and <u>vapour</u> from <u>stoves</u>.
Held: that an injunction was granted. It was <u>immaterial</u> that the shop served a working-class area and <u>supplied a public need</u>.

durchdringen – Geruch – Dampf – Herd
unwesentlich
öffentliche Bedürfnisse erfüllen

Example – Bliss v *Hall (1838) –:*

The defendant <u>carried on</u> the trade of a candle-maker in certain premises near to the <u>dwelling house</u> of the plaintiff and his family. Certain '<u>noxious</u> and foul smells' were emitted from the defendant's premises and the plaintiff sued him for nuisance. The defence was that, for three years before the plaintiff occupied the dwelling house in question, the defendant had exercised the trade <u>complained of</u> in this present establishment.
Held: that this was no defence to the <u>complaint</u> and judgment was given for the plaintiff.

betreiben
Wohnhaus
schädlich

sich dagegen beschweren
Beschwerde

---

e) Variety

Verschiedenartigkeit

The modes of <u>annoyance</u> are infinitely varied: <u>bell-ringing</u>, <u>circus performances</u>, the excessive use of radio, <u>stenches</u>, <u>filth</u> or opening a sex-shop in a <u>residential area</u> may all be nuisances.

Belästigung – Glockengeläute
Zirkusveranstaltung – Gestank
Dreck – Wohngebiet

Example – Christie v *Davey (1893) –:*

The plaintiff was the occupier of a <u>semi-detached house</u> and she and her daughter gave <u>pianoforte</u>, violin and

Doppelhaushälfte
Klavier

singing lessons in the house four days a week for 17 hours in all. There was also music and singing at other times, and occasional musical evenings. The defendant, a woodcarver and a versatile amateur musician, occupied the adjoining portion of the house and he found the activities of the plaintiff and her family annoying. In addition to writing abusive letters, he retaliated by playing the concertina, horn, flute, piano and other musical instruments, blowing whistles, knocking on trays or boards, hammering, shrieking or shouting, so as to annoy the plaintiffs and hinder their activities.

Held: that what the plaintiff and her family were doing was not an unreasonable use of the house, and could not be restrained by the adjoining tenant. However, the adjoining tenant was himself restrained from making noises to annoy the plaintiff, the court being satisfied that such noises had been made wilfully for the purpose of annoyance.

Holzschnitzer – vielseitig
angrenzende Hälfte
störend
beleidigend – sich rächen –
Ziehharmonika
(Triller)-Pfeife – Tablett
Brett – kreischen

ärgern
absichtlich
Störung

f) Several wrongdoers

Schädiger/Rechtsverletzer

A nuisance may result from the act of several wrongdoers. If, for instance, A, B and C are the persons involved, any of them may be proceeded against. The plaintiff may sue all jointly or separately, for example A, for the total damage. If this is done, A will have a right to a contribution from B and C.

verklagen
gemeinsam
Ausgleichsanspruch

g) Continuity

Dauer/Beständigkeit

The duration of the act complained of has an influence upon the remedy which is appropriate and the court will not often grant an injunction in respect of a temporary nuisance because damages are an adequate remedy. Moreover, a temporary interference may be too trivial to be actionable. The general rule is that a single event is not a nuisance and the plaintiff must show that there is some degree of repetition of the offending act.

Dauer

unmaßgeblich
einmaliges Ereignis
darlegen – *hier:* Ausmaß

Example – Bolton v Stone (1951) –:

A cricket field was near a highway and it was proved that only six to ten cricket balls during thirty-five years had been known to have been hit into the road. No one had previously been injured until the plaintiff was struck by a ball.

Held: that this event did not occur often enough and therefore was not a nuisance.

---

h) Malice or evil motive

Böswilligkeit – schlechte/niedrige Motive

Sometimes malice or evil motive may become the foundation of the offending act.

Grundlage

To shout, shriek, whistle and bang trays may be a reasonable use of your own property, but if it is done with the express purpose of spoiling your neighbour's musical evening, it may be a nuisance, as we saw in *Christie v Davey* (1893).

kreischen – „auf die Pauke hauen" (= Tabletts zerschlagen)

verderben

An evil motive is illustrated in our next case.

Example –Hollywood Silver Fox Farm v Emmett (1936) –:

The plaintiffs were breeders of silver foxes and erected a notice board on their land inscribed: "Hollywood Silver Fox Farm". The defendant owned a neighbouring field, which he was about to develop as a building estate, and he regarded the notice board as detrimental to such development. He asked the plaintiffs to remove it, and when this request was refused, he sent his son to discharge a 12-bore gun close to the plaintiff's land, with the object of frightening the vixens during breeding. The result of this activity was that certain of the vixens did not mate at all, and others, having whelped, devoured their young. The plaintiff brought this action alleging nuisance and the defence was that Emmett had a right to shoot as he pleased on his own land.

Held: that an injunction would be granted to restrain Emmett. His evil motive made an otherwise innocent use of land a nuisance.

Züchter – errichten

Gebäudeanwesen
schädlich

abfeuern
12-Kaliber-Gewehr
Fähen – züchten
sich paaren
werfen – verschlingen

---

i) **Prescription**

hier: ständige Rechtsausübung

It is possible <u>to acquire</u> the right to commit a private nuisance by prescription. This means: when a nuisance has been in <u>continuous</u> existence for not less than twenty years, the right <u>to carry on</u> the act may be acquired.

erlangen

fortwährend
weitermachen

This is one defence which we shall deal with later on. But let us first answer the question: who may sue and be sued?

3. The parties to an action

The occupier of the property affected by the nuisance is the person who may bring the action. As a rule, no other person injured on the property has a claim in nuisance.

Example – Malone v Laskey (1907) –:

The defendants owned a house which they leased to a firm named Witherby & Co., who <u>sub-let</u> it to the Script Shorthand Company. The plaintiff's husband was employed by this company, and was allowed to occupy the house as an <u>emolument</u> of his employment. A <u>flush cistern</u> in the lavatory of the house was unsafe, the <u>wall brackets</u> having been loosened by the vibration of the defendants' electric generator next door. The plaintiff told Witherby & Co. of the situation, and they wrote to the defendants, who sent two of their <u>plumbers</u> to repair the cistern free of charge. The work was carried out in a negligent manner and, four months later, the plaintiff was injured when the cistern <u>came loose</u>. The plaintiff sued the defendants (a)in nuisance, and (b)in <u>negligence</u>.

Held: that there was no claim in nuisance against the defendants. The plaintiff was not a tenant, and only the tenant could sue in nuisance, but not other persons present on the premises, though such persons may have a claim where the nuisance is a public nuisance.

untervermieten

Entlohnung – Spülungskasten
Stützmauern

Klempner

sich lösen
Fahrlässigkeit

A <u>landlord</u> may, however, sue in some cases, for example, where a permanent injury is caused or will be caused to his property.	Grundeigentümer (der nicht Besitzer sein muss = Verpächter, Vermieter)
The person to be sued is the one who created the nuisance, i.e. the occupier of the property from which the nuisance <u>emanated</u>.	ausgehen von/herrühren
But a landlord also may be liable if he created the nuisance and then leases the property, or if he authorises a <u>tenant</u> to commit or continue the nuisance.	Mieter/Pächter

Example – Harris v *James (1876) –:*	
A landlord was *held* liable for the nuisance created by his tenant's <u>blasting</u> operations at a <u>quarry</u> because he had let the property for that purpose. The tenant, therefore, <u>inevitably</u> created a nuisance.	Sprengung – Steinbruch unvermeidlich

4. Defences

It is, of course, a defence to <u>rebut</u> the <u>allegation</u> that a nuisance was caused and to prove that the act complained of is not an unreasonable interference with the use or enjoyment of land.	widerlegen – Behauptung
The law <u>recognises</u>, as mentioned above, that, in everyday life, generally there must be some element of "give and take", e.g. noise caused by the <u>carrying out</u> of <u>repairs</u>. But repairs carried out in the middle of the night might not be reasonable.	*hier:* berücksichtigen/anerkennen Vornahme – Reparaturen
On considering the following defences, you will notice (*I hope*) some <u>similarities</u> with the defences to the trespass to land. Both torts disturb the occupier of land. The main difference between them is that trespass of land is a *direct* interference, <u>whilst</u> nuisance is an indirect one.	Ähnlichkeiten während
Defences to nuisance are:	
a) *consent of the plaintiff*,	
b) *<u>statutory authority</u>*,	gesetzliche Erlaubnis

which means that it is a defence to show that a statute authorises the act or omission in question (we will come back to this when we deal with the general defences in tort at the end of this chapter),

c) *triviality*,

Geringfügigkeit

where the damage caused was <u>minute</u> or minimal. The <u>maxim</u> here is *de minimis non curat lex* (the law does not concern itself with <u>trifles</u> = cf. "give and take"!),

winzig

Maxime/Grundsatz

Kleinigkeiten

d) *prescription* (cf.p. 21 above),

which will be <u>clarified</u> by the following leading case.

erklären/durchschaubar machen

Example – Sturges v *Bridgman (1879) –:*
The defendant, a <u>confectioner</u> and baker in Wigmore Street, London, used a <u>pestle</u> and <u>mortar</u> for some twenty years on his premises. The plaintiff, a doctor, built <u>consulting rooms</u> in his garden next to the confectioner's premises. Noises and vibration interfered with the plaintiff's practice and, accordingly, he sued the defendant in nuisance. *Held*: that although the defendant could acquire a <u>prescriptive</u> right to create a nuisance, the nuisance in this case arose only when the doctor's consulting room was built.

Konditor

Stößel – Mörser

Behandlungszimmer

ersessen/dinglich

e) *lawful use of land*,

rechtmäßig

where the defendant may prove that his use of land does not constitute a so-called nuisance, which means: where the law gives a person a legal right to do something, no <u>ill-will</u> in the doing of it will turn that right into a wrong; this was the position in the next case.

böser Wille

Example – Bradford Corporation v *Pickles (1895) –:*
Water <u>percolated</u> in undefined channels beneath Pickles' land and flowed <u>therefrom</u> to land belonging to the appellant corporation. The corporation used this water for their city's supply. <u>Actuated</u> by a desire to force the

durchsickern

von da

auslösen/bewegen

corporation to buy his land at his own price, Pickles <u>obstructed</u> the <u>flow</u> of water by sinking <u>shafts</u> into it. The corporation sought an injunction to restrain him from his <u>mercenary</u> behaviour.

Held: that no injunction would <u>lie</u> because a previous decision of the House of Lords had laid down that, <u>whereas</u> it is a nuisance to obstruct the flow of water, when it runs from one's own land to another's in defined channels, it is not a nuisance to <u>extract</u> merely percolating water – indeed, if this were the law it would provide a <u>disincentive</u> to land <u>drainage</u>. This kind of <u>obstruction</u> was therefore something which Pickles had a right to do. As *Lord Halsbury*, LCJ said, what he did was "*a lawful act, however ill the motive might be*" and he therefore "*had a right to do it*".

	verstopfen – Durchfluss – Schaft/Stamm
	gewinnsüchtig
	zulässig sein
	während
	herleiten
	Abschreckungsmittel – Entwässerung – Behinderung

f) *reasonableness*,

which is always a good defence; what is reasonable is based on the conduct of the ordinary man.

Angemessenheit/Billigkeit

5. Remedies

a) <u>Abatement</u>

Beseitigung/Minderung

The injured party may <u>abate</u> the nuisance, that is <u>remove</u> it, <u>provided that</u> no unnecessary damage is caused and that no injury arises to an innocent third party, e.g. a tenant. This remedy is a kind of <u>self-help</u>, which is <u>invoked</u> when the nuisance can be terminated without entering another person's land. It applies to over-hanging trees or roots but it must be noted that the branches which are cut off still belong to the owner of the tree. If the nuisance cannot be abated without <u>entering</u> the other's land, permission must be obtained, <u>unless</u> there is an <u>emergency</u>.

beseitigen – entfernen – vorausgesetzt, dass

Selbsthilfe – anrufen/sich berufen auf

betreten
falls nicht/es sei denn – Dringlichkeit/Notfall

b) Damages

Damages are the usual common law remedy in tort, thus also for nuisance.

c) Injunction

An injunction is an equitable remedy. It is an order of the court restraining further acts constituting the nuisance. In order to obtain an injunction, it is necessary to prove that the nuisance is likely to <u>recur</u> and do irreparable damage to the plaintiff.

sich wiederholen

6. Difference between trespass and nuisance

We have already stated that the torts of trespass to land and nuisance are similar in that they both <u>affect</u> land, trespass to land in a direct manner and nuisance indirectly. Yet there are some other differences which can be <u>summarised</u> as follows:

betreffen

zusammenfassen

Trespass (to land)	Nuisance
• Actionable *per se*	• Requires proof of damage
• Wrongful *entry* of an object or person on another's land	• No entry necessary
• May consist of one act only	• Usually more than one act is necessary
• Trespass is only a civil tort	• *Public* nuisance is a tort *and* a crime

Diagram 39

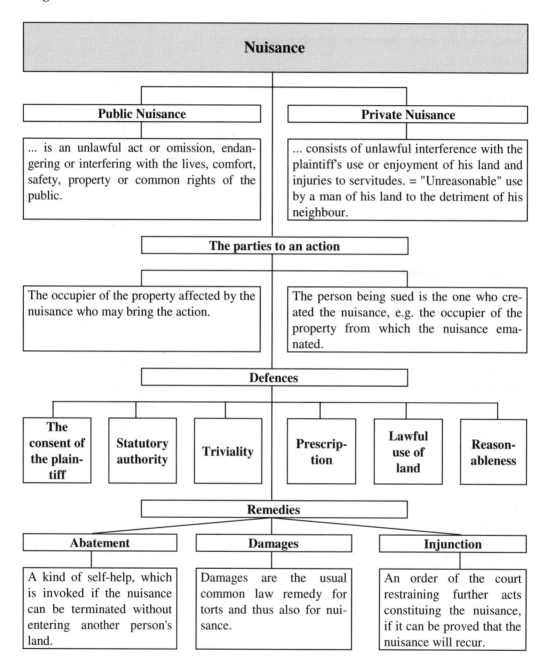

Nuisance

Public Nuisance

... is an unlawful act or omission, endangering or interfering with the lives, comfort, safety, property or common rights of the public.

Private Nuisance

... consists of unlawful interference with the plaintiff's use or enjoyment of his land and injuries to servitudes. = "Unreasonable" use by a man of his land to the detriment of his neighbour.

The parties to an action

The occupier of the property affected by the nuisance who may bring the action.

The person being sued is the one who created the nuisance, e.g. the occupier of the property from which the nuisance emanated.

Defences

| The consent of the plaintiff | Statutory authority | Triviality | Prescription | Lawful use of land | Reasonableness |

Remedies

Abatement

A kind of self-help, which is invoked if the nuisance can be terminated without entering another person's land.

Damages

Damages are the usual common law remedy for torts and thus also for nuisance.

Injunction

An order of the court restraining further acts constituing the nuisance, if it can be proved that the nuisance will recur.

IV. Negligence

Fahrlässigkeit/fahrlässige Schadenszufügung

1. Introduction

In the law of torts, negligence has two meanings:

(1) Firstly it is a kind of fault, which lies in the commission of certain torts, e.g. trespass or nuisance. Negligence, in the sense of "negligent misrepresentation", is also a kind of tort, in contrast to "innocent misrepresentation".
In this sense, negligence means exactly the same as „Fahrlässigkeit" in German.

Verschuldensform – Begehung

im Gegensatz zu

(2) More important is the second special meaning of negligence. It is an independent tort, being a breach of a legal duty of care which results in damage, undesired by the defendant, to the plaintiff (according to *Winfield & Jolowicz*). In this sense negligence can be translated into German as „fahrlässige Schadens-zufügung".

selbstständig – Verletzung einer rechtlichen Sorgfaltspflicht – Schaden herbeiführen – nicht vorsätzlich

In legal practice today, of all the actions in tort, it is negligence which is the most frequent.
Most by far of the actions in tort are brought in negligence and, even if other torts are involved in a particular case, negligence is frequently pleaded as well.
The tort of negligence is a relatively recent creation of English law.
Although its origins are to be found in trespass and trespass on the case, the action was developed and formulated by the courts only in the nineteenth century.

Gerichtspraxis

häufig

bei weitem – Klage einreichen wegen

geltend machen

jung/neu

allgemeine Schadensersatz-klage wegen rechtswidriger oder fahrlässig begangener Handlungen, durch die dem Kläger Schaden entstanden ist

Negligence, as an independent tort may be said to have found its precise outlines only in the House of the Lords' decision of 1932 in the case of *Donoghue* v *Stevenson*, which may be regarded as one of the most famous decisions in English civil law.

genaue Konturen – erst

The meaning of negligence as an independent tort is the only aspect that will be dealt with in the following passages, apart from the case of *Donoghue* v *Stevenson*.

2. Elements of the tort

Merkmale

The plaintiff suing in negligence must prove the following elements for a successful action:

(a) that the defendant owed a duty of care to the plaintiff,

schulden – Sorgfaltspflicht

(b) that there had been a breach of that duty by the defendant, and

Pflichtverletzung

(c) that, as a result, the plaintiff had suffered damage.

a) The duty of care

aa) *The standard of care*

Standard/Norm

For the tort of negligence, a person is only liable in negligence if he has breached a duty of care owed to the injured party. In the famous case *Le Lievre* v *Gould* (1895), *Lord Esher* said: "A man is entitled to be as negligent as he pleases towards the whole world, if he owes no duty to them."

haftbar

verletzen

verletzt/geschädigt

berechtigt – so nachlässig, wie es ihm gefällt

This is true and it is good law. On your own private property, having given no one permission to be there and having no knowledge of any other person's presence, you can do what you like there. You can drive your car there, you can shoot a rabbit (if you have a gun licence ...), and hit a golf ball anywhere you please. You do not owe a duty to anyone and you can be as negligent as you please. Negligence is not a foundation of liability unless the person whose conduct is impeached is under a legal duty to take care. But sometimes it is difficult to decide when such a duty of care arises in real life. This was the question dealt with, besides some others, in *Donoghue* v *Stevenson*.

Kaninchen

Haftung

anklagen

This case is of such fundamental importance not only for the development of negligence as an independent tort as such and not only for the evolution of the English law of tort, but also for the evolution of English civil law itself. If you have not as yet tasted the blood of English (civil) law, you may either do it now or else after having read the following excerpts from the decision in this case ("stolen" from *Tony Weir*, A Casebook on Tort, pages 33 – 39).

nicht nur

noch nicht – Blut lecken

andernfalls

Exzerpt/Auszug

Example("The Paisley Snail") – Donoghue v Stevenson (1932) –:

Action by consumer against manufacturer in respect of personal injury

According to Mrs Donoghue (née McAllister), she went to Minchella's café in Paisley with a friend, who ordered her a bottle of ginger beer. After taking the cap off the bottle, which was made of opaque stone rather than transparent glass, Minchella, the friend, poured some of the ginger beer over some ice-cream in a tumbler, and Mrs Donoghue partook thereof. As some ginger beer was still left in the bottle, her friend emptied it into her tumbler. A nauseating foreign body floated out – possibly something that had once been a snail... Mrs Donoghue was taken ill, poisoned by the drink or sickened by the thought of it, or both.

    geborene

    Verschlusskappe
    undurchsichtig
    gießen
    Becher – zu sich nehmen

    ekelerregend

Mrs Donoghue claimed that Stevenson, who had bottled the ginger beer and sold it to Minchella, owed a legal duty of care *to her*: he should have had a system for keeping snails out of the bottles and for inspecting the bottles before they were filled, and his breach of duty in these respects had caused her illness.

Stevenson replied that even if she managed to prove the facts she alleged, he was not liable in law, so there was no point in going to trial, but *Lord Moncrieff* decided to hear the evidence, and Stevenson appealed. The Inner House (Scotland's Court of Appeal) allowed Stevenson's appeal, and dismissed the claim. Mrs Donoghue appealed to the House of Lords, and her appeal was allowed, so that the case could proceed to trial (*though in fact it never did*).

Held (by the House of Lords as follows):

Lord Atkin: My Lords, the sole question for determination in this case is legal: Do the averments made by the pursuer in her pleading, if true, disclose a cause of action? I need not restate the particular facts. The question is whether the manufacturer of an article of drink sold by him to a distributor, in circumstances which prevent the distributor or the ultimate purchaser or consumer from discovering by inspection any defect, is under any legal duty to the ultimate purchaser or consumer to take reasonable care that the article is free from defect likely to cause injury to health. I do not think a more important problem has occupied your Lordships in your judicial capacity: important both because of its bearing on public health and because of the practical test which it applies to the system under which it arises ... The law ... appears to be, that in order to support an action for damages for negligence the complainant has to show that he has been injured by the breach of a duty owed to him in the circumstances by the defendant to take reasonable care to avoid such injury. In the present case we are not concerned with the breach of the duty; if a duty exists, that would be a question of fact which is sufficiently averred and for present purposes must be assumed. We are solely concerned with the question whether, as a matter of law in the circumstances alleged, the defender owed any duty to the pursuer to take care.

    Behauptung – Kläger (=*schottisch*)
    hier: rechtfertigen – wiederholen/
    neuformulieren – Hersteller
    Wiederverkäufer
    hindern

    wahrscheinlich
    Gesundheitsschädigung
    richterliche Funktion
    Einfluss

    um zu
    Beschwerdeführer

    vortragen
    vermuten/voraussetzen
    Beklagter (*schottisch*)

It is remarkable how difficult it is to find in the English authorities statements of general application defining the relations between parties that give rise to the duty... And yet the duty which is common to all the cases where liability is

    entstehen lassen – trotzdem/dennoch

established must logically be based upon some element common to the cases where it is found to exist. To seek a complete logical definition of the general principle is probably to go beyond the function of the judge, for the more general the definition the more likely it is to omit essentials or to introduce non-essentials. The attempt was made by *Brett* M.R. in *Heaven v Pender* (1883), in a definition to which I will later refer. As framed, it was demonstrably too wide, though it appears to me, if properly limited, to be capable of affording a valuable practical guide.

At present I content myself with pointing out that in English law there must be, and is, some general conception of relations giving rise to a duty of care, of which the particular cases found in the books are but instances. The liability for negligence, whether you style it such or treat it as in other systems as a species of "culpa", is no doubt based upon a general public sentiment of moral wrongdoing for which the offender must pay. But acts or omissions which any moral code would censure cannot in a practical world be treated so as to give a right to every person injured by them to demand relief. In this way rules of law arise which limit the range of complainants and the extent of their remedy. The rule that you are to love your neighbour becomes in law, you must not injure your neighbour; and the lawyer's question, "Who is my neighbour?" receives a restricted reply. *You must take reasonable care to avoid acts or omissions which you can reasonably foresee would be likely to injure your neighbour. Who then, in law is my neighbour? The answer seems to be – persons who are so closely and directly affected by my act that I ought reasonably to have them in contemplation as being so affected when I am directing my mind to the acts or omissions which are called in question.* This appears to me to be the doctrine of *Heaven v Pender*, as laid down by *Lord Esher* (then Brett M.R.) when it is limited by the notion of proximity introduced by *Lord Esher* himself and *A.L. Smith* L.J. in *Le Lievre v Gould* (1893). *Lord Esher* says: "That case established that, under certain circumstances, one man may owe a duty to another, even though there is no contract between them. If one man is near to another, or is near to the property of another, a duty lies upon him not to do that which my cause a personal injury to that other, or may injure his property." So *A.L. Smith* L.J.: "The decision of *Heaven v Pender* was founded upon the principle, that a duty to take due care did arise when the person or property of one was in such proximity to the person or property of another that, if due care was not taken, damage might be done by the one to the other." I think that this sufficiently states the truth if proximity be not confined to mere physical proximity, but be used, as I think it was intended, to extend to such close and direct relations that the act complained of directly affects a person who the person alleged to be bound to take care would know would be directly affected by his careless act. That this is the sense in which nearness or "proximity" was intended by *Lord Esher* is obvious from his own illustration in *Heaven v Pender* of the application of his doctrine to the sale of goods. "This" (i.e. the rule he has just formulated) "includes the case of goods, etc., supplied to be used immediately by a particular person or persons, or one of a class of persons, where it would be obvious to the person supplying, if he thought, that the goods would in all probability be used at once by such persons before a reasonable opportunity for discovering any defect which might exist, and where the thing supplied would be of such a nature that a neglect of ordinary care or skill as to its condition or the manner of supplying it would probably cause danger to the person or property of the person for whose use it was supplied, and who was about to use it. It would exclude a case in which the

übersteigen
je...desto
unterlassen/auslassen –
Nebensächlichkeiten
wie – verfassen
offensichtlich
gewähren/bieten
sich damit zufrieden geben

sind nur Beispiele
bezeichnen
zweifellos

Moralkodex – tadeln

hier: Kreis – Ausmaß

begrenzt

berücksichtigen/in Betracht ziehen

Nähe

festlegen

sich beschweren über

offensichtlich – Beschreibung

Vernachlässigung/Außerachtlassung

30

goods are supplied under circumstances in which it would be a <u>chance</u> by whom they would be used, or whether they would be used or not, or whether they would be used before there would probably be means of observing any defect, or where the goods would be of such a nature that a <u>want</u> of care or skill as to their condition or the manner of supplying them would not probably produce danger of injury to person or property." I <u>draw</u> particular <u>attention</u> to the fact that *Lord Esher* <u>emphasizes</u> the necessity of goods having to be "used immediately" and "used at once before a reasonable opportunity of <u>inspection</u>." This is obviously to exclude the possibility of goods having their condition altered by <u>lapse of time</u>, and <u>to call attention</u> to the proximate relationship, which may be too <u>remote</u> where inspection even by the person using, certainly by an intermediate person, may reasonably be <u>interposed</u>. With this necessary <u>qualification</u> of proximate relationship as explained in *Le Lievre* v *Gould*, I think the judgement of *Lord Esher* expresses the law of England; without the qualification, I think the majority of the Court in *Heaven* v *Pender* were justified in thinking the principle was expressed in too general terms. There will no doubt arise cases where it will be difficult to determine whether the <u>contemplated</u> relationship is so close that the duty arises. But in the class of case now before the Court I cannot <u>conceive</u> any difficulty to arise. A manufacturer puts up an article of food in a container which he knows will be opened by the actual consumer. There can be no inspection by any purchaser and no reasonable preliminary inspection by the consumer. Negligently, in the course of preparation, he allows the contents to be mixed with <u>poison</u>. *It is said that the law of England and Scotland is, that the poisoned consumer has no remedy against the negligent manufacturer. If this were the result of the authorities I should consider the result a <u>grave defect</u> in the law, and so contrary to principle that I should <u>hesitate</u> long before following any decision to that effect which had not the authority of this House.* I would point out that, in the assumed state of the authorities, not only would the consumer have no remedy against the manufacturer, he would have none against any one else, for in the circumstances alleged there would be no evidence of negligence against any other than the manufacturer; and, except in the case of a consumer who was also purchaser, no contract and no <u>warranty of fitness</u>, and in the case of the purchase of a specific article under its patent or trade name, which might well be the case in the purchase of some articles of food or drink, no warranty protecting even the purchaser-consumer. There are other instances than of articles of food and drink where goods are sold intended to be used immediately by the consumer, such as many forms of goods sold for cleaning purposes, where the same liability must exist. The doctrine supported by the decision below would not only deny a remedy to the consumer who was injured by consuming bottled beer or chocolates poisoned by the negligence of the manufacturer, but also to the user of what should be a harmless <u>proprietary</u> medicine, an <u>ointment</u>, a soap, a cleaning fluid or cleaning powder. I <u>confine myself</u> to articles of common household use, where everyone, including the manufacturer, knows that the articles will be used by other persons than the actual ultimate purchaser – namely, by members of his family and his servants, and in some cases his guests. I do not <u>think</u> so <u>ill of</u> our jurisprudence as to suppose that its principles are so <u>remote</u> from the <u>ordinary needs</u> of civilized society and the <u>ordinary</u> <u>claims</u> it makes upon its members as to deny a legal remedy where there is so obviously a <u>social wrong</u>.

It will be found, I think, on examination that there is no case in

Zufall

Mangel

Aufmerksamkeit ziehen auf –
betonen

Untersuchung

Zeitablauf/Fristablauf –
aufmerksam machen auf –
entfernt
einschieben – Beschränkung

betrachten

begreifen/vorstellen

Gift

schwer
zögern

Gewährleistung der Eignung

gesetzlich geschützt
Salbe
sich beschränken

schlecht denken über
entfernt
gewöhnliche Bedürfnisse –
gewöhnliche Ansprüche
soziales Fehlverhalten

which the circumstances have been such as I have just <u>suggested</u> where the liability has been <u>negatived</u>. There are numerous cases, where the relations were much more remote, where the duty has been held not to exist ...

My Lords, if your Lordships accept the view that this pleading discloses a relevant cause of action you will be affirming the proposition *that by <u>Scots</u> and English law <u>alike</u> a manufacturer of products, which he sells in such a form as to show that he intends them to reach the ultimate consumer in the form in which they left him with no reasonable possibility of intermediate examination, and with the knowledge that the absence of reasonable care in the preparation or putting up the products will result in an injury to the consumer's life or property, owes a duty to the consumer to take that reasonable care.*

It is a proposition, which I <u>venture</u> to say, no one in Scotland or England who was not a lawyer would for one moment doubt. It will be an advantage to make it clear that the law in this matter, as in most others, is <u>in accordance</u> with <u>sound common sense</u>. I think that this appeal should be <u>allowed</u>.

Lord Macmillan: ... The law takes no <u>cognizance</u> of <u>carelessness</u> in the abstract. It concerns itself with carelessness only where there is a duty to take care and where <u>failure</u> in that duty has caused damage. In such circumstances carelessness <u>assumes</u> the legal quality of negligence and <u>entails</u> the consequences in law of negligence. What, then, are the circumstances which give rise to this duty to take care? In the daily contacts of social and business life human beings are <u>thrown into</u>, or <u>place themselves</u> in, an <u>infinite</u> variety of relations with their <u>fellows</u>; and the law can refer only to the standards of *the reasonable man* in order to determine whether any particular relation gives rise to a duty to take care as between those who stand in that relation to each other.

... To <u>descend</u> from these generalities to the circumstances of the present case, I do not think that *any reasonable man or any twelve reasonable men* would hesitate to hold that, if the appellant establishes her allegations, the respondent has <u>exhibited</u> carelessness in the conduct of his business. For a manufacturer of <u>aerated water</u> to store his empty bottles in a place where snails can get <u>access</u> to them, and to fill his bottles without taking any <u>adequate precautions</u> by inspection or otherwise to ensure that they contain no <u>deleterious</u> foreign matter, may reasonably be characterized as carelessness without applying too exacting a standard. But, as I have pointed out, it is not enough to prove the respondent to be careless in his process of manufacture. *The question is: Does he owe a duty to take care, and to whom does he owe that duty?* Now I have no <u>hesitation</u> in <u>affirming</u> that a person who <u>for gain</u> engages in the business of manufacturing articles of food and drink intended for <u>consumption</u> by members of the public in the form in which he issues them is under a duty to take care <u>in the manufacture</u> of these articles. That duty, in my opinion, he owes to those whom he intends to consume his products. He manufactures his <u>commodities</u> for a container so that the contents cannot be <u>tampered with</u> I regard his control as remaining effective until the article reaches the consumer and the container is opened by him. The intervention of any exterior agency is intended to be excluded, and was in fact in the present case excluded ...

The <u>burden of proof</u> must always be upon the injured party to establish that the defect which caused the injury was present in the article when it left the hands of the party whom he sues, that the defect was occasioned by the carelessness of that party, and that

---

darlegen
verneinen

schottisch – gleichermaßen

wagen

im Einklang – „gesunder Menschenverstand" – stattgeben

Erkenntnis – Nach-, /Fahrlässigkeit

hier: Vernachlässigung
annehmen
nach sich ziehen

hineinwerfen – sich begeben
unendlich – Mitmenschen

übergehen/darauf kommen

zeigen/offenlegen

Sprudelwasser
Zugang
angemessene Vorsichtsmaßnahmen
gesundheitsschädlich

Zögern – bekräftigen/bestätigen
mit Gewinnerzielungsabsicht
Verbrauch

bei der Herstellung

Waren
heimlich öffnen/manipulieren

Beweislast

the circumstances are such as <u>to cast upon</u> the defender a duty to take care not to injure the pursuer. There is no presumption of negligence in such a case as the present, nor is there any justification for applying the maxim *res ipsa loquitur*.[1]
Negligence must be both <u>averred</u> and proved ... This appeal should be allowed.

aufbürden

„die Sache spricht für sich selbst"
behaupten

Lord Thankerton: ... A man cannot be charged with negligence if he has no obligation to exercise <u>diligence</u> ... Unless the consumer can establish a special relationship with the manufacturer, it is clear, in my opinion, that neither the law of Scotland nor the law of England will hold that the manufacturer has any duty towards the consumer to exercise diligence ... But here there was a special relationship because the manufacturer in placing his manufactured article of drink upon the market, has intentionally so excluded <u>interference with</u>, or <u>examination</u> of, the article by any intermediate <u>handler</u> of the goods between himself and the consumer that he has, of his own <u>accord</u>, brought himself into direct relationship with the consumer, with the result that the consumer is entitled to rely upon the exercise of diligence by the manufacturer to secure that the article shall not be <u>harmful</u> to the consumer ... (=Appeal allowed)

Sorgfalt

Einwirkung auf – Untersuchung
hier: am Produktionsvertrieb
Beteiligter – Einverständnis

schadhaft/schädlich

Lord Buckmaster dissented on the ground that there were only two exceptions to the principle that "the breach of the defendant's contract with A to use care and skill in and about the manufacture or repair of an article does not itself give any cause of action to B when he is injured by reason of the article proving to be <u>defective</u>" (*per Lord Sumner* in *Blacker* v *Lake & Elliot Ltd* (1912), namely, where the article was dangerous in itself or had a defect known to the manufacturer. The majority decision was "simply to <u>misapply</u> to tort a doctrine applicable to sale and purchase".

fehlerhaft

falsch anwenden

Lord Tomlin also dissented.

Quotation

Zitat

> There may be in the cup
> A spider steep'd, and one may drink, depart,
> And yet partake no venom, for his knowledge
> It is not infected; but if one present
> The abhorr'd ingredient to his eye, make known
> How he hath drunk, he cracks his gorge, his sides
> With violent hefts. I have drunk, and seen the spider. [2]

(Shakespeare, The Winter's Tale, II.i.37.)

– End of the excerpt from *Tony Weir's* "A casebook on tort" –

---

[1] "The thing speaks for itself"; i.e.: evidence of negligence in the absence of an <u>explanation</u> by the defendant.

Erklärung/Rechtfertigung

[2] *Dazu die Übersetzung von Dorothea Tieck:*

> *Wohl kann sich eine Spinne*
> *Verkriechen in den Becher, und man trinkt;*
> *Man geht, und spürt kein Gift; nicht angesteckt*
> *Ward das Bewusstsein, aber hält uns einer*
> *Die ekelhafte Zutat vor, und sagt uns,*
> *Was wir getrunken, sprengt man Brust und Seiten*
> *Mit heft'gem Würgen: - ich trank und sah die Spinne.*

This decision was a <u>landmark</u> in the evolution of the English law of tort, <u>providing</u> the <u>foundations</u> for a general duty of care in negligence. The "neighbour principle" <u>enunciated</u> by *Lord Atkin* is sometimes <u>equated</u> with <u>proximity</u>, but this does not necessarily mean that the plaintiff must be in a close physical or <u>spatial</u> relationship to the defendant.

Meilenstein
liefern – Grundlage
verkünden/aussprechen
gleichsetzen – Nähe

räumlich

On the other hand, it is essential to note that the <u>extent</u> of a duty of care is limited by the test of *foreseeability of harm*; where the harm could not have been foreseen, it is said to be "too remote".

Ausmaß
Vorhersehbarkeit – Schaden

The "neighbour principle" and "reasonable foreseeability" have been used in many different situations. For instance, a duty of care has been held to be owed to in the following cases:

Example – Grant v Australian Knitting Mills Ltd. (1936) –:

The plaintiff <u>contracted</u> <u>dermatitis</u> through wearing woollen <u>underpants</u> which had been manufactured by the defendants. The <u>disease</u> was caused by <u>invisible excess</u> of <u>sulphites</u> which had been negligently left in the <u>underwear</u> during the manufacturing process. The defendant <u>contended</u> that *Donoghue* v *Stevenson* could be <u>distinguished</u> on the ground that the ginger beer was to be consumed <u>internally</u> whereas the underpants were to be <u>worn</u> <u>externally</u>.
Held: that the defendants were liable. No distinction can be logically drawn between a <u>noxious</u> thing taken internally and a noxious thing applied externally.

hier: sich zuziehen – Hautent-zündung – Unterhose

Krankheit– unsichtbar – Übermaß – schwefel-saures Salz/Sulfit
Unterwäsche
vorbringen
unterscheiden/abweichen von
innerlich
tragen – äußerlich

schädlich/ungesund

Example – Sayers v Harlow <u>Urban District Council</u> (1958) –:

The defendants owned and <u>operated</u> a <u>public lavatory</u>. The plaintiff, having paid for admission, entered a <u>cubicle</u>. Finding that there was no <u>handle</u> on the inside of the door and no means of opening the cubicle, the plaintiff had tried for some 10 to 15 minutes to <u>attract attention</u>. Having

Stadtbezirksrat

betreiben – öffentliche Toilette
Kabine
Griff

auf sich aufmerksam machen

failed to do so, and wishing to catch a bus to London in the next few minutes, she tried to see if there was a way of <u>climbing</u> <u>out</u>. She placed one foot on the seat of the lavatory and rested her other foot on the toilet roll and <u>fixture</u>, holding the <u>pipe</u> from the <u>cistern</u> with one hand and resting the other hand on the top of the door. She then realised it would be impossible to climb out and she <u>proceeded</u> to come down, but as she was doing so, the toilet roll <u>rotated</u> owing to her weight on it and she <u>slipped</u> and injured herself. She sued the defendants for negligence. In the county court, the defendants were found negligent, but, as the plaintiff was in no danger <u>on</u> <u>that account</u>, and as she chose <u>to embark</u> on a dangerous act, she must <u>bear the consequences</u>.

Held (by the Court of Appeal): that her act was not a *novus actus interveniens*[1], and the damage was not too remote as a consequence of the defendant's negligence. She was 36 years of age, and in her <u>predicament</u>, her act was not unreasonable, though if she had been an old lady it might have been. However, the damages recoverable by the plaintiff would be <u>reduced</u> by one-quarter in respect of her <u>share</u> of the responsibility for the damage.

herausklettern

Befestigung – Rohrleitung – Spülkasten

sich anschicken
sich drehen
ausrutschen

in diesem Fall
hier: sich einlassen auf
die Konsequenzen tragen

lat.: „neu eintretende Handlung"

Zwangslage

vermindern
Anteil

Example – Condon v Basi (1985) –:

During a football match, the defendant <u>recklessly</u> <u>tackled</u> the plaintiff, breaking his leg. The defendant was <u>sent off</u> by the referee.

Held: that the defendant was liable in negligence, the <u>foul</u> <u>tackle</u> <u>falling below the standard</u> of care reasonably expected in any match.

rücksichtslos – angreifen

vom Platz verweisen

Faulspiel – unter der Norm/dem Standard liegen

Example – Ogwo v Taylor (1988) –:

O, a fireman, was injured by <u>scalding</u> caused by <u>hose</u> <u>water</u> and flames while <u>fighting a fire</u> in the <u>loft</u> of T's house.

Verbrennung – Spritzwasser
ein Feuer bekämpfen/löschen – Dachboden

---

[1] A <u>fresh</u> <u>act</u> of someone other than the defendant which intervenes between the alleged wrong and the damage in question = *Unterbrechung des Kausalzusammenhanges durch ein dazwischen tretendes Ereignis.*

neue Handlung

Held: T was liable, as his negligence had created a foreseeable risk and there had been no <u>break in the chain of</u> causation.

Unterbrechung der Ursachen-kette/des Kausalzusammen-hanges

Before deciding that a duty of care was owed, a judge will ask himself many questions, for example:

- Was the harm reasonably foreseeable?
- What was the proximity of relationship between the parties?
- Would it be <u>just and reasonable</u> to <u>impose</u> a duty?

gerecht und vernünftig – auferlegen

If the court <u>confirms</u> that the defendant owed a duty to the plaintiff, the action will only succeed, as mentioned already, if there is a breach of this duty and if the plaintiff has <u>proved</u> damage.

bestätigen

beweisen

However, not every type of damage caused by the defendant's <u>negligent act</u> is always <u>recoverable</u>, as one can see from the following cases.

fahrlässige Handlung – erstattungsfähig

bb) Exceptions

(1) <u>Pure economic loss</u>

rein wirtschaftlicher Verlust

Much of the <u>controversy</u> about the extent of the duty of care in the tort of negligence has <u>arisen</u> in cases which have involved the problem of "economic loss". This expression (as stated by *Winfield & Jolowicz*) "<u>is liable to mislead</u>": if a car is <u>destroyed</u>, that is *economic* in the sense that the owner's <u>assets</u> are thereby diminished, but, <u>in legal terms</u>, it is classified as <u>damage to property</u> and the owner is entitled to its value as damages.

Kontroverse/Meinungs-verschiedenheit – entstehen/hervortreten

ist (durchaus) missverständlich zerstören

Vermögen – im Rechtssinne

Sachschaden

Even if the loss is <u>unquestionably</u> only financial <u>in nature, no difficulty is felt about allowing</u> its <u>recovery</u> if it is a consequence of <u>physical injury</u> or <u>damage to</u> the plaintiff's <u>property</u>. As we have learnt in *Donoghue v Stevenson*, the plaintiff could have recovered <u>lost earnings</u> and <u>medical expenses</u>.

fraglos/unzweifelhaft – dem Wesen nach – macht es keine Schwierigkeiten, zu gestatten – Ersatz – Körperverletzung – Sachbeschädigung

Verdienstausfall – Arztkosten

The <u>key principle</u> is that there is a distinction between "pure economic loss" and economic loss which is consequent upon physical damage to person or property. Economic loss which results from physical damage is recoverable.

Grundprinzip

Example – Spartan Steel & Alloys Ltd. v *Martin & Co. (Contractors) Ltd. (1973) –:*

The defendant <u>contractor</u>, in the course of <u>digging up</u> a road, negligently cut a <u>power cable</u>, <u>causing</u> the plaintiff's <u>smelting works</u> to be <u>shut down</u>. At the time of the <u>power cut</u>, there <u>was a "melt" in progress</u> and, to stop the <u>steel solidifying</u>, it had to be drawn out in the <u>furnace</u>. This reduced its value by £368. The plaintiffs claimed the <u>reduction value</u> of the <u>melt</u> and for the profit which would have been made had the process been <u>completed</u>. They also claimed for the loss of profit from four further <u>melts</u> which would have <u>been processed</u> <u>but for</u> the fourteen hour power cut.

Held: that the plaintiffs should recover the reduction in the value of the solidified melt and the profits they would have made from *its* sale. However, they obtained nothing for the loss of profits on the four further melts which could not have been processed before the <u>electricity</u> was <u>restored</u>: that was pure economic loss independent of the <u>physical damage</u>.

hier: Bauunternehmer – aufgraben – Stromkabel – verursachen
Schmelzwerk – stilllegen– Stromunterbrechung – fand ein Schmelzvorgang statt – Stahl fest werden lassen – Schmelzofen

Minderwert – Schmelzmasse beenden

Schmelzvorgänge – ausgeführt werden – ohne

Stromverbindung
wiederhergestellt
Sachschaden

The reason why pure economic loss is not recoverable is that allowing such claims may result in "liability in an <u>indeterminate</u> amount for an indeterminate time to an indeterminate class" [as stated by *Cardozo*, C.J. in *Ultramares Corporation* v *Touche* (1931)].

unbestimmt

(2) Negligent misstatement

fahrlässige Falschauskunft

<u>Formerly</u>, the general rule was that a person was liable for negligent acts but not for negligent <u>statements</u>. Thus in *Candler* v *Crane, Christmas & Co.* (1951), it was held that an <u>accountant</u> who negligently prepared certain <u>accounts</u> for a particular transaction was under no liability in tort in

früher
Äußerung

Buchhalter – Rechnung

respect of those accounts, even though a plaintiff, <u>in reliance on</u> the accounts, invested money in the company and suffered <u>financial loss</u> as a consequence.	im Vertrauen auf finanzieller Verlust
This case was overruled by the following decision (which we have already dealt with[1], in the context of "negligent misrepresentation").	

> *Example – Hedley Byrne & Co. Ltd.* v *Heller & Partners Ltd. (1964) –:*
>
> H.B. contacted A's bankers, H. & P. (the defendants) for references. H. & P. gave a favourable report of A's credit-worthiness. H. & P. <u>headed</u> the document "without responsibility". H.B. acted on the <u>misleading report</u>, gave <u>substantial credit</u> and suffered heavy loss when A went into <u>liquidation</u> shortly afterwards. H.B. sued H. & P. in negligence.
>
> *Held* (by the House of Lords*): that the defendant bankers (H. & P.) would have been liable in negligence if they had not expressly <u>disclaimed</u> liability. "Where in a sphere in which a person <u>is</u> so <u>placed</u> that others could reasonably rely on his judgement or his skill or on his ability to make careful inquiry, a person takes it on himself to give information or advice to, or allows his information or advice <u>to be passed on to</u> another, who, as he knows or should know, will <u>place reliance</u> on it, then a duty of care will arise" (per *Lord Morris*). But if information is given "without responsibility" this duty of care will not arise.

Beside the example box:

- betiteln/ausfertigen
- irreführende Auskunft –
- beträchtlicher Kredit
- Konkurs
- ausschließen
- gestellt sein
- weitergeben
- darauf vertrauen

The <u>*ratio*</u> of *Hedley Byrne* can be summarised[2] as follows:	Urteilsgründe
One can recover the loss caused by negligent misstatement, so long as	
• a special relationship exists (e.g. between solicitor and client)	
• the plaintiff <u>relies on</u> the defendant's <u>skill</u> and knowledge, and	verlassen/vertrauen auf – Geschicklichkeit
• it was reasonable for him to rely on the <u>advice</u>.	Rat(schlag)

---

[1] Cf. vol. 1, p. 181 f.

[2] You can also use the old form: "summarized"

In *Caparo Industries PLC* v *Dickmann* (1990), the House of Lords held that the auditors of a company's accounts did not owe a duty of care in negligence to either a shareholder or a potential shareholder. *Lord Bridge* stated that to be liable, the auditors must know who is relying on the statement and to what use it is being put.

Rechnungs-/Abschlussprüfer – Rechnungslegung

potenziell/möglich

wofür es gebraucht wird

On the other hand, a gratuitous agent might owe a duty of care where the circumstances make it clear that considered advice is being sought.

unentgeltlich tätig werdender Beauftragter – wohlüberlegter Rat
suchen

Our next case is based on this principle.

Example – Chaudry v Prabhakar (1988) –:

The plaintiff asked a friend who had some knowledge of cars, though not a mechanic, to find a suitable car that had not been involved in an accident. The defendant found her a car which he recommended but which was subsequently discovered to have been involved in a serious accident, and was poorly repaired and unroadworthy.

dürftig repariert – nicht verkehrssicher

Held (by the Court of Appeal): that the defendant was liable, but *Stocke*r L.J. stated that: "in the absence of other factors giving rise to such a duty, the giving of advice sought in the context of family, domestic or social relationships will not in itself give rise to any duty in respect of such advice." In such situations there would not be reasonable reliance.

entstehen lassen
innerhalb

Vertrauen

---

(3) Nervous shock

Nervenschock

According to modern authorities on the law of negligence, the term "nervous shock" is understood to refer to recognisable psychiatric illness, or as recognisable and severe physical damage to the human body and system. This psychiatric or physical harm might be caused by a sudden appreciation, by sight or sound, of a horrifying event. To be recoverable, the damage must not just have been

erkennbar – psychische Krankheit – körperlicher Schaden
verursachen
Erkennen – Sehen – Hören – schreckliches Ereignis

reasonably foreseeable, but the plaintiff must be a <u>close relative</u> of the <u>victim</u>, an <u>unwilling</u> participant in the event or a passive, unwilling <u>witness</u>, and <u>be proximate in both time and space</u>.

naher Verwandter
Opfer – unfreiwillig
Zeuge – in zeitlicher und räumlicher Nähe stehen

In this context, the decision in *McLoughlin* v *O'Brian* (1983) should be considered carefully. A mother visited a hospital to see her husband and her daughters, who had been injured in a serious <u>road accident</u>, which happened two hours before. As a result of what she saw combined with the horrific news of the death of one of her daughters, she <u>suffered</u> severe nervous shock. The House of Lords held that, although distance and time were factors to be considered, they were *not* <u>legal restrictions</u>. The plaintiff was entitled to damages for nervous shock, even though she was not present at the accident, because it was a reasonably foreseeable consequence of the defendant's negligence.

Verkehrsunfall

erleiden

rechtliches Hindernis

But foreseeability of nervous shock alone is not enough. In addition to reasonable foreseeability the following factors must be considered: the relationship between the <u>primary victim</u> and the plaintiff, the proximity of the plaintiff in time and space to the scene of the accident and the means by which the shock is caused. This so-called "<u>aftermath test</u>" was <u>adopted</u> by *Lord Wilberforce* in the *McLoughlin* case and <u>applied</u> in the following case.

Hauptopfer

Nachwirkungstest
beschließen
anwenden

> *Example* – *Alcock* v <u>*Chief Constable of South Yorkshire*</u> *(1992) –:*
>
> Actions for nervous shock were brought against the police <u>arising from</u> the Hillsborough football stadium <u>disaster</u>. 95 people were <u>crushed</u> to death in the tragedy which was shown in a live television broadcast. Claims were brought by relatives and friends of the victims who had suffered psychiatric illness as a result of their experiences. A number of them had been in other parts of the stadium from where they had witnessed the events and others had

Polizeipräsident

entstehen aus – Unglück/
Katastrophe – zerquetschen

seen the disaster live on television. Some of the plaintiffs had identified bodies at the <u>mortuary</u> and others suffered solely from being told the news. The plaintiffs based their claim on the argument that <u>the sole test</u> for a duty in nervous shock was reasonable foreseeability.

Held: that this argument was <u>to be rejected</u> and the plaintiffs' actions were therefore dismissed. Only those people who were close relatives and who were temporally and <u>spatially</u> close to the accident or its <u>immediate aftermath</u> can claim for nervous shock.

Leichenhalle

das einzige Kriterium

zurückweisen

räumlich – unmittelbare Nachwirkung

b) Breach of duty

Defendants will be in breach of duty if they have acted negligently, which means that they have not acted in a reasonable way but <u>carelessly</u>. So the question arising is how a "reasonable man" would have acted in the defendant's position. According to *Baron Alderson* [in *Blyth* v *Birmingham Waterworks Co.* (1856)], *"negligence is the <u>omission</u> to do something which a reasonable man, <u>guided upon</u> those <u>considerations</u> which <u>ordinarily regulate</u> the <u>conduct of human affairs</u>, would do, or doing something which a <u>prudent</u> and reasonable man would not do."*

nachlässig/unsorgfältig

Unterlassung – von Überlegungen geleitet werden – normalerweise regeln Verhalten in menschlichen Angelegenheiten – vorsichtig/klug

The standard of a reasonable man, of course, <u>varies</u> with each individual situation but, as a general rule, the standard is that of a person who uses <u>ordinary care</u> and skill. In other words: all our actions are compared to those of an ordinary reasonable man, who is neither careless nor <u>overly careful</u>.

What is <u>appropriate</u> will depend on the circumstances of each particular case. What to one judge may <u>seem far fetched</u> may seem to another natural and probable [as stated by *Lord Macmillan* in *Glasgow Corporation* v *Muir* (1943)].

sich ändern

gewöhnliche Sorgfalt

übertrieben sorgfältig

geeignet/angemessen

als weit hergeholt betrachten

A duty of care is owed to each person individually, and consequently, a breach of duty and taking the <u>precautions</u>

Vorsichtsmaßnahmen

41

necessary to avoid the risk of <u>doing harm</u> to another person are to be differentiated between in each case. How this is done by the courts will be illustrated by the following examples.

Schaden zufügen

Example – Paris v *Stepney <u>Borough Council</u> (1951) –:*

Gemeinde

The defendants knew that the plaintiff was blind in one eye. He was working in conditions which involved some risk of eye injury but the <u>likelihood</u> of this injury was not sufficient <u>to call upon</u> the defendants to provide <u>goggles</u> to a normal two-eyed workman. The plaintiff was <u>rendered</u> totally blind when a chip of metal entered his good eye.

Wahrscheinlichkeit
veranlassen – Schutzbrille
machen

Held: that the duty of employers was owed to each particular employee and they were negligent in failing to provide goggles to the plaintiff. In this case, the risk to a two-eyed workman was the loss of one eye but the plaintiff risked the much greater injury of total blindness.

This decision <u>reveals</u> that the obligations of a potential defendant may <u>increase</u> where the risk to a plaintiff is greater than normal.

aufzeigen
steigen/wachsen

Example – Carmarthenshire <u>County Council</u> v Lewis (1955) –:

Kreisrat

A <u>mistress</u> <u>in charge</u> of the appellants' <u>nursery school</u> was about to take David, who was about three and three-quarter years of age, and, a little girl out for a walk, but she left the classroom briefly and during the time that she was away, about ten minutes, she visited the lavatory and <u>attended</u> to a child who had fallen down and cut himself. When she returned, she found that David had left the classroom and made his way out of the school playground through an <u>unlocked</u> <u>gate</u> and down a <u>lane</u> into a busy highway where he caused a <u>lorry</u> <u>to swerve</u> so that it <u>struck</u> a telegraph pole. The driver of the lorry was killed and his widow, the respondent, brought an action in damages for negligence.

Lehrerin – beschäftigt bei – Kindergarten

sich kümmern um

unverschlossen – Tor – Fahrspur
Lkw – ausweichen
aufprallen

Held: that although the mistress had not been negligent,

the respondent should succeed, as the appellants had failed to give any explanation that would <u>discharge</u> the <u>presumption</u> <u>of negligence</u> that arose from the escape of the child on to the road, and such an accident as happened should have been in the <u>contemplation</u> of any reasonable person. It was not necessary that the precise result should have been foreseen.

widerlegen/entlasten
Fahrlässigkeitsvermutung
Erwägung

In this case, the County Council had been negligent in <u>allowing</u> a situation <u>to arise</u> where the child had the possibility to leave the school building.

zulassen – entstehen

Example – Bolam v *Friern <u>Hospital Management Committee</u> (1957) –:*

Krankenhausverwaltung

The plaintiff agreed <u>to undergo</u> <u>electro-convulsive therapy</u> (E.C.T.) during which he suffered a <u>fracture to the pelvis</u>. The <u>issue</u> was whether the doctor was negligent in failing to give a <u>relaxant drug</u> before the treatment, or in failing to provide <u>means of restraint</u> during the procedure. Evidence was given of the practices of various doctors in the use of relaxant drugs before E.C.T. treatment. One <u>body</u> of medical opinion favoured the use of relaxant drugs but another body of opinion took the view that they should not be used because of the risk of fractures.

Held: that the action failed. A defendant is not negligent if he acts in accordance with the practice accepted at the time as proper by a responsible body of professional opinion skilled in a particular form of treatment.

sich unterziehen –
Elektroschocktherapie
Beckenbruch
Entscheidung
Entspannungsmedikament
Sicherungsmaßnahmen

hier: Gruppe

From this specialized medical case, one can see that the appropriate test for judging the acceptable standard of professional behaviour is not that of the ordinary man: the defendant is judged by the standard of the ordinary <u>skilled</u> person exercising and <u>professing</u> to have that special skill. Thus: a <u>doctor</u> must show the skill of a reasonably competent doctor, a <u>surgeon</u> must show the skill of reasonably competent surgeon, etc.

geschickt/erfahren
fachlich ausgebildet sein
praktischer Arzt
Chirurg

Example – Ashton v *Turner and Another (1980)–:*

After spending the evening together drinking heavily, the plaintiff persuaded his friend to join him in a <u>burglary</u>. They were disturbed and <u>chased</u>; their car crashed at high speed and the plaintiff – the passenger – sustained serious injuries. The friend was <u>convicted</u> of burglary, dangerous driving and driving with more than the permitted amount of alcohol in his blood and the plaintiff sued him, *inter alia,* in negligence.

Held: that, as a matter of <u>public policy</u>, the law would, in certain circumstances, refuse to recognise the existence of a duty of care owed by one participant in a crime to another participant in the same crime in respect of an act done in connection with the commission of that crime and this was such a case. In any case, the maxim *volenti non fit injuria* applied and <u>afforded</u> the friend a complete defence.

„Einbruchdiebstahl"
jagen

verurteilen

lat.: unter anderem

Grundprinzipien von Recht und Ordnung

lat.: „wer in eine Gesetzes-verletzung einwilligt, wird vom Gesetz nicht geschützt" [1] – er-lauben

---

Example – Hill v *Chief Constable of West Yorkshire (1988) –:*

The plaintiff was the mother of the last victim of a <u>serial murderer</u>, the "Yorkshire Ripper". She claimed damages on the basis that the police had negligently failed <u>to apprehend</u> the murderer before her daughter was killed.

Held: that <u>notwithstanding that</u> harm was reasonably foreseeable, there was <u>insufficient</u> proximity between the police and the victim. The House of Lords <u>further</u> stated that a general duty of care to protect all members of the public from the consequences of crime would be <u>impracticable</u> and, on grounds of public policy, <u>deeply damaging</u> to police operations[2].

Serienmörder

verhaften

ungeachtet dessen, dass
unzureichend
weiterhin

nicht durchführbar – äußerst schädlich

Whereas in the *McLoughlin case* (see above p. 40) the consideration of public policy led to liability of the

---

[1] *Vgl. auch: „Mitgegangen, mitgefangen, mitgehangen"... (Simrock, Die deutschen Sprichwörter, Reclam-Nachdruck 1995, Nr. 7044)*

[2] After the judgment of the European Court of Human Rights in *Osman* (1998) and of the House of Lords in *Barret* v *Enfield LBC* (1999), this decision can no longer be considered good law!

defendant without the generally required proximity, in this case public policy is <u>capable</u> of constituting a separate and independent ground <u>for holding</u> that liability in negligence should not be <u>imposed</u>.

fähig

zu entscheiden

auferlegen

Example – Kirkham v *Chief Constable of the Greater Manchester Police (1990) –:*

The <u>deceased</u>, the plaintiff's husband, while suffering from <u>clinical depression</u>, had been arrested and charged with an <u>offence</u>. The plaintiff told the police that her husband was a <u>suicide risk</u> but, after he had been <u>remanded in custody</u>, the police failed <u>to follow the procedure</u> for <u>notifying</u> the prison authorities that he had <u>suicidal</u> tendencies. At the <u>remand</u> centre, the deceased was treated like a normal prisoner and he committed suicide there. The plaintiff claimed damages for negligence.

Held: that her action would be successful as the police, by failing <u>to pass on</u> relevant information, had been in breach of their duty of care. The defence of *volenti non fit injuria* failed because, in the light of the deceased's mental condition, his suicide had not been a truly <u>voluntary act</u>. The maxim *ex turpi causa non oritur actio* [1] did not apply as suicide is no longer an <u>affront</u> to the <u>public conscience</u>.

Verstorbener

klinische Depression

Vergehen – Selbstmordrisiko

Haftfortdauer ankündigen

der Gepflogenheit nachgehen – benachrichtigen – selbstmörderisch – Haftanstalt

weitergeben

freiwillige Handlung

lat.: siehe Fußnote!

Affront/Beleidigung – allgemeines Rechtsempfinden

In this case, the *volenti* and *ex turpi* rules were not <u>applicable</u> because, though not legally insane, Kirkham was clinically depressed and of <u>diminished responsibility</u>.

anwendbar

verminderte Schuldfähigkeit

Example – White v *Jones (1995) –:*

The plaintiffs were <u>disinherited</u> by their father in his will after a family <u>row</u> in 1986. Six months later, a <u>reconciliation</u> took place and, in July 1986, the father gave his solicitors (the defendants) instructions to <u>draw up a new will</u> giving his

enterben

Streit – Versöhnung

ein neues Testament aufsetzen

---

[1] No action can be brought where the parties are guilty of illegal or immoral conduct = *Wer sich selbst ungesetzlich oder unmoralisch verhält, hat keinen Grund zu klagen.*

daughters £9,000 each. The solicitors <u>delayed</u> <u>carrying out</u> the father's request and, after a month, he renewed his instructions. The solicitors had still failed to act <u>by the time</u> the father, who was 78, died in September 1986.
Held: a remedy under the *Hedley Byrne* principle was <u>extended</u> to such a situation and the sisters were entitled to recover damages from the defendants for negligence.

sich verspäten – ausführen

währenddessen

ausweiten

This decision, concerning professional persons (as the defendants) – cf. above *Bolam* v *Friern Hospital...*, p. 43 – shows that a solicitor owes a duty of care to a disappointed <u>beneficiary</u>.

Begünstigter

A professional like a solicitor, according to the House of Lords, has to "act with <u>due expedition</u> and care" on behalf of his clients. In other words, the principle of this case is: reliance on a statement of promise by the plaintiff is not essential to establish a duty of care; the <u>assumption</u> of responsibility by a solicitor towards a client extends to the <u>intended</u> beneficiary.

angemessene Eile

Vermutung
beabsichtigt

c) Damage suffered as the result of negligence

aa) The "<u>but-for</u>" rule

ohne

Although a plaintiff must prove damages, not all damages are recoverable if they are too remote. The courts always have to decide whether the breach of duty was the <u>cause,</u> or a *material* cause of the damage. This decision is generally based on the so-called "*but-for*" test, which means: "If the damage would not have happened *but for* a particular fault, then that fault is the cause of the damage (cf. above *Spartan Steel...*v *Martin,* p. 37). If it would have happened all the same, fault or no fault, the fault is not the cause of the damage" [*Lord Denning* in *Cork* v *Kirby MacLean Ltd.*(1952)].

Ursache
wesentlich

bb) Foreseeability

Moreover, a defendant is only liable for damage which a reasonable man could have foreseen.

Example – The "Wagon Mound"; Overseas Tankship (UK) Ltd. v Morts Dock & Engineering Co. (1961) –:

Owing to the carelessness of the defendants, a large quantity of <u>fuel oil</u> was <u>discharged</u> from their ship into Sydney Harbour. The oil was carried by wind and <u>tide</u> to the plaintiff's <u>wharf</u> about 600 feet away, where <u>welding</u> on another ship was being <u>carried out</u>. After <u>making enquiries</u>, the plaintiffs were advised that it was safe to continue with the welding operations on their wharf. Two days later, the oil caught fire and the wharf and the ships being repaired were damaged in the <u>blaze</u>. The oil also <u>congealed</u> on the <u>slipways</u> and <u>interfered with</u> the plaintiffs' use of the <u>slips</u>. Because there was a breach of duty and direct damage, at <u>trial</u> and at appeal judgement was given for the plaintiff.

Held (by the Privy Council): that that decision was to be <u>reversed</u>. The fact that some of the damage suffered (the damage to the slipways) was foreseeable did not make the defendants liable for the fire damage which was unforeseeable. The test for <u>remoteness of damage</u> was whether the kind of damage sustained was reasonably foreseeable.

(Schiffsname)

Heizöl – auslaufen
fließen/fluten
Werft – Schweissarbeit
durchführen – Auskünfte einholen

loderndes Feuer
gerinnen – Helling[1] – stören
ebenfalls: Helling
Hauptverfahren

aufheben

Entfernungsgrad des Folgeschadens

This famous leading case establishes the test for liability in negligence and is based, *inter alia*, on the reasonable foreseeability of the damage happening as a result of the negligent act. As the <u>then</u> Lord Chancellor *Viscount Simmonds* put it: "After the event even a <u>fool</u> is <u>wise</u>. But it is not the <u>hindsight</u> of a fool, it is the <u>foresight</u> of the reasonable man which alone <u>determines</u> responsibility".

damalig(er)
Narr/Dummkopf – klug
nachträgliche Einsicht – Weitblick/Voraussicht – bestimmen

---

[1] „Helling" ist eine Vorrichtung im Hafen, um Schiffe vom Stapel laufen zu lassen.

Having read that *"The Wagon Mound"* case was decided by the *Privy Council*, you may have possibly remembered, considering "the doctrine of precedent", that the decisions of the Judicial Committee of the Privy Council are not binding, but only of <u>persuasive</u> <u>authority</u> in English courts.

einschlägige (nicht bindende) Vorentscheidung

Notwithstanding this, the new rule <u>propounded</u> in this case has been followed in important cases, for instance by the House of Lords in *Hughes* v *Lord Advocate* (1963) and by the Court of Appeal in the following case:

vorschlagen/anbieten

Example – Doughty v *Turner Manufacturing Co. Ltd. (1964) –:*
D was employed by the T.M. Co. A fellow employee of D let <u>slip</u> into a <u>cauldron</u> of <u>molten metal</u> an <u>asbestos cement cover</u>. At that time, it was unknown that asbestos cement coming into contact with the molten metal would cause an explosion. An explosion resulted and D was injured. No similar accident had been known to occur previously.   *Held*: that the accident (though a direct result of the action of the defendant's <u>servant</u>) was not reasonably foreseeable and, therefore, the defendants were not liable.

entgleiten – großer Kessel – geschmolzenes Metall – Asbestzementplatte

Angestellter

cc) <u>Causation</u> by the defendant's act

Verursachung

In this context, it is repeated and must be stressed that the plaintiff must suffer and prove damage caused by a negligent act of the defendant which injured the plaintiff himself or his property.

Example – Wilsher v *Essex Area Health Authority (1988) –:*
When the infant plaintiff was <u>born prematurely</u> he was suffering from various illnesses. In the defendant's baby <u>unit</u> he was given <u>excess</u> <u>oxygen</u> and it was later

zu früh geboren

Station – übermäßig – Sauerstoff

discovered that he had an <u>incurable</u> condition of the <u>retina</u>. This condition could have been caused by excess oxygen; it also occurred in <u>premature babies</u> suffering from the plaintiff's illnesses. During the plaintiff's action for negligence, the medical evidence was <u>inconclusive</u> as to the true cause of the plaintiff's condition.

Held: that here should be a new trial as (contrary to the view of the courts below) the plaintiff had not discharged the burden of proving the <u>causative link</u> between the defendants' negligence and his injury.

unheilbar – Netzhaut

Frühgeburt

unschlüssig

Kausalzusammenhang

The plaintiff's claim failed because he could not prove that the hospital's negligence was the *material* cause of the damage to his <u>eyesight</u>.

Augenlicht

dd) <u>Res ipsa loquitur</u> [1]

lat.: Anscheinsbeweis

The general rule of the law of torts is that a plaintiff must prove that the defendant has been negligent. This <u>proof</u> is <u>furnished</u> if the plaintiff <u>demonstrates</u> that it was more <u>likely</u> than not that the damage was caused by the defendant's negligence.

Beweis erbringen
nachweisen – wahrscheinlich

In cases, however, where the act or omission <u>obviously</u> <u>indicates</u> negligence, the <u>burden of proof</u> <u>moves</u> to the defendant, who must show that, in fact, he was not negligent.

The *"res ipsa loquitur"* rule has been applied, for instance, where

(1) <u>bags</u> of sugar fell on the plaintiff from an <u>upper floor</u> of the defendant's warehouse. As sugar bags do not normally fall from the sky, negligence of the defendant was indicated [*Scott* v *London & St. Katherine's Dock Co. (1865)*].

(2) <u>swabs</u> were left in a patient's body after an operation [*Mahone* v *Osborne (1939)*].

offensichtlich
anzeigen/indizieren –
Beweislast – sich verlagern

Sack – oberes Stockwerk

Wattebausch/Tupfer

---

[1] Cf. above p. 33, footnote 1.

(3) a customer <u>slipped</u> on yoghurt which had been <u>spilled</u> on the floor of a supermarket [*Ward* v *Tesco Stores Ltd. (1976)*].

ausrutschen – verschütten

ee) <u>*Multiple*</u> *causation of damage*

mehrfach(e)

Where there has been a problem of multiple causation, the courts have <u>taken different views</u>.

verschiedene Ansichten vertreten – schießen auf

If, for instance, A and B shoot C at the same time and the double injury results in C's death, the "*but-for*" rule leads to the result that neither shot is the substantial cause of C's death. Where, however, two independent events cause the damage, and the second defendant's act produces the same damage as that caused by the first defendant, the first event should <u>be treated as</u> the cause.

angesehen werden als

Example – *Baker* v *Willoughby (1970)* –:

In a road accident caused by the defendant's negligence, the plaintiff suffered an injury to his left leg. Before the trial of his negligence action, the plaintiff was the victim of an <u>armed robbery</u> at his place of work. He suffered <u>gunshot</u> <u>wounds</u> to his left leg and, as a result of his injuries, his leg had to be amputated. The defendant admitted negligence but argued that his responsibility ended when the plaintiff was shot and, therefore, all losses from the date of the shooting <u>flowed from</u> the robbery.
Held: that the defendant's argument was to be <u>rejected</u> on the ground that it produced a manifest injustice and that he remained liable for the full extent of the plaintiff's damage.

bewaffneter Überfall – Schuss-verletzung

herrühren von

zurückweisen

Thus, the second event was not considered by the court as a *novus actus interveniens*.

In a later case, however, it was held that if the second event had <u>occurred</u> naturally and had been <u>unconnected</u> with the first event, it may be unfair to make the defendant responsible for that second event also.

passieren – ohne Zusammenhang

50

> *Example – Jobling v Associated Dairies Ltd. (1981) –:*
>
> In 1973, in the course of his employment and as a result of his employers' negligence, a man suffered a slipped disc; his earning capacity was reduced by 50 per cent. Nearly four years later he was found to be suffering from a spinal disease, unrelated to his accident, and by the time (1979) that his claim came to trial, this disease had rendered him totally incapable of any work.
>
> *Held:* that the employers' liability was limited to loss of earnings up to the time when the disease resulted in total incapacity.

bei Verrichtung seiner Arbeit
Arbeitgeber – ausgerenkte Gelenkscheibe
Prozent
Rückenleiden
ohne Bezug

Verdienstausfall

d) Contributory negligence as a defence

mitwirkende Fahrlässigkeit (Mitverschulden) – Verteidigungsmittel

The defendant's liability for damages will be reduced if he can show that the plaintiff did not, in his own interest, take reasonable care of himself and therefore contributed to his own injury.

According to *The Law Reform (Contributory Negligence) Act 1945* [s1(1)] the amount recoverable is reduced "to such an extent as the court thinks just and equitable having regard to the claimant's share in the responsibility for the damage."

In practice, the court usually awards damages and then reduces the award by the percentage for which the plaintiff is deemed to be responsible.

Betrag
halten für
Kläger – Anteil
zusprechen
hier: Schadensersatzsumme – Prozentsatz – halten für

Usually the maximum reduction is 25 per cent when injuries could have been avoided if the plaintiff had taken due care.

As we have seen already (cf. above, p. 34) in *Sayers* v *Harlow UDC* (1958), the woman who was trapped in a toilet was held to be contributorily negligent by stepping on a toilet-roll holder when trying to escape.

Contributory negligence is often considered in road traffic accidents.

vermeiden – pflichtgemäße Sorgfalt

gefangen

> *Example – Capps v Miller (1989) –:*
>
> The plaintiff, a motor-cyclist, suffered head injuries as a result of the defendant's negligent driving. The plaintiff's <u>crash helmet</u>, which was <u>unfastened</u>, fell off before his head hit the road.
>
> *Held* (by the Court of Appeal): that although the sole responsibility for the accident lay with the defendant, the plaintiff´s failure to secure his helmet had contributed to the injury.

Schutzhelm – unbefestigt

In this context, it is important to note that <u>a distinction is drawn</u>, in law, between <u>blame</u> for an accident itself and blame for the injuries that result from that accident. In this case, Miller was 100% <u>to blame</u> for the collision between his car and Capps' moped but held to be only 90% to blame for the injuries sustained by Capps. The court further considered that the reduction would have been greater if a helmet had not been <u>worn</u> at all.

eine Unterscheidung machen
Schuld

verschulden

getragen

A child is generally never found guilty of contributory negligence.

e) The <u>Occupiers'</u> Liability Acts

(Grundstücks)besitzer

A <u>particular sector</u> of liability in negligence is codified. It is the occupier's liability to visitors who injure themselves or damage their property while staying on the occupier's <u>premises</u>.

The *Occupiers' Liability Act 1957* provides [s2(1)] that the occupier of premises, or the landlord, if responsible for repairs to the premises, has a common law duty of care to see that all <u>lawful</u> visitors will be reasonably safe when using the premises.

Lawful visitors are all people with <u>express or implied</u> permission to enter the property, for example a guest, the postman, the milkman or the <u>paper-boy</u>. Thus, lawful visitors are "neighbours" in the sense of the "neighbour-principle" stated by *Lord Atkin* in *Donoghue v Stevenson* (cf.

Teilbereich

Räumlichkeiten/Gebäude

rechtmäßig

ausdrücklich oder stillschweigend

Zeitungsjunge

p. 28 f.). To these visitors the occupier owes a general and personal duty of care.

Unlawful visitors, such as <u>burglars</u> for instance, are <u>trespassers</u> to whom the occupier does not owe the full duty of care. For these trespassers the *Occupiers' Liability Act 1984* provides limited protection. A general duty of care is nevertheless owed by the occupier if:

 Einbrecher
 Besitzstörer/Rechtsverletzer

(1) he is aware of the danger or has reasonable grounds to believe that it exists (e.g. <u>gun traps</u>),

 Selbstschussanlage

(2) he knows or has reasonable grounds to believe that there are others in the <u>vicinity</u> of the danger, or who may come into the vicinity, and

 Nähe

(3) the risk is such that he may reasonably be expected to offer the other persons some protection.

The occupier is discharged from liability if he has put up a clear warning sign (unless the trespasser is a young child). Moreover the general defence to negligence *volenti non fit iniuria* (cf. above, p. 44) is also included in the 1984 Act [s1(6)].

Diagram 40

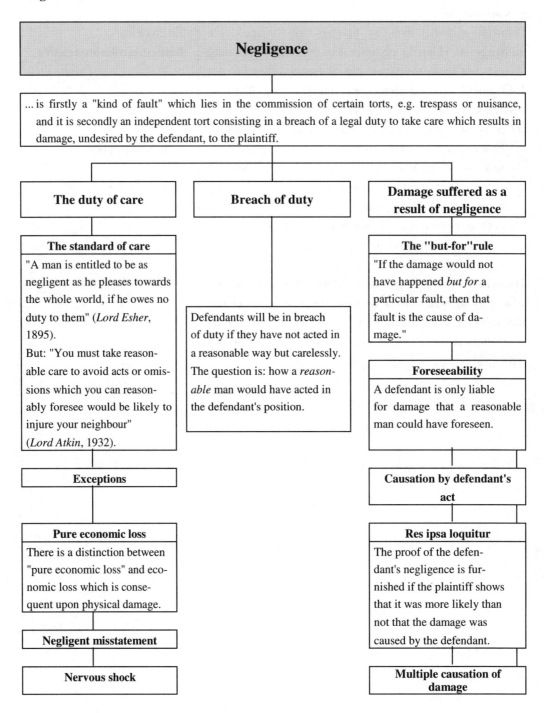

Negligence

... is firstly a "kind of fault" which lies in the commission of certain torts, e.g. trespass or nuisance, and it is secondly an independent tort consisting in a breach of a legal duty to take care which results in damage, undesired by the defendant, to the plaintiff.

The duty of care

Breach of duty

Damage suffered as a result of negligence

The standard of care

"A man is entitled to be as negligent as he pleases towards the whole world, if he owes no duty to them" (*Lord Esher*, 1895).
But: "You must take reasonable care to avoid acts or omissions which you can reasonably foresee would be likely to injure your neighbour" (*Lord Atkin*, 1932).

Defendants will be in breach of duty if they have not acted in a reasonable way but carelessly. The question is: how a *reasonable* man would have acted in the defendant's position.

The "but-for"rule

"If the damage would not have happened *but for* a particular fault, then that fault is the cause of damage."

Foreseeability

A defendant is only liable for damage that a reasonable man could have foreseen.

Exceptions

Causation by defendant's act

Pure economic loss

There is a distinction between "pure economic loss" and economic loss which is consequent upon physical damage.

Res ipsa loquitur

The proof of the defendant's negligence is furnished if the plaintiff shows that it was more likely than not that the damage was caused by the defendant.

Negligent misstatement

Nervous shock

Multiple causation of damage

V. Defamation

Diffamierung/Ehrverletzung/ Verleumdung

1. Definition and meaning

Defamation may be defined as the publication of a statement which reflects badly on a person's reputation and tends to lower him in the estimation of right-thinking members of society generally. Although one of the fundamental human rights is freedom of speech, the tort of defamation protects an individual's private interest in his reputation. For defamation to be actionable, two preconditions are necessary:

Veröffentlichung
ein schlechtes Licht werfen auf – Ruf/Leumund – herabsetzen – Achtung – rechtschaffen denkend
Redefreiheit

(1) The statement must be published to a third party, which means that there is no defamation if the statement is only published to the plaintiff. It would be defamation, however, if a third party heard the defamatory words, even by accident. Postcards can easily be read by other people. Thus, they are deemed to be published, even if the postman (or people other than the recipient) has not actually read them.

diffamierend
zufällig
als veröffentlicht gelten

(2) "Would the words tend to lower the plaintiff in the estimation of right-thinking members of society generally?" This was the question put by *Lord Atkin* in the following case.

Example – Sim v Stretch (1936) –:

When Edith Saville, a maid who had left the plaintiff's employment, went to work for the defendant, he sent a telegram to the plaintiff saying: "Edith has resumed service with us today. Please send her possessions and the money you borrowed also her wages to Old Barton. Sim." The plaintiff alleged that the telegram suggested that he was in pecuniary difficulties and had had to borrow money from his housemaid.

wiederaufnehmen

geliehen – Lohn

in Geldschwierigkeiten

Held: that the words in question were not reasonably capable of a defamatory meaning.

In defamation, the test of what "right-thinking" members of society think appears to be determined by what they *should* think <u>rather than</u> what in fact they *do* think.

eher als

Example – Byrne v Deane (1937) –:

A golf club had some <u>gambling machines</u> unlawfully kept in the club house. These were removed by police after somebody had informed them of their illegal presence. Soon after this, a <u>verse</u> appeared on the notice board of the club which ended with the lines: "But he who gave the game away, may he <u>byrne</u>[1] <u>in hell</u> and <u>rue the day</u>." The plaintiff brought an action for <u>libel</u>, alleging that by these words the defendants meant that he was guilty of <u>underhand</u> <u>disloyalty</u> to his fellow members.

Held: that the plaintiff's claim failed. It could not be defamatory to "allege of a man ... that he has reported certain acts, wrongful in law, to the police ..."

Glücksspielmaschinen

Vers/Reim

in der Hölle verbrennen (to burn) – den Tag verwünschen – schriftliche Ehrverletzung

heimlich – Untreue/ verräterische Haltung

So Byrne's action was <u>dismissed</u> because right-thinking members of society would have <u>approved of</u> a person informing the police of an illegal practice.

abweisen
zustimmen

The defendant's statement must be shown to be <u>referring</u> to the plaintiff, but need not be a specific reference. The test is to ask whether ordinary sensible observers would believe that the plaintiff was being referred to.

sich beziehen auf

Example – Morgan v Odhams Press Ltd. (1971) –:

The newspaper, *The Sun*, alleged that a girl had been kidnapped by a <u>dog doping</u> <u>gang</u> because she was <u>threatening</u> to inform the police of their activities. At the relevant time the girl had been staying at the plaintiff's flat and the plaintiff produced six witnesses who swore

Hunde einschläfern – Bande
drohen

---

[1] The English pronunciation of the name Byrne is the same as that one of the verb "to burn", which means „*(ver)brennen*".

56

that they understood from the article that he was connected with the gang.

Held: that the story was capable of a defamatory meaning. There was no rule that the article should contain some kind of key to indicate the plaintiff, the question was whether readers who knew of the circumstances would reasonably have understood the article as referring to the plaintiff.

The tort of defamation does not require an intention of the defendant to refer to the plaintiff with his statement.

Example – Hulton & Co. v Jones (1910) –:

The *Sunday Chronicle*, which was owned by the appellants, published an article in which appeared statements defamatory of a person described as 'Artemus Jones', a churchwarden at Peckham. The writer of the article and the editor of the paper both believed 'Artemus Jones' to be a purely fictitious personage. A barrister, the respondent, who was not a churchwarden and did not live in Peckham, happened to have the same name as the imaginary churchwarden and brought an action for libel. He admitted that neither the author, the editor nor the appellants intended to defame him, but succeeded in showing that some of his friends thought that he was the subject of the article.

Held: that the respondent was entitled to damages as it was no defence for the appellants to contend that the defamation was unintentional.

Kirchenvorsteher

fiktiv

imaginär – schriftliche Beleidigung

geltend machen

Cases like this may today make use of the defence of "unintentional defamation" under s4 of the *Defamation Act 1952*. The defendant is not liable of damages if he was not aware that his statement could have a defamatory character and if he acted with reasonable care in publishing the statement. Moreover, he must be ready to publish a rectification combined with an apology.

unabsichtlich

Richtigstellung – Entschuldigung

2. Innuendo

A statement may be defamatory <u>by implication</u>, even though the words are not defamatory in their ordinary sense, if it can be shown that another person's reputation has been <u>affected</u>. It is sufficient if the statement was understood by others to have a defamatory meaning.

> *Example – Cassidy* v *Daily Mirror Newspapers Ltd. (1929) –:*
>
> The defendants published a photograph of Mr Cassidy with a woman, below which was an announcement of their <u>engagement</u>. The information on which the defendants based their statement came from Mr Cassidy alone and they had made no effort <u>to verify</u> it from any other source. Mr Cassidy was already married, although he lived apart from his wife. However, he did occasionally stay with his wife at her flat. She brought an action in libel claiming that readers who knew her as Mr Cassidy's wife would <u>assume</u> that she had been <u>lying</u> about being married to him.
> *Held:* that the defendants were liable. The story would be understood by others as referring to the plaintiff and the newspaper's <u>complete ignorance</u> of the circumstances could not prevent the statement from having a defamatory meaning.

It is furthermore defamation if the plaintiff relies on an innuendo where the words are not defamatory in their natural and ordinary meaning but may be defamatory when combined with <u>extrinsic</u> facts known to others about the situation.

> *Example – Tolley* v *J.S. Fry & Sons Ltd. (1931) –:*
>
> The plaintiff was a leading amateur golfer. Without his knowledge or consent, the defendants issued an advertisement showing the plaintiff playing golf with a packet of their chocolate <u>protruding</u> from his pocket. A

versteckte Andeutung/
beleidigende Unterstellung

stillschweigend

beeinträchtigen/beeinflussen

Verlobung

bestätigen lassen

vermuten
lügen

völlige Unkenntnis

äußerlich

herausragen

caddy was depicted as saying in a limerick that the chocolate advertised was as excellent as the plaintiff's drive. The plaintiff brought an action for libel and alleged that the advertisement meant that the plaintiff had, for gain and reward, agreed to its publication, and thereby prostituted his reputation as an amateur golf player.
Held: the plaintiff would succeed as the advertisement was capable of bearing the meaning alleged in the innuendo.

Schlägerträger beim Golf – abbilden/zeichnen – Limerick[1]

Treibschlag beim Golf

mit Gewinnerzielungsabsicht

Entlohnung

preisgeben/verkaufen

stützen

3. Libel and slander

schriftliche Beleidigung – mündliche Ehrverletzung

The tort of defamation is divided into two categories, libel and slander.

a) Libel

A libel is a defamatory statement which is published in some permanent form. The usual form is writing or printing. It also can be broadcasted on radio or television, or it could be in painting or as a cartoon, or on record, as an audio tape, CD or in the Internet.

senden

Karikatur (gezeichnet)

The action for libel is an action *per se*, which means that the plaintiff does not have to prove specific damages.

Anspruch eigener Art

b) Slander

Slander is the publication of a defamatory statement in a non-permanent form, usually by words and gestures.

Geste

Slander is not actionable *per se*. Thus, the plaintiff must prove specific damages, if none of the four following exceptions applies:

---

[1] *Limerick ist ein „typischer britischer", fünfzeiliger Vers mit dem Reimschema aa bb a sowie „lang, lang, kurz, kurz, lang".*
Example:
There was an old lawyer called Rainer,
who thought English law could be finer.
So he soon undertook
to write this new book,
although a lawyer is not a rhymer!

(1) an <u>allegation</u> that a person has committed a crime,	Behauptung
(2) an allegation of <u>unchastity</u> of a woman,	Unkeuschheit
(3) an allegation against the plaintiff in respect of his office, profession, trade or business,	
(4) an allegation that a person has an existing <u>infectious disease</u> (e.g. <u>leprosy</u>, <u>venereal disease</u> or AIDS).	infektiöse Krankheit – Lepra – Geschlechtskrankheit

4. Defences

a) <u>Justification</u>

Wahrheitsbeweis

It is a defence, by showing that the statement was completely or substantially true.

b) <u>Absolute privilege</u>

absolutes Vorrecht

The following statements <u>carry complete protection</u> from actions in defamation:

vollen Schutz genießen

- statements in Parliamentary or judicial proceedings,
- statements between solicitor or barrister and client,
- state communications,
- statements between husband and wife.

c) <u>Qualified privilege</u>

qualifiziertes Vorrecht

The following statements carry similar protection from actions for defamation, unless it can be shown that the maker of the statement acted out of <u>malice</u>, such as an <u>improper</u> motive or <u>out of spite</u>:

Böswilligkeit – schmutzig/ unehrenhaft – aus reiner Bosheit

- reports on Parliamentary or judicial proceedings, and
- statements made to protect an interest.

An example of the latter would be a company director reporting to the <u>chairman</u> of the company about the misbehaviour of an <u>employee</u>.

Präsident
Arbeitnehmer

d) Fair comment

People in public life, such as politicians, sport or film stars, etc. <u>receive praise</u> and must accept criticism. Provided that the comments concern their public activities, and are not made out of malice, they are not actionable in defamation.

Beifall bekommen

Diagram 41

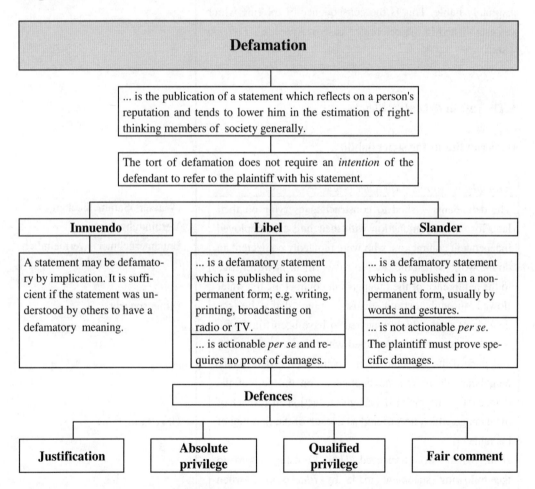

Defamation

... is the publication of a statement which reflects on a person's reputation and tends to lower him in the estimation of right-thinking members of society generally.

The tort of defamation does not require an *intention* of the defendant to refer to the plaintiff with his statement.

Innuendo	**Libel**	**Slander**
A statement may be defamatory by implication. It is sufficient if the statement was understood by others to have a defamatory meaning.	... is a defamatory statement which is published in some permanent form; e.g. writing, printing, broadcasting on radio or TV.	... is a defamatory statement which is published in a non-permanent form, usually by words and gestures.
	... is actionable *per se* and requires no proof of damages.	... is not actionable *per se*. The plaintiff must prove specific damages.

Defences

Justification	**Absolute privilege**	**Qualified privilege**	**Fair comment**

VI. <u>Strict liability</u>

strenge (verschuldenunabhängige) Haftung/Gefährdungshaftung

1. General rule of liability in tort

A person is generally liable in tort when his or her act is done intentionally or negligently.

In some cases, however, a person may be liable when he or she acts neither intentionally nor negligently. In these cases, the law has imposed a strict limit on a person's activities, and if this limit is exceeded, the defendant is strictly or absolutely liable. This is the consequence of the rule which was established in the celebrated case of *Rylands* v *Fletcher* (1868).

2. The rule in *Rylands* v *Fletcher*

a) Preconditions for strict liability

Example – Rylands v *Fletcher (1868) –:*

The defendants wished to construct a <u>reservoir</u> on their land for use in <u>conjunction</u> with their mill and employed independent <u>contractors</u>, who were <u>reputedly</u> competent, to do the work. When the reservoir was filled, however, due to the negligence of the independent contractors, the water flowed through certain disused <u>mine shafts</u> on the defendants' land which appeared to have been filled with earth but were in fact connected with the mines owned by and underneath the land of the plaintiff, the defendants' neighbour. There was no negligence on the part of the defendants. The plaintiff brought an action in respect of the damage which he suffered as a result of the <u>flooding</u> of his mine.

Held: that he would succeed. Their Lordships approved the following statement made by *Blackburn* J when expressing the view of the Court of Exchequer Chamber: "We think that the true rule of law is, that the person who, <u>for his own purposes</u>, brings on his land and collects and

(Wasser-)Sammelbecken
Verbindung
Bauunternehmer – vermeintlich

Minenschacht

Überflutung

für eigene Zwecke

keeps there any thing <u>likely</u> <u>to do mischief</u> if it <u>escapes</u>, must <u>keep it in</u> <u>at his peril</u>; and if he does not do so, is *prima facie* answerable for all the damage which is the natural consequence of its escape. He can excuse himself by showing that the escape was owing to the plaintiff's default; or, perhaps, that the escape was the consequence of <u>*vis major*</u>, or the Act of God."

wahrscheinlich – ein Übel zufügen – (ent)fliehen/ freisetzen – sich im eigenen Risikobereich halten – auf den ersten Anschein

höhere Gewalt

<u>Note</u>: The plaintiff in the first instance was *Fletcher*, who succeeded with his action. *Rylands* was the defendant and became the appellant and *Fletcher* the respondent. As the decision of the House of Lords dates back to before 1974 (cf. vol. 1, chapter four, p. 73), the names of the <u>litigants</u> had been <u>inverted</u> in the appellate court.

Beachte!

Prozessparteien – umkehren

To <u>simplify</u> this rule established by *Blackburn* J we can say: *"A person who for his own purposes brings onto his land anything likely to do mischief if it escapes, must keep it in at his <u>peril</u>."*

vereinfachen

Gefahr

If the "dangerous" thing escapes and damage was foreseeable, the owner of the land will be liable for all the consequences, even if he took all due care and was not negligent.

Thus, to create liability under this rule, the thing causing the damage must have been brought onto the land. In other words, if the damage had occurred there naturally, the owner would not have been liable. Moreover, it must be foreseeable that the thing could cause damage (e.g. fireworks, wild animals, chemicals, gas).

According to *Blackburn* J (and confirmed by *Lord Cairns* in the decision of the House of Lords), the rule <u>covers</u>: *"The person whose grass or corn is <u>eaten down</u> by the escaping <u>cattle</u> of his neighbour, or whose mine is flooded by the water from his neighbour's reservoir, or whose cellar is invaded by the <u>filth</u> of his neighbour's <u>privy</u>, or whose <u>habitation</u> is made <u>unhealthy</u> by the <u>fumes</u> and <u>noisome</u> <u>vapours</u> of his neighbour's <u>alkali</u> works ..."*

anwendbar sein/auf-/abdecken
auffressen
Vieh

Schmutz – Abort
Wohnung – ungesund – Rauch – schädlich – Dampf – Alkali (Laugensalz)

Example – Emanuel (H. and N.) Ltd. v *Greater London Council (1971) –:*	
An arrangement was made whereby a firm of independent contractors, engaged by the <u>Ministry of Works</u>, would remove two war-time bungalows and all materials and <u>rubbish</u> from a <u>site</u> owned by the defendant council. The contractors started a fire to burn unwanted materials. <u>Sparks</u> <u>blew</u> onto the plaintiffs' property and the resulting fire caused damage. *Held:* that the council, as occupier, was strictly liable under the rule in *Rylands* v *Fletcher* for the escape of fire caused by the negligence of anyone other than a stranger. The contractors were on the land with the council's <u>leave</u>, and although the contractors were forbidden by the terms of their contract from starting fires on the land, the council could reasonably have anticipated that they might start a fire.	Arbeitsministerium Abfall – Grundstück Funken *hier:* fliegen Erlaubnis

The essential fact is that there must be an "*escape*" of the dangerous thing from the defendant's land.

Example – Read v *J. Lyons & Co. Ltd. (1947) –:*	
The plaintiff was employed as an inspector in the defendant's <u>munitions factory</u>. In the course of her employment, she was injured by the explosion of a <u>shell</u> that was being manufactured on the premises. There was no allegation of negligence on the part of the employers. *Held*: that, as there had been no "escape" of the thing that <u>inflicted</u> the injury, *Rylands* v *Fletcher* was inapplicable, and, in the absence of negligence, the plaintiff's claim failed.	Munitionsfabrik Patrone/Geschoss zufügen

As *Lord Cairns* has stressed, it must be shown that there was "<u>non-natural use</u>" of the land <u>to found</u> the defendant's liability. This requirement has been established as part of the rule. The courts have interpreted "natural" to mean something which is ordinary and usual, and non-natural use is <u>equated</u> with an extraordinary use or activity.

unnatürlicher (unüblicher) Gebrauch – begründen

gleichsetzen

> *Example – Rickards* v *Lothian (1913) –:*
>
> By a malicious act, an unknown third party blocked a domestic <u>water system</u>. The water overflowed and caused damage to the plaintiff's premises on the floor below.
>
> *Held:* that there was no liability under *Rylands* v *Fletcher* because the <u>supply of water</u> via a normal domestic instal-lation was a natural use of land.

Wasserleitung

Wasserversorgung

In this decision, *Lord Moulton* defined non-natural use as "some special use, bringing with it <u>increased danger</u> to others".

gesteigerte Gefahr

To summarise the preconditions for the application of the rule in *Rylands* v *Fletcher* one can say:

(1) a person must bring onto his land for his own purpose some dangerous thing, which is not naturally there;

(2) the dangerous thing must escape from the land, and

(3) must <u>cause damage </u>("without damage no liability").

Schaden verursachen

b) Exceptions (defences)

If the preconditions described above are fulfilled, the occupier of the land is strictly liable but the following defences are available:

(1) the plaintiff <u>consented</u> to the dangerous thing being kept there, and the defendant was not negligent;

einwilligen

(2) the escape <u>was due to</u> the act of a stranger;

veranlasst werden durch

(3) the event was an "Act of God", which could not have been foreseen or prevented;

(4) the defendant was under a <u>statutory duty</u> to do some-thing, and he was not negligent in carrying out his duty.

gesetzliche Pflicht

Example – Cambridge Water & Co. Ltd. v Eastern Counties Leather (1994) –:	
The defendants, an old established <u>leather</u> manufacturer, used PCE, a chemical <u>solvent</u> in their <u>tanning process</u>. PCE <u>evaporates</u> quickly in the air but is not readily <u>soluble</u> in water. In the course of the process, before a change of method in 1976, <u>continual</u> small <u>spillages</u> had gradually built up a pool of PCE under their premises. The solvent <u>seeped</u> into the <u>soil</u> below and <u>contaminated</u> the <u>aquifer</u> from which the plaintiffs drew their water. At first instance, the claim in *Rylands* v *Fletcher* was dismissed because it was held that there was no non-natural use of the land. The <u>nuisance action</u> failed because, at the time the <u>contamination</u> was taking place, it was not foreseen that the quantities of the chemical would <u>accumulate</u>, or that if they did, there would be any significant damage.	Leder Lösungsmittel – Gerbprozess verdampfen – löslich immer wiederkehrend – das Vergossene/Übergelaufene durchsickern – Boden – verseuchen – Wasserbehälter Besitzstörungsklage – Verseuchung ansammeln
Held: that the claims in negligence and nuisance failed for <u>lack of foreseeability</u>. The action in *Rylands* v *Fletcher* also failed because the defendants had not known, and could not reasonably have foreseen, that the <u>seepage</u> would cause the <u>pollution</u>.	Mangel der Vorhersehbarkeit das Durchsickern Umweltverschmutzung

The <u>key principle</u> of this case is that foreseeability of damage should be regarded as a <u>prerequisite</u> of liability under the rule in *Rylands* v *Fletcher*.

Therefore, strict liability for things likely to do mischief only arises if the defendant knew, or should have reasonably foreseen, that those things <u>might cause</u> damage if they escaped.

Schlüsselprinzip
Vorbedingung/Voraussetzung

könnten verursachen

Diagram 42

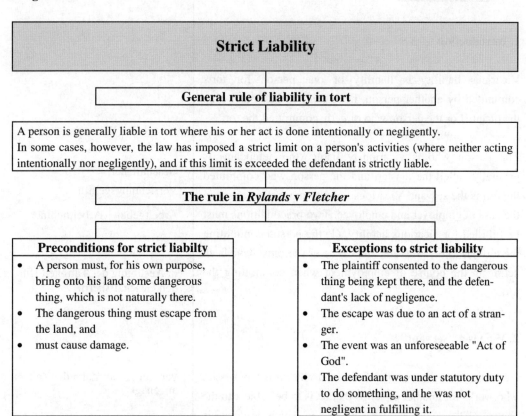

Strict Liability

General rule of liability in tort

A person is generally liable in tort where his or her act is done intentionally or negligently.

In some cases, however, the law has imposed a strict limit on a person's activities (where neither acting intentionally nor negligently), and if this limit is exceeded the defendant is strictly liable.

The rule in *Rylands* v *Fletcher*

Preconditions for strict liabilty

- A person must, for his own purpose, bring onto his land some dangerous thing, which is not naturally there.
- The dangerous thing must escape from the land, and
- must cause damage.

Exceptions to strict liability

- The plaintiff consented to the dangerous thing being kept there, and the defendant's lack of negligence.
- The escape was due to an act of a stranger.
- The event was an unforeseeable "Act of God".
- The defendant was under statutory duty to do something, and he was not negligent in fulfilling it.

VII. Vicarious liability

Haftung für einen Dritten

1. Introduction

Vicarious liability is liability of one person for torts committed by another person, i.e. a third person other than the plaintiff or the person who directly committed the tort[1].

The person who is vicariously liable (the defendant) is generally called the master, and the person who committed the tort is the servant. Vicarious liability most often arises in the case of employer and employee. Two preconditions must be fulfilled for vicarious liability: (1) the person committing the tort has to be a servant, and (2) he or she must have been acting in the course of employment when committing the tort.

Geschäftsherr –
Verrichtungsgehilfe

Arbeitgeber – Arbeitnehmer

in Ausübung der Tätigkeit (für den Geschäftsherrn)

2. Who is a "servant"?

According to a time-worn definition, a *servant* is any person who works for another on terms that he is to be subject to the control of that other as to the manner in which he does his work ("control test"). Thus, for instance, chauffeurs and apprentices are undoubtedly servants.
Self-employed skilled workers, such as electricians, carpenters and dressmakers who come to work in people's houses are independent contractors.
In contrast to servants who work under a contract *of* service, they work under a contract *for* services! As briefly indicated previously, a further test which may produce straightforward answers in some cases is that of "control" (of the master); the crucial factor being the degree of control exercised by the employer over the way the work is done. In modern working conditions, however, this control test does not usually prove conclusive.

veraltet („vom Zahn der Zeit angenagt")

„Weisungsbefugnistest"
Lehrling

selbstständig – Facharbeiter – Elektriker – Zimmermann – Schneider – freie (Werk)Unternehmer
Arbeits-/Dienstvertrag –
Werkvertrag
unkompliziert/klar

entscheidend – Grad/Ausmaß
Art/Weise

zwingend beweisen

---

[1] Comparable with the liability of *§ 831 BGB* in German law.

There are many contracts of service in which the employer does not, or cannot, control the way in which the work is done. For example, a <u>surgeon</u> working for the <u>National Health Service</u>[1] would not <u>fit</u> the control test. Therefore the <u>emphasis</u> on the control test has been reduced, and instead of relying on a single test, the courts now consider a <u>wide range</u> of factors in each particular case.

Chirurg – staatlicher Gesundheitsdienst – geeignet sein für
Betonung/Bedeutung
breites Spektrum

In this context, it is <u>worthwhile</u> mentioning that the <u>express</u> intentions of the parties as to the <u>classification</u> of their working relationship may be an important factor but it is not <u>conclusive</u>.

der Mühe wert – ausdrücklich
hier: Bezeichnung

abschließend/zwingend

Example – Ferguson v *John Dawson & Partners (Contractors) Ltd. (1976) –:*

The plaintiff, a <u>building worker</u>, was injured when he fell off a <u>roof</u> at the defendant's <u>construction site</u>. Contrary to regulations, there was no <u>guard rail</u> on the roof. If he had been an independent contractor he would have been responsible for his own safety and unable to sue the company. At the time of <u>hiring</u>, the plaintiff was expressed <u>to be a "labour only sub-contractor"</u>, although he was an <u>unskilled labourer</u> and subject to the control of the site agent.
Held: that the employers were liable. Despite the <u>label</u> that the parties had given to the employment relationship, in all other respects the plaintiff was treated as an employee working under a contract of service.

Bauarbeiter
Dach – Baustelle
Leitplanke

einstellen
nur als Subunternehmer arbeiten – ungelernter Arbeiter

Bezeichnung

---

3. In the course of employment

Of course a master cannot be made liable for every tort which his servants commit, but only for wrongs committed in connection with their master's business.

---

[1] *Der National Health Service sieht grundsätzliche kostenlose (free of charge) Heilbehandlung für alle sich in Großbritannien aufhaltenden Personen vor.*

But the extent of what falls within the "course of employment" is fairly wide: if a bus driver negligently injures someone while driving a bus, his employer will be vicariously liable. Not all situations are so straightforward, however. An employer is liable if the employee commits a tort in the course of his employment, even though the latter performs his duty in a manner expressly forbidden by the employer.

Ausmaß – ziemlich weitreichend

letzterer – seine Pflicht erfüllen

Example – Limpus v *London General Omnibus Co. (1862) –:*

The driver of one of the defendants' omnibuses obstructed one of the plaintiff's omnibuses to prevent it passing. His action caused injury to one of the plaintiff's horses and severe damage to his omnibus. The defendants' driver had been instructed that "he must not on any account race with or obstruct another omnibus, or hinder or annoy the driver or conductor thereof".

Held: that nevertheless, the defendants should make good the plaintiff's loss as they were liable for such of their driver's reckless and improper conduct as could be said to have occurred within the course of his employment.

blockieren
überholen

auf keinen Fall – um die Wette fahren – ärgern
Schaffner
wieder gutmachen

rücksichtslos

Example – Harrison v *Michelin Tyre Co. Ltd. (1985) –:*

An employee, whose duties included pushing a truck within a passage marked by chalk lines, deliberately moved the truck outside the lines as a "practical joke" and the plaintiff was injured. The plaintiff sued the company, arguing that the employee's negligence was within the course of employment. The company contended that the employee was "on a frolic of his own".

Held: that two mutually exclusive questions should be asked. (1) Although unauthorised or prohibited, was the employee's action incidental to his employment? If "Yes", the defendant was liable. (2) Was it so divergent from the employment as to be plainly alien to and wholly distinguishable from the employment? If "Yes", the defendant was not liable. On the basis of the facts, the

einen Wagen schieben
Schlagschnur/Kreidestrich
„um einen Streich zu spielen"

Scherz

gelegentlich
abweichend
fremd

answer to question (1) was "Yes", so that the employers were vicariously liable.

4. Liability for independent contractors

As already mentioned, an employer generally is not liable for the torts of independent contractors, unless:

(1) they were <u>expressly</u> <u>hired</u> to commit a tort;

ausdrücklich – „anheuern"

(2) the work necessarily created a dangerous situation;

(3) the work <u>obstructed</u> the highway, thereby creating a <u>public nuisance</u>;

behindern
öffentliche Störung

(4) the employer delegated a duty <u>imposed</u> by statute or common law.

auferlegen

Independent contractors are employed to do specific <u>tasks</u> but can choose the method of carrying out the work. An employee, on the other hand, is under the control of his employer as to what he must do, and how to do it.

Aufgaben

Note: Where liability is strict (independent of negligence), as in the case under the rule in *Rylands* v *Fletcher* (s.a., p. 62), a defendant will also be liable for acts of an independent contractor.

5. Employer's <u>indemnity</u>

Entschädigung/Regress

An employer who has been held vicariously liable for an employee's negligence is entitled to seek an indemnity from the employee to recover any damages paid.

Example – Lister v *Romford Ice & Cold Storage Co.*
(1957) –:

The appellant was a <u>lorry driver</u> employed by the respondents and, while he was <u>backing</u> his lorry into the yard of a <u>slaughterhouse</u>, to which he had been sent to collect <u>waste</u>, he negligently ran into and injured his father, who was also employed by the respondents for the same work. The father obtained judgement for damages

Lastwagenfahrer
zurücksetzen
Schlachthaus
Abfall

against the respondents on the ground that they were vicariously liable for the appellant's negligence.

Held: that the appellant had been in breach of his duty to the respondents to take due care, and they were entitled to recover in damages from the appellant the amount for which they had been held liable to his father.

Diagram 43

Vicarious liability

Vicarious liability means to be liable for torts committed by another person, i.e. a third person other than the plaintiff or the person who directly committed the tort. The person who is vicariously liable (the defendant) is called the master, and the person who committed the tort is called the servant (e.g. employer and employee).

Preconditions

Person acting must be a servant	Acting in the course of employment
A servant is any person who works for another on terms that he is to be subject to the control of the other person ("control-test"). Besides the control test, the courts have to consider a wide range of factors in each particular case.	The extent of the course of employment is fairly wide. A master is liable if the servant commits a tort in the course of his employment, even though the latter performs his duty in a manner expressly forbidden by the employer.

VIII. Further reading[1]

Adams, Law for business students; *Barker & Padfield*, Law; *Bermingham*, Nutcases: Tort; *Boucher & Corns*, GCSE Law, Casebook; *Brown*, GCSE Law; *Cooke*, Law of Tort; *Cracknell*, Torts (Cracknell's law students' companion); *Denham*, Law – a modern introduction; *Geldart*, Introduction to English law; *Giliker & Beckwith*, Tort; *Hepple, Howarth & Matthews*, Tort, Cases and Materials; *Harpwood*, Principles of Tort Law; *Harris*, An introduction to law; *Harvey & Marston*, Cases and Commentary on Tort; *Hedley*, Tort; *James'* Introduction to English law; *Jones*, Textbook on Torts; *Kidner*, Casebook on Torts; *Lunney/Oliphant*, Tort Law; *Lyall*, An introduction to British law; *Markesinis/Deakin*, Tort Law; *Rose*, (Blackstone's) Statutes on contract, tort and restitution; *Salmond & Heuston*, Law of torts; *Smith & Keenan's* English law; *Stapelton*, Product liability; *Tayfoor*, Tort (Law cartoons); *Templeman & Pitchfork*, Obligations: The law of tort, Textbook – Casebook – Revision work book; *Tiernan*, Nutshells: Tort; *van Gerven/Lever/Larouche*, Cases, Materials and Text on National, Supranational und International Tort Law; *Weir*, A Casebook on Tort; *Winfield & Jolowicz*, On Tort.

---

[1] Edition, place of publication and year of publication are quoted in the bibliography.

Chapter Eight

The <u>law of property</u>

Sachenrecht

I. Nature and <u>concept</u> of "<u>property</u>"

gedankliche Erfassung/
Konzept – Eigentum

According to *William Geldart* "there is perhaps nothing more difficult than to give a precise and <u>consistent</u> meaning to the word *property*".

feststehend

There are many possible translations of this word into German.

In the specialist dictionary by *Dietl/Lorenz*, for example, you can find: *„Eigentum, Eigentumsrecht; Vermögen, Vermögensgegenstand, Vermögenswert(e); (bebautes oder unbebautes) Grundstück; Grundbesitz, Grund und Boden, Landbesitz; (charakteristische) Eigenschaft"*. The similarly excellent, but not so <u>comprehensive</u> dictionary by *Romain* offers: *„Eigentum, eigentumsähnliches Recht, absolutes Recht; Vermögen, Vermögensgegenstand; Grundstück; Sache"*...

umfangreich

What can we do <u>to elucidate</u> this <u>muddle</u> of different translations and meanings? "The first thing we do, let's kill all the lawyers?" No, this would <u>certainly not</u> solve our problem.

klarstellen/aufhellen – Tohuwa-
bohu/Wirrwarr

sicherlich nicht

First, we should consider that in English law the notion of "property" has different meanings.

For example "property" means *„Eigentum"* in the sense of <u>ownership</u>, meaning "the <u>entirety</u> of <u>the powers of use and disposal</u> allowed by the law" (as once expressed by the <u>legal historian</u> *Pollock* in his "First Book of Jurisprudence"). "Property" as "ownership" is therefore comparable with the German notion *„Eigentum"* in *§ 903 BGB*, where it means the <u>legal domination</u> over a thing.

Eigentum(srecht) – Gesamtheit
– Gebrauchs- und Verfügungs-
befugnis
Rechtshistoriker

rechtliche Herrschaft

In this sense, ownership is to be differentiated from <u>possession</u>, which means <u>the domination in fact</u> over a thing.

Besitz
tatsächliche Herrschaft

II. "<u>Real property</u>" and "<u>personal property</u>"

„Eigentum an unbeweglichen Sachen" – „Eigentum an beweglichen Sachen"

1. Introduction (development)

English law divides property into "real property" and "personal property", which is similar to but not completely identical to the differentiation made in German law. Real property includes only <u>freehold interests</u> in land, and personal property <u>comprises</u> all other <u>proprietary rights</u>, whether in land or <u>chattels</u>.

Grundeigentumsansprüche
umfassen – Eigentümerrechte
bewegliche Sachen

This classification is not identical to the <u>obvious</u> distinction between <u>immoveables</u> and <u>moveables</u>, and <u>takes its roots from</u> the medieval <u>law of lease</u> and the old <u>system of actions</u>.

offensichtlich
unbewegliche Sachen – bewegliche Sachen – seinen Ursprung haben in – Lehnsrecht – Aktionensystem (Klagesystem)

Actions in respect of property <u>once</u> fell into two categories: with the *action in rem* (cf. vol. 1, chapter one, p. 35) ("real action"), in English law one could sue for the <u>restitution</u> of a specific thing (*in natura*).

einst

Herausgabe

An *action in personam* ("personal action") <u>sounds in</u> damages only; i.e. the defendant could choose between specific restitution or paying money in damages.

gehen auf

In medieval law, an *action in rem* was only permitted for the restitution of <u>land</u>. Thus only land could be "real property". All other <u>assets</u> were "personal property".

Grundstück/Grund und Boden
Vermögenswerte

So far, the distinction corresponds to that between moveables and immoveables but this <u>convenient</u> classification was <u>disturbed</u> by the "<u>lease for a term of years</u>".

herkömmlich
stören/durcheinander bringen – Pacht auf Zeit

Only property in land entitled the plaintiff to an *action in rem*.

Although a <u>lease of land</u> was an <u>interest</u> in immoveable property, the *action in rem* was not <u>available</u> for the <u>dispossessed</u> <u>tenant</u>. Leases were regarded as *personal business arrangements* <u>whereby</u> one person allowed another the use of his land for a certain period <u>in return for</u> a <u>rent</u>. These transactions were personal contracts and, therefore, created rights *in personam* between the parties, and not rights *in rem*.	Landpacht – Anspruch verfügbar/zulässig besitzlos/besitzgestört – Pächter – Geschäftsabschluss – wodurch als Gegenleistung – Pachtzins
Thus, <u>leaseholds</u> <u>fell under the heading</u> of personal property or chattels but, because they were so closely connected with the land, they are often referred to as "<u>chattels real</u>", to be distinguished from "<u>chattels personal</u>" or "<u>pure personalty</u>", for example a watch, a bicycle or a pencil.	Pachtgrundstück – bezeichnet werden „beschränkte Rechte an Grundstücken" – persönliche Habe/persönliches Vermögen[1] – bewegliches Vermögen/Fahrnis

2. Modern law

Since the land law reforms of 1925 (mainly the *Law of Property Act 1925)*, the distinction between "real property" and "chattels real" as a part of "personal property" has lost much of its importance, since chattels real are <u>granted</u> <u>equality of status</u> very close to "real property". In particular, they now entitle the plaintiff to an *action in rem*.	„Sachenrechtsgesetz" gleichstellen
Pure personality – in other words, any property apart from land – is divided into two groups known as "<u>choses in possession</u>" and "<u>choses in action</u>".	bewegliche Sachen – Forderungsrecht
"Choses in possession" <u>denote</u> <u>chattels</u>, such as a watch, a bicycle or a pencil, furniture, jewellery etc., which are <u>tangible</u> objects and can be physically possessed and enjoyed by their owners.	bezeichnen – bewegliche Sachen (i.S.d. deutschen Rechts) – körperlich
"Choses in action" are <u>intangible</u> forms of property which are not subject to physical possession, and their owners are usually <u>compelled</u> to bring an action if they wish to <u>enforce</u> their rights over property of this kind.	unkörperlich gezwungen erzwingen/durchsetzen

---

[1] *Eigentum oder andere Rechte an beweglichen Sachen.*

Examples of choses in action are <u>debts</u>, <u>shares</u> in companies, other <u>negotiable instruments</u>, intellectual property rights such as <u>patents</u>, <u>trade marks</u> and <u>copyrights</u>. An owner of these rights would certainly regard them as his property.

Schulden/Forderungen – Aktien/Anteile – umlauffähige Wertpapiere
Patentrechte – Warenzeichen – Urheberrechte

With all the above mentioned forms of personal property we have to note that, <u>up to now</u>, we have only been considering the main rights which one has over one's *own* things. It is possible, however, to have <u>rights over things of another</u>.

bis jetzt

Rechte an fremden Sachen

We have just become familiar with the expression lease, which is the right <u>to possess</u> another's land <u>for a period of time</u> in return for a rent. In addition, it is possible to become the owner of a *servitude* over the land of another, e.g. a <u>right of way</u>, a <u>right to light</u> or a <u>right to the support buildings</u>.

besitzen – für gewisse Zeit

Dienstbarkeit – Wegerecht – Lichtrecht – Recht, Gebäude instandzuhalten

A servitude may also be a right to take something from the land of another, e.g. the <u>right to fish</u>.

Fischereirecht

The first group of rights are called *easements*, the second *profits à prendre*.

Grunddienstbarkeit
Nutzungs-(Entnahme-)recht am fremden Grundstück

Further, a person may <u>raise a loan</u> on the <u>security</u> of his property, either real or personal, and the <u>lender</u> has certain rights over the property so used as a security if the loan is not repaid.

ein Darlehen aufnehmen – Sicherheit – Darlehensgeber

III. Ownership and possession

1. Ownership

As indicated above, ownership is the most <u>comprehensive</u> right or collection of rights which a person can have over a thing.

umfassend

The owner of a thing is the person who has, <u>to the greatest extent</u>, the rights of <u>use and enjoyment</u>, <u>destruction</u>, and <u>disposition</u>. These rights, of course, are <u>limited by the general rules of law which protect the rights of others</u>, by certain <u>limited rights</u> which the owner or his <u>predecessors</u>

in höchstem Maß
Gebrauch und Nutzung – Zerstörung – Verfügung

Vorgänger

may have created in favour of others and (as is frequently the case with land) by rules imposed by statute. The owner of a field does not cease to be the owner simply because the public or a neighbour has the right to use a footpath across it. Nor is ownership infringed by the *Access to Neighbouring Land Act 1992*, which allows a person a right of access to neighbouring land in order to carry out certain types of repair and maintenance work on his own land.

auch nicht

beeinträchtigen – Zugang – Nachbargrundstück

Instandhaltung

If an owner's bicycle is stolen by a thief, the owner's rights as such remain intact; the thief acquires no right to the bicycle against the owner.

The owner's possession and with it his actual ability to exercise his rights is, however, for the time being gone. He must therefore recover the bicycle before he can be said to be back in possession of it.

gegenwärtig

„man sagt, er sei"

2. Possession

Whereas ownership is a right or a collection of rights over a thing, possession is, as already mentioned, a matter of fact.

Tatsache

Possession may be either unlawful, as we saw in the case of the thief who has wrongful possession, or lawfully acquired without, however, being connected to ownership.

unrechtmäßig

An owner who hires a bicycle to another gives him the possession but he does not cease to be the owner. The same is true of a person who brings the bicycle to another so that the latter repair it for him. Such voluntary transfers are called bailments and the person who so acquires possession is the bailee. The owner is thus the bailor. In none of these cases is the right of ownership infringed but it is possible that the contract between the parties creates rights in favour of the bailee which prevent, for the duration of the contract, the bailor from exercising his ownership rights. In a bailment for a fixed term, for example, the bailee can have possession to the exclusion of the bailor, and,is, therefore, the only person who could sue a

vermieten

das Gleiche gilt für
letzterer
Verwahrung
Verwahrer/Fremdbesitzer – Hinterleger

verletzen

bestimmte Zeit

third party for <u>wrongful interference</u>. This is different from German law, where the bailor as the indirect possessor has the same rights against a third party as the actual possessor himself. A bailee can sue a third party in tort for loss or damage to the thing, <u>even though</u> the bailee is not liable to the bailor for the loss or damage.

verbotene Eigenmacht/Besitz-störung

selbst wenn

> *Example – The Winkfield (1902) –:*
>
> This was an <u>Admiralty action</u> arising because a ship called the "Mexican" was negligently <u>struck</u> and sunk by a ship called the "Winkfield". The "Mexican" was carrying mail from South Africa to England during the <u>Boer War</u>.
> The <u>Postmaster-General</u> made a claim for damages in respect of the estimated value of parcels and letters for which no claim had been made or instructions received from the senders. The Postmaster-General undertook to distribute the amount recovered when the senders were found. An <u>objection</u> was made that the Postmaster-General represented the Crown and was not liable to the senders (see now *Crown Proceedings Act 1947*).
> *Held*: that as a bailee in possession, the Postmaster-General could recover damages for the loss of the goods <u>irrespective of</u> whether or not he was liable to the bailors.

Klage in Seerechtssachen
rammen

Burenkrieg
Postminister

Einwendung

Gesetz über Zivilverfahren der Krone

unabhängig davon

If one tries to analyse the concept of possession, we find two elements. First it <u>involves</u> actual power of control over the thing possessed.
Secondly it involves <u>an intention to maintain</u> that control <u>on the part of</u> the possessor.
Only the person who has this actual control is the "possessor". Thus, a servant who receives a thing from his master for the master's use (e.g. a chauffeur) <u>is deemed not to be</u> the possessor.
He is (as in German law) only a <u>possessory servant</u>.

enthalten

Absicht/Wille – aufrechterhal-ten – auf Seiten

gilt nicht als

Besitzdiener

Although ownership is the most <u>comprehensive</u> right over a thing, possession is a fact which has great legal significance, and to which rights <u>are attached</u>.

umfassend

verbunden sein

As in German law[1], actual possession in English law gives a presumption of ownership and, except in cases where ownership is determined by public registration, it is difficult to prove one's own ownership if the thing is in the possession of another.

Eigentumsvermutung

Moreover, possession is not merely evidence of ownership, but – subject to the right of the ownership – is itself entitled to legal protection.
The finder of a thing is entitled to it against all persons other than the true owner.

Eigentumsnachweis
vorbehaltlich
Rechtsschutz

Example – Hannah v *Peel (1945) –:*

The plaintiff, a lance-corporal in the Royal Artillery, was stationed in a house which was owned by, but had never been actually occupied by, the defendant. During his stay, the plaintiff accidentally discovered a valuable brooch in a wall crevice in an upstairs room. The real owner of the brooch could not be traced and the parties disagreed as to which of them should have it.
Held: that the plaintiff was entitled to the brooch as the defendant had never been in physical possession of the house and had no knowledge of the existence of the brooch until it was found by the plaintiff.

Obergefreiter (militärischer Dienstgrad „weit unten")

Brosche – Mauerspalte
gefunden werden

Finally, we may note that even wrongful possession, if continued for a sufficent length of time, can mature into lawful ownership. Wrongful possession of a moveable thing for six years, or of land for twelve years, destroys the previous owner's right to recover the thing or the land by legal action.

unrechtmäßiger Besitz
reifen/erwachsen

wiedererlangen

---

[1] *Cf. § 1006 BGB.*

Diagram 44

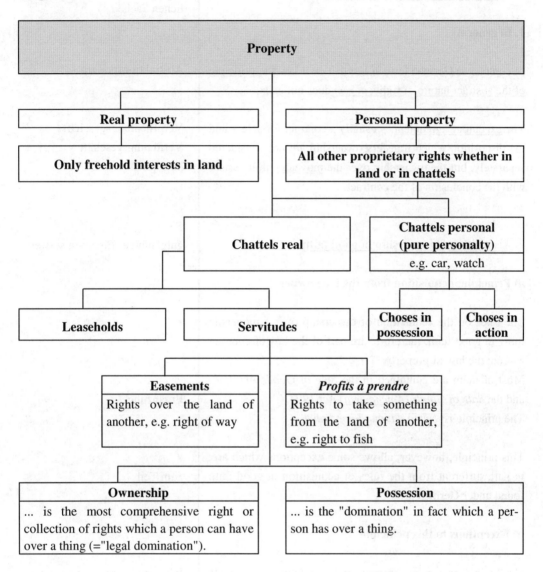

IV. Acquisition of personal property	Eigentumserwerb an beweg-lichen Sachen
1. In general	
In contrast to German law, in English civil law the <u>principle of the abstract nature of rights</u> *in rem* does not exist.	Abstraktionsprinzip *not existant in Ell*
The <u>executory agreement,</u> – usually a contract for sale – and the <u>disposition</u> which transfers ownership are not considered separately, but the ownership over the <u>moveable</u> thing arises with the <u>conclusion of the contract.</u>	Verpflichtungsgeschäft Verfügungsgeschäft beweglich
2. Acquisition of ownership in good faith	gutgläubiger Eigentumserwerb
a) Principle: acquisition from the true owner	
The rules on the acquisition of ownership over a moveable thing in good faith, therefore, are part of the law of contract and not the <u>law of property.</u> Most of them are contained in the *Sale of Goods Act 1979* and the *Sale of Goods (Amendment) Act 1994.* The principle is: *Nemo dat quod non habet*[1].	Ergänzung
This principle, however, allows some exceptions which are, <u>in part,</u> different from the rules of acquisition in good faith found under German law.	zum Teil
b) Exceptions to this principle	
(1) As in German law, money and <u>negotiable instruments</u> <u>made out to bearers</u> can always be acquired in good faith from a <u>non-owner.</u>	Inhaberpapiere = *IHI.* auf den Inhaber ausgestellt Nichteigentümer

---

[1] Lat.: No one can give that which he does not own = „*Niemand kann geben, was er nicht hat*".

(2) Another exception to the *nemo dat* principle is based on the concept of estoppel. If an owner, by certain statements, gives the (deceptive) impression that another is entitled to dispose of a thing, he cannot rely, as against a bona fide transferee, on the fact that no actual power of disposal had been given (estoppel by representation).

Unzulässigkeit der Rechtsaus-übung – den (falschen) An-schein erwecken

veräußern – sich berufen auf – gutgläubiger Erwerber – Verfügungsmacht („Duldungsvollmacht")

The same holds true if the owner acts in such a negligent way that the impression given by him is that a particular person has actually been entitled to dispose (estoppel by negligence).

gelten

verfügungsberechtigt („An-scheinsvollmacht")

He who relies on estoppel by negligence, however, has to prove that the owner has breached his duty of care towards him, the bona fide transferee. It will often be difficult to furnish this proof.

liefern

The concept of estoppel in this context has been codified in s21(1) of the *Sale of Goods Act 1979*:

"... where goods are sold by a person who is not the owner, and who does not sell them under the authority or with the consent of the owner, the buyer acquires no better title to the goods than the seller had, unless the owner of the goods is by his conduct precluded from denying the seller's authority to sell."

Anspruch
es sei denn
ausgeschlossen – Befugnis

(3) Another possibility of acquisition in good faith is given by s23 of the *Sale of Goods Act 1979*: ***"Sale under voidable title***. *When the seller of goods has a voidable title to them, but his title has not been avoided at the time of the sale, the buyer acquires a good title to the goods, provided he buys them in good faith and without notice of the seller's defect of title."*

Anspruch/Eigentumsrecht

hier: anfechten

(4) S24 of this Act provides for the
seller in possession after sale: *"Where a person having sold goods continues or is in possession of the goods, or of the documents of title to the goods, the delivery or transfer by that person, or by a mercantile agent acting for him, of the goods or documents of title under any sale, pledge, or other*

Handelsvertreter
Verpfändung

disposition thereof, to any person receiving the same in good faith and without notice of the previous sale, has the same effect as if the person making the delivery or transfer were expressly authorised by the owner of the goods to make the same."

(5) In s25 of this Act there follows provision for the **buyer in possession after sale***: "Where a person having bought or agreed to buy goods obtains, with the consent of the seller, possession of the goods or the documents of title to the goods, the delivery or transfer by that person, or by a mercantile agent acting for him, of the goods or documents of title, under any sale, pledge, or other disposition thereof, to any person receiving the same in good faith and without notice of any lien or other right of the original seller in respect of the goods, has the same effect as if the person making the delivery or transfer were a mercantile agent in possession of the goods or documents of title with the consent of the owner."*

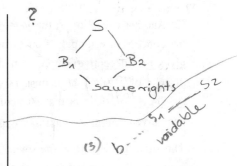

Pfandrecht

In this context, one should <u>note</u> that the <u>acquiring party</u> under a "<u>hire-purchase-agreement</u>" is not a buyer in the sense of s25 of the *Sale of Goods Act 1979*. Hire-purchase means <u>hire</u> with an <u>option to purchase</u> (which corresponds to the modern concept of leasing). <u>Therefore someone, even though he has an option to purchase, who has not in fact exercised that option and purchased the goods, cannot be called a buyer.</u>
The same applies to a <u>purchaser</u>, who, as a consumer, buys goods under a <u>conditional sale agreement</u>.

beachten – Erwerber
Kaufmietvertrag

Miete – Kaufoption

Käufer
Kauf unter Eigentumsvorbehalt

A <u>counter-exception</u> is provided by the *Hire-Purchase Act 1964* regarding the acquisition of a motor vehicle by a consumer. According to this Act, the purchaser of a motor vehicle is a "buyer" in the sense of s25 *Sale of Goods Act 1979*, even though he is in possession of the vehicle <u>on the basis</u> of a hire-purchase agreement or a conditional sale agreement.

Gegenausnahme – Abzahlungs-Gesetz

aufgrund

[handwritten margin note, left: power of attorney / Vollmacht]

[handwritten margin notes, top right: ? ; S ; B₁ ; B₂ ; same rights ; S₂ ; (3) b voidable ; has the same rights and duties (debts) ; S → B₁ → B₂]

Note: As we have learnt from <u>section</u> IV, under English law, the acquisition of personal property is not separated from the <u>contractual executory agreement</u> as it is under German law. Thus, fewer problems in dealing with the acquisition of ownership of moveable things arise under the English law of property (=*Sachenrecht*, in the sense of the German civil law): the issues which arise are to be found in the law of contract, with which we have dealt relatively <u>thoroughly</u> in chapter six. The English law of property, as <u>reflected</u> in numerous textbooks, is mainly a "law of *real* property" or "<u>land law</u>", <u>supplemented</u> by a special "law of trusts" (which forms our next chapter). This explains why in this section there are few cited cases, in contrast to the sections which follows.

hier: Abschnitt

vertragliches Verpflichtungs-geschäft

gründlich
sich widerspiegeln

Grundstücks-/Bodenrecht
Grundstücksübertragung/
Grundstücksverkauf – ergänzen

Diagram 45

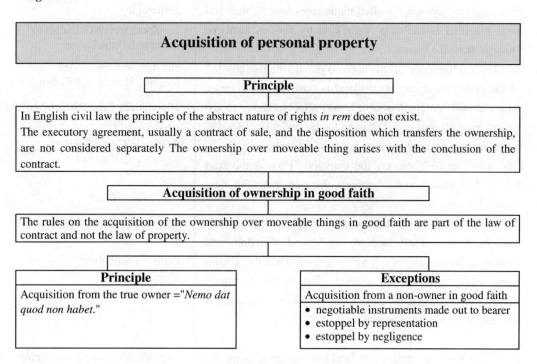

Acquisition of personal property
Principle
In English civil law the principle of the abstract nature of rights *in rem* does not exist. The executory agreement, usually a contract of sale, and the disposition which transfers the ownership, are not considered separately The ownership over moveable thing arises with the conclusion of the contract.
Acquisition of ownership in good faith
The rules on the acquisition of the ownership over moveable things in good faith are part of the law of contract and not the law of property.

Principle	**Exceptions**
Acquisition from the true owner ="*Nemo dat quod non habet.*"	Acquisition from a non-owner in good faith • negotiable instruments made out to bearer • estoppel by representation • estoppel by negligence

V. Law of real property – land law

Grundstücksrecht

1. Introduction: what is "land" ?

"Land" is, in the words of *Sir Edward Coke*, "of all elements the most ponderous and immovable"; land endures, all other property perishes, changes or is lost in the course of time. It follows that rights and interests which can be enjoyed in land are necessarily more complex than others.

gewichtig – überdauern
verderben
daraus folgt – Rechte und Ansprüche – notwendigerweise

Since the Norman Conquest (cf. vol. 1, chapter one, p. 24), it has been a fundamental legal commonplace that full ownership of land is possible for no one save the Crown. William the Conqueror considered himself owner of all land in England and parcelled it out to his barons who became his tenants. They commonly called themselves land owners and were regarded as "holding" their land by various forms of "tenure" from the Crown.

juristische Binsenwahrheit
außer

parzellieren
gemeinhin
Landbesitzrecht/Grundbesitz/
Pachtverhältnis/Lehen

It is beyond the scope of this book to pursue the rise and fall of the system of tenure but all land is now held by a single tenure called "common socage", and all obligations to the Crown have disappeared. But even today, under English law, a person does not own land; he holds an estate in land.

aus dem Rahmen fallen – ver-
folgen – Höhen und Tiefen

allgemeines Erb-/Dienstlehen

Recht am Grundstück
Pacht, Lehen

The term "*tenure*" answers the question "How is the land held?" The term "*estate*" answers the question "For how long is the land held?"

The term "estate" arose because in legal theory the Crown is still the owner of all land in the United Kingdom and English citizens can only have a part of what the Crown owns. This is called an "estate". The matter is purely traditional and theoretical since the Crown has no rights over the "estate" of a private person.

entstehen – Rechtstheorie

Bürger – teilhaben
vollkommen

In 1925, a thorough updating of land law was undertaken and was thought to have been achieved by the following statutes: the *Law of Property Act 1925*, the *Settled Land Act 1925*, the *Administration of Estates Act 1925*, the *Land Charges Act 1925* and the *Land Registration Act 1925*.

hier: Verbesserung – vornehmen

„Landordnungsgesetz"
Grundstücksbelastung

By s. 205 (1)(ix) of the *Law of Property Act 1925* the answer to the question "what is land?" is given as follows:

"Land includes land of any tenure, and <u>mines and minerals</u>, | Bergminen und Bodenschätze
whether or not held apart from the surface, buildings or parts of buildings (whether the division is horizontal, vertical or made in any other way) and other <u>corporeal</u> | körperliche, dingliche Rechte an Grundstücken – Erbpacht-
<u>hereditaments</u>; also a <u>manor</u>, an <u>advowson</u>, and a rent and other incorporeal hereditaments, and an <u>easement</u>, right, privilege, or benefit in, over, or <u>derived from</u> land; but not | land (inkl. Haus) – (kirchliches) Recht, Pfründe zu besetzen – Dienstbarkeit – herrühren von
an <u>undivided share</u> in land; and 'mines and minerals' | ungeteilter Anteil
include any <u>strata</u> or <u>seam</u> of minerals or substances in or under any land, and powers of working and getting the same | Schicht – Flöz (Nutzschicht im Bergbau)
but not an undivided share thereof; and 'manor' includes a <u>lordship</u>, and <u>reputed</u> manor or lordship; and 'hereditament' | Herrschaft(sbesitz) – vermeintlich – gesetzliche Erbfolge
means any real property which on an <u>intestacy</u> occurring |
before the commencement of this Act might have <u>devolved</u> | zufallen
upon an <u>heir</u>." | Erbe

Knowing this comprehensive description of land, we should now <u>pose</u> the question "how far does land <u>extend</u>?" In | stellen – ausbreiten/reichen
Roman law there was the principle *"Cuius est solum eius est usque ad caelum et ad inferos"*[1].

However, this principle has, of course, been <u>restricted</u> by | einschränken
modern law.

Example – Bernstein (Lord) v *Skyviews & General Ltd.*
(1978) –:

The defendant company used an aircraft to fly over the plaintiff's <u>country house</u> for the purpose of photo- | Landhaus
graphing it.
Held: that the plaintiff's action for trespass would fail, since the rights of a landowner in the <u>air space</u> above his | Luftraum

---

[1] Lat. = Whosoever owns the soil also owns everything above it as far as the heaven and everything below as far as to the depths of the earth.= „Wem der Boden (das Land) gehört, dem gehört alles bis zum Himmel und bis in die Tiefe der Erde".

land are restricted to such height as is necessary for the ordinary use and enjoyment of his land and the <u>structures</u> upon it, and the defendant's flight was hundreds of feet above the ground. Apart from common law, the defendant was protected by s40(1) of the *Civil <u>Aviation Act 1949</u>*, which exempted certain flights by aircraft from actions in trespass or nuisance. The taking of photographs cannot of itself constitute an act of trespass.

Beschaffenheit/Gebäude

Luftfahrtgesetz

Our next case deals with the depth of the earth.

Example – Attorney-General of the Duchy of Lancaster v *G.E. Overton (Farms) Ltd. (1982) –:*

A large <u>hoard</u> of Roman coins was found buried in a field belonging to the defendants. The plaintiff claimed the <u>find</u> as <u>treasure trove</u> because: (1) the coins contained some silver; and (2) it could be <u>inferred</u> that they had been buried by somebody who later intended to reclaim them. The defendants contended that, as the coins contained only a small amount of silver, they were <u>base metal</u> and, therefore, could not be treasure trove. A <u>coroner's</u> <u>inquest</u> found for the plaintiff, but a first appeal was allowed by *Dillon* J. The plaintiff appealed.

Held: that in order for the coins to be treasure trove, they should contain a <u>substantial</u> amount of gold or silver. The coins were therefore the property of the defendants.

Hort
Fund
Schatzfund
schließen/folgern

unedles Metall
Untersuchungsrichter – Nachforschung

wesentlich

Thus, the principle which can be concluded from this decision is: if the original owner is unknown, chattels discovered on the land, belong to the landowner unless they are treasure trove.

2. <u>Estates</u> and <u>interests</u> in land

unbeschränktes dingliches
Recht – beschränktes dingliches
Recht (an fremdem Grund-
stück)

The difference between an estate and an interest is that the owner of the estate is entitled to the enjoyment of the whole of the property, either in possession or receiving rents, whereas the owner of an interest has a limited right in or over the land of another.

a) Estates

At common law estates can be either *estates of freehold estates, less than freehold* or *estates of leasehold*.

von unbestimmter Dauer –
von bestimmter Dauer – von
bestimmbarer Dauer

The *Law of Property Act 1925* reduced the number of estates (having been possible at common law) which can exist over land, to two:
An *estate in fee simple absolute in possession* and *a term of years absolute*.

unbeschränktes Grundeigentum/
unbeschränkter Besitz – Erb-
pacht

aa) An estate in 'fee simple' absolute in possession

The technical meaning of this expression may be clarified by an analysis of its technical terms.

besondere (berufsspezifische)
Ausdrucksweise

The word "fee" implies that the estate is an estate of inheritance.

Erbschaft

The word "simple" denotes that the estate is not a fee tail, which would be an estate limited to certain lineal decendants only of the grantee. "Simple" thus means that the estate is capable of passing on to the *general heirs* of the grantee.

beschränktes Eigentumsrecht
(durch Erbfolge) – Abkömmling in gerader Linie – Erwerber – weitergehen – (alle)
gesetzliche(n) Erben

The word "absolute" distinguishes a fee simple which will continue forever, from a fee which may be determinable on the happening of a certain event.

bestimmbar

Eintritt eines bestimmten
Ereignisses

"In possession" signifies that the grantee is entitled to immediate possession and this does not imply merely physical possession, but also the right to receive rents and profits for an unlimited time.

Einkünfte/Pacht-/Mietzins
Erträge

After all, one can say that a tenant of an "estate in fee simple absolute in possession" is in the same position as an owner. His rights, therefore, also extend up to the sky and down to the depths of the earth.

Berechtigter

> *Example – Graham* v *K.D. Morris and Sons Pty. Ltd. (1974) –:*
>
> At frequent intervals, the <u>jib</u> of the defendants' <u>crane</u> <u>projected</u> over the plaintiff's land.
> *Held*: that the invasion of the plaintiff's air space by the projection of the crane jib was a trespass and not just a nuisance.

Ausleger – Kran
schleudern

bb) A term of years absolute

A term of years absolute is what is normally understood as <u>leasehold</u>. The essential characteristic is that a term of years has a maximum period <u>of certain duration</u>.

dingliches Pacht-/Nutzungs-
recht auf Zeit – von gewisser
Dauer

(1) The nature of leaseholds

The major characteristics of a *term of years* are that the <u>lessee</u> is given exclusive possession of the land and that the period for which the term is <u>to endure</u> is fixed and definite.

„Pächter"
andauern

It is, to a limited extent, open to the parties, who are the <u>landlord</u> and the <u>tenant</u>, to decide whether their agreement should be a lease or a <u>licence</u>, though the words used by the parties are not <u>decisive</u>. If there is no right to exclusive possession, then there is a mere licence and not a lease. For example, a guest in a hotel does not normally have a lease because the proprietor <u>retains</u> general control over the room.

Verpächter – Pächter
Nutzungsrecht
entscheidend

behalten

> *Example – Shell-Mex and BP Ltd. v Manchester Garages Ltd. (1971) –:*
>
> The plaintiffs, by an agreement contained in a document called a licence, let the defendants into occupation of a <u>petrol filling station</u> for one year. The parties had some <u>disagreements</u> during this time and, at the end of the year, the plaintiffs asked the defendants to leave. The defendants refused, claiming that the agreement gave them a <u>business tenancy</u> protected by the *Landlord and*

Tankstelle
Meinungsverschiedenheit

gewerbliches Mietverhältnis

Tenant Act 1954, Part II, which deals with the method of terminating business tenancies. This method had not been followed by the plaintiffs.

Held (by the Court of Appeal): that it was open to parties to an agreement to decide whether that agreement should constitute a lease or a licence, but the fact that it was *called* a licence was not <u>conclusive</u>. However, in this case it *was* a licence because the plaintiffs retained, under the agreement, the right to visit the premises whenever they liked and to exercise general control over the layout, decoration and equipment of the filling station. These rights were <u>inconsistent</u> with the grant of a tenancy.

> zwingend

> unvereinbar

The expression "term of years" is misleading <u>in that</u> it includes weekly, monthly, <u>quarterly</u> or yearly <u>tenancies</u> (called *periodic tenancies*), as well as long leases for 99 or 999 years which are <u>common</u> in practice.

Other types of tenancies are *tenancies at will* and *tenancies at sufferance*.

> insoweit als
> vierteljährlich – Miet-/Pacht-verhältnis – Miet-/Pachtver-hältnis auf Zeit
> üblich
> jederzeit fristlos kündbares Miet-/Pachtverhältnis – Nut-zungsverhältis nach Ablauf der Pachtzeit

Under a *tenancy at will*, the tenant is permitted to stay in possession, <u>on the understanding</u> that there are to be negotiations for a new lease. A *tenancy at will* may also arise by agreement where a person takes possession of property with the owner's consent. Such an arrangement like that can be brought to an end by either party without giving notice.

However, for the courts it does not matter what the tenancy is named by the parties. They will look at the transaction in order to <u>ascertain</u> its true nature.

> mit der Maßgabe

> bestimmen

| *Example – Binions v Evans (1972) –:* |

Mr Evans was employed as a chauffeur by the Tredegar Estate, which owned a number of houses. His father and grandfather had also worked for the estate. Mr Evans died in 1965 and the trustees of the <u>estate</u> allowed Mrs Evans to continue to reside in a cottage which belonged to the estate, free of rent and rates for the <u>remainder</u> of her life.

> *hier:* Vermögen

> Rest

In 1968, the trustees made a formal agreement with Mrs Evans, the defendant in this case, who was then aged 76. The agreement <u>purported</u> to create a <u>tenancy at will</u> in order to provide her with a temporary home for the rest of her life, free of rent, without any rights <u>to assign</u>, <u>sub-let</u> or <u>part with possession</u>. Two years later, the trustees sold the cottage and other properties to Mr and Mrs Binions, the plaintiffs, expressly subject to the tenancy of Mrs Evans and, because of that tenancy, the trustees accepted a lower price. A copy of the trustees' agreement with Mrs Evans was given to the purchasers. Shortly afterwards, the purchasers tried <u>to evict</u> Mrs Evans on the ground that her tenancy, being at will, was liable to <u>determination</u> at any time. She refused <u>to vacate</u> and the court was asked to decide whether her occupation was in the nature of a tenancy at will or a mere licence.

Held (by the Court of Appeal): that the interest of the defendant was not a tenancy at will, although it had been so described in the agreement. When the trustees created a right in her favour to live in the cottage for the rest of her life, it could not have been a tenancy at will liable to be terminated at any time. It was, therefore, a mere licence, though equity would not permit the plaintiffs to revoke it as long as the defendant was not in breach of the licence. The plaintiffs held the cottage on a <u>constructive trust</u> to give effect to the agreement with Mrs Evans.

ausdrücken/vorgeben – jederzeit fristlos kündbares Mietverhältnis

abtreten – untervermieten

Besitz teilen

zur Räumung zwingen

Beendigung

den Besitz räumen

gesetzliches Treuhand-verhältnis

A *tenancy at sufferance* means that a tenant stays on the land after the <u>expiry</u> of his term without the consent of the owner. No rent is payable under such a tenancy but the tenant must <u>compensate</u> the owner by payment for the use of the land.

Ablauf

entschädigen

(2) The creation of leaseholds

In order to give rise to a *legal* estate, a lease must either be created by deed or be one which takes effect in possession for a term not exceeding three years at the best rent reasonably obtainable.

All other kinds of leases, which are informal in nature, <u>give rise</u> only to equitable interests (see below).

entstehen lassen

In equity, if a person entered into possession without a formal lease by deed, and then has paid rent or carried out repairs, there is what is called an act of <u>part performance</u>. Equity will insist that the owner of the property execute a formal lease by deed. The maxim "*Equity looks upon as done that which ought to be done*"[1] applies.

Teilerfüllung

Example – Walsh v *Lonsdale (1882) –:*

The defendant agreed in writing <u>to grant</u> a seven years' lease of a <u>mill</u> to the plaintiff at a rent payable one year <u>in advance</u>. The plaintiff entered into possession without any <u>formal lease</u> having been <u>granted</u>, and he paid his rent <u>quarterly</u> and not in advance. <u>Subsequently</u> the defendant demanded a year's rent in advance, and as the plaintiff refused to pay, the defendant <u>distrained</u> on his property. At common law, the plaintiff was a tenant from year to year because no formal lease had been granted, and, as such, his rent was not payable in advance. The plaintiff argued that the legal remedy of <u>distress</u> was not available to the defendant.

Held: that as the agreement was of the kind that the court could grant specific performance, and as equity <u>regarded</u> as done that which ought to be done, the plaintiff was bound to the same terms as if a lease had been granted. Therefore the distress was valid.

gewähren

Mühle

im Voraus

Mietvertragsurkunde – erstellen/aufsetzen – vierteljährlich – später

pfänden

Beschlagnahme/Pfandrecht

betrachten

---

(3) The relationship between landlord and tenant

In any lease, the parties may sign <u>express covenants</u> which are binding on them. Apart from these covenants, there are certain implied obligations on the landlord, who is also called the <u>lessor</u>, and on the tenant, who is the <u>lessee</u>.

ausdrückliche Vereinbarung

Vermieter/Verpächter – Mieter/Pächter

---

[1] *Equity betrachtet das als getan, was getan werden soll.*

(a) Landlord's obligations

The following are the main duties owed by the landlord to the tenant:

(1) The landlord has <u>to ensure</u> that the tenant receives "*<u>quiet enjoyment</u>*" of the land. This does not mean that there will be no noise, but that the lessor guarantees to the tenant that no third party will lawfully be able to disturb the tenant's use of the land.

sicherstellen – ungestörter Besitz(genuss)

(2) There is an implied obligation that a furnished house which is <u>let</u> must be <u>fit</u> for <u>human habitation</u> at the time of the letting. The *Landlord and Tenant Act 1985* provides that houses let at an annual rent of less than £52 (£80 in Greater London) must be fit for human habitation and <u>maintained</u> in that state during the tenancy.

vermietet – geeignet – menschliches Wohnen

aufrechterhalten

(3) Some statutes and cases now impose limited obligations on the landlord to repair.

(b) Tenant's obligations

The main duties of the tenant are:

(1) to pay the rent;

(2) to pay <u>rates and taxes</u>, except those which are legally the landlord's obligation;

Gebühren und Steuern

(3) not to commit <u>waste</u>: the property must not be deliberately or negligently damaged.

Verschwendung/Vernachlässigung

(c) Express covenants

From the wide <u>scope</u> of possible express covenants the two most <u>common</u> are:

Rahmen/Bereich

üblich

(1) *The covenant not to <u>assign</u> or <u>sub-let</u>.*

<u>In the absence</u> of such a covenant, a tenant may assign his whole interest in the lease to a third person or he may sub-let the premises for a term shorter than his own.

übertragen – untervermieten
bei Nichtvorhandensein

(2) *The covenant to repair*

In long leases, the tenant usually agrees to make repairs if they are necessary. In short leases, the landlord frequently <u>assumes</u>

übernehmen

the liability for external repairs and the tenant assumes the liability for any internal repairs.

Example – O'Brien v Robinson (1973) –:

The plaintiff was the tenant of a flat to which s32 of the _Housing Act_ 1961 (giving an implied covenant to repair) applied. In 1965, the plaintiff had complained about stamping on the ceiling above but it was found that the landlord had not been given notice that the ceiling was defective. In 1968, the ceiling fell down and the plaintiff was injured.

Held (by the House of Lords): that the defendant landlord was not liable for breach of covenant.

Wohnraumgesetz

hier: schadhafte Stelle – Decke

---

b) Interests

Besides these two legal estates, the legislation of 1925 created five _legal interests_, which are rights in or over the land belonging to another person.

These are:

aa) Servitudes

which may be either _easements_ or _profits à prendre_. An easement may be defined as the right to _use_ the land of another person in some way.

The most important easements are rights of way, rights to light, rights to abstract water and rights of support for buildings.

A _profit à prendre_ is the right _to take_ something _from_ the land of another, e.g. a right to fish in another's river, a grazing right for cattle, a right to cut firewood or to cut turf.

bb) Rent-charges

A rent charge is an annual sum of money payable out of land, the due payment of which is secured by a right of distress that is not the result of the tenure between the parties, but is either expressly reserved or allowed by the _Rent-charges Act 1977_.

Dienstbarkeiten

Grunddienstbarkeit – Nutzungs-/Entnahmerecht

Wegerecht – Lichtrechte Wasser(be)nutzungsrechte – Gebäudeinstandhaltungsrechte

Fischereirecht
Weiderecht – Vieh – Brennholz schlagen – Torf stechen
Rentenschuld (Grundstücks-belastung, die zu regelmäßigen Leistungen verpflichtet)
Pfändungsrecht – Pachtverhält-nis
ausdrücklich vorgesehen

cc) Charges by way of legal mortgage
which we will consider separately below.

dd) Land tax

ee) Rights of entry

Rights of entry are means by which a lease is forfeited if the tenant is in breach of its term. An estate may also be forfeited if the terms of a rent-charge, to which it is subject have been broken.

Belastung – Grundpfandrecht

Grundsteuer
Recht auf Inbesitznahme
verwirkt sein/verfallen

betreffen/dazugehören

c) Equitable interests

When dealing with *legal* estates and *legal* interests we mentioned that these rights arise from common law or statute. Consequently, *equitable* interests have their origin in equity.
All estates, interests or charges over land, which do not belong to those outlined above [under *a)* and *b)*], are equitable interests, and need the establishment of a trust (cf. next chapter). A life interest, for instance, is an equitable interest. A trust is also the precondition for a *remainder* and a *reversion*.
A remainder differs from a reversion in that:

- a remainder originates in grant or assurance and does not arise by operation of law (as does a reversion), and
- the interest, limited to follow the preceding or "particular estate", passes to some third party and not to the original grantor (which would happen in the case of a reversion).

Begründung eines Trust-Verhältnisses – dingliches Recht an fremdem Grundstück auf Lebenszeit – Anwartschaftsrecht – Heimfallrecht[1]

Bewilligung – Zusicherung
gesetzlicher Rechtsübergang
voraus-/vorhergehend
hier: Besitzrecht – übergehen auf – Veräußerer

---

[1] *Eigentum des langfristigen Verpächters nach Ablauf des Nutzungsverhältnisses.*

Diagram 46

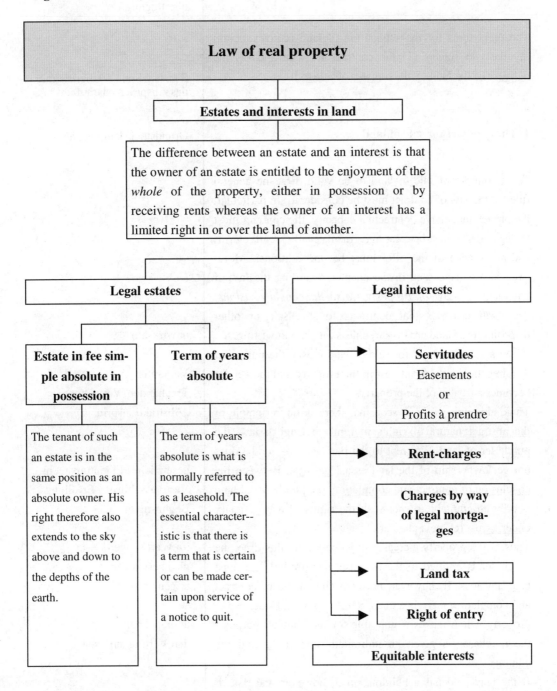

Law of real property

Estates and interests in land

The difference between an estate and an interest is that the owner of an estate is entitled to the enjoyment of the *whole* of the property, either in possession or by receiving rents whereas the owner of an interest has a limited right in or over the land of another.

Legal estates | Legal interests

Estate in fee simple absolute in possession

Term of years absolute

The tenant of such an estate is in the same position as an absolute owner. His right therefore also extends to the sky above and down to the depths of the earth.

The term of years absolute is what is normally referred to as a leasehold. The essential character-- istic is that there is a term that is certain or can be made cer- tain upon service of a notice to quit.

Servitudes
Easements
or
Profits à prendre

Rent-charges

Charges by way of legal mortga-ges

Land tax

Right of entry

Equitable interests

VI. The sale of land – <u>conveyancing</u>

(Anspruch auf) Grundstücks-übertragung

The procedures for the acquisition of land (conveyancing) involve two stages: (1) the contract for sale and (2) the <u>delivery</u> of the land by the <u>transfer of title to</u> it.

Bereitstellung – Übertragung des Anspruchs darauf

1. The <u>contract for sale of land</u>

Grundstückskaufvertrag

For a contract of sale of land to be valid, first the general rules of the law of contract must be considered. In particular, the parties must have contractual capacity, the contract must be legal, there must be clear agreement on all essential terms and acceptance of the offer must be unconditional. Moreover, as we have seen in the chapter regarding the law of contract, the *Law of Property (Miscellaneous Provisions) Act 1989* provides that contracts for the sale or other dispositions of land are <u>invalid</u> unless they are in writing.

unwirksam

When a valid contract for sale of land exists, the purchaser acquires the equitable interest in the property and the <u>vendor</u> becomes a <u>trustee</u> of the property.

Verkäufer
Treuhänder (Verwalter)

Thus, although we have seen that there is no "<u>principle of the abstract nature of rights in rem</u>" in English law, the purchaser of land (different to the purchaser of goods) does not get ownership of the land as a <u>legal title</u>. Between the <u>conclusion of contract</u> and <u>completion</u>, the purchaser of land is only an <u>equitable owner with the rights of a beneficiary under a trust</u> (cf. next chapter).

„Abstraktionsprinzip"

gesetzliches Eigentumsrecht
Vertragsschluss – Erfüllung
Begünstigter

Thus, if the property <u>increases in value</u> within this time, the purchaser is entitled to the increase and <u>similarly</u> he must <u>bear</u> any loss. If, however, between conclusion of contract and completion there is a change in the physical state of the property which makes it <u>unusable</u> for the contract purpose, the purchaser is given an unlimited right <u>to rescind the contract</u>.

im Wert steigen
gleichermaßen
tragen

unbrauchbar
den Vertrag auflösen

except If the land sold has a building on it, however, the risk of destruction by fire falls upon the purchaser from the time of the conclusion of the contract.

For the sale of land it is usual to use a standard form of contract prepared by "The Law Society" (Do you remember what this is? - If not: cf. footnote[1]!)

Under an *open* contract, that is a contract which does not set out the terms of the sale, but merely specifies the names of the parties, the description of the property and the price, there is a very important condition implied by law that the vendor must show title for at least fifteen years (s23 of the *Law of Property Act 1969*), beginning with a good "*root of title*".

| | Eigentumsrecht nachweisen |
| | urkundlicher Eigentumsnachweis („Wurzel des Eigentumsrechts") |

A root of title may be defined as a document which shows with whom the whole legal and equitable interests in the land lie. Sometimes it can be necessary to go back even more than fifteen years.

The vendor has to prepare an *abstract of title*, listing all the relevant documents concerning the land and the rights connected with it. The vendor must also show all facts which have affected the legal estate in the last fifteen years. This is called "*deducing title*". Then follows the "*investigation of title*" by the purchaser.

It should be noted that all the above mentioned matters are attended to by the parties' solicitors.

When the investigation of title is finished, the conveyance can take place.

Verzeichnis der Grundeigentumsurkunden – auflisten

beeinflussen

Nachweis der Rechtsnachfolge

Prüfung der Eigentums- und Belastungsverhältnisse

vornehmen/ausführen

„Auflassung"/Grundstücksübertragung

2. Conveyance

Conveyance nowadays means nothing more than a deed, which has to be signed, sealed and delivered to take effect. The conveyancing is concluded when the previous owner of the land, the vendor, delivers this deed to the acquirer, the purchaser, with the words: "I deliver this as my deed".

wirksam werden

abgeschlossen

übergeben

---

[1] The professional body for solicitors! – See vol. 1, chapter three.

Berufsverband

3. The stages of a __transfer of land__

Grundstücksübertragung

The process of transferring land involves the following stages –

(1) The preparation of the contract by the parties' solicitors.

(2) The exchange of contracts between the parties' solicitors, when the purchaser pays a __deposit__, usually 10% of the purchase price. The transaction has then become binding on both parties.

Anzahlung

(3) Delivery by the vendor's solicitor of an "__abstract of title__".

Zusammenfassung der Grundeigentumsurkunden

(4) Examination of this title by the purchaser's solicitor and the checking of __the abstract__ against the actual deeds for __accuracy__.

Übersicht/Verzeichnis

Genauigkeit

(5) After all __outstanding questions__ have been solved, a conveyance is prepared by the purchaser's solicitor which is sent to the vendor's solicitor for __approval__.

offenstehende Fragen

Zustimmung

(6) Just before completion, the purchaser's solicitor will make the necessary __searches__ in the __Land Charges Register__ and similar local registers.

Nachforschungen – „Grundstücksbelastungsregister" (ähnlich Abt. II und III des deutschen Grundbuchs)

(7) Finally, an appointment is made for completion, at which the purchaser hands over the money and the vendor hands over the conveyance, which he has signed, together with the title deeds concerning the property. Completion (conveyancing) is usually carried out at the office of the vendor's solicitor.

4. Registered land

The above described procedure refers to unregistered land, where the __need__ to examine the title is to some extent __cumbersome__ and expensive.

Bedürfnis

beschwerlich

The *Land Registration Act 1925* provides that the title to land can be examined and __registered__ with the state and that this is followed by the __issue__ of a certificate guaranteeing ownership.

eintragen

Ausfertigung

Where there is a sale of registered land, the certificate is handed over and the name of the new owner registered.

A transfer, rather than a conveyance, is prepared.

This is a less complicated procedure than the one underlined above for unregistered land and the legal fees for the transaction are also less. | hervorheben

The *Land Registration Act 1997* now applies and its major aim is to increase the rate at which unregistered land is brought on to the register of title, kept by the Land Registry. | Grundbuch – Grundbuchamt

VII. Mortgages of land → speak → 109 | Grundpfandrechte

1. Introduction

A loan of money may be obtained in several ways. | Darlehen

The borrower may have a rich friend who lends gratis or at a certain percentage per annum. If such a friend does not exist, he may obtain a loan from a stranger. But strangers may insist on some form of security. The security may be *personal* or *real*. | Entleiher/Darlehensnehmer — Sicherheit

Personal security usually requires a third party (a guarantor), who undertakes to repay the loan in case the borrower is not able to do so. | Bürge

Real security requires some form of property, either personal property or real property.

The borrower may, for example, secure the loan by giving the lender possession of his gold watch. When the loan is repaid with interest on the date agreed, the property (e.g. the watch) is returned to the borrower. | Verleiher/Darlehensgeber — mit Zinsen

If the borrower is lucky, however, he may own land. In this case, he will be able to secure his debt on his real property. But real property, such as land and houses, cannot be delivered like personal property. Land and houses as securities must be conveyed, which entails the preparation of a formal deed. | Schuld — übergeben — übertragen

The best way of securing a debt on land is by way of a *mortgage*. This strange word derives from Norman-French | Pfandrecht and means "dead <u>pledge</u>". Thus, mortgage is the transaction by which a borrower (the <u>mortgagor</u>) obtains a loan from another person (the <u>mortgagee</u>) on the security of property.

„toter Bürge"
Hypothekenschuldner
Hypothekengläubiger

Since the *Law of Property Act 1925*, there are two forms of mortgages of land, legal mortgages and equitable mortgages.

2. <u>Legal mortgages</u>

gesetzliche (Grund)pfandrechte

Legal mortgages appear in two forms: <u>mortgages by demise</u> and <u>the charge by way of legal mortgage</u>.

durch Vertrag bestelltes Grundpfandrecht – Belastung durch gesetzliches Grundpfandrecht

a) Mortgages by demise

The mortgage by demise is effected by creation of a <u>lease</u>. Suppose A is the <u>owner of land in fee simple</u>. A wishes to borrow money from B; so A becomes the mortgagor and B the mortgagee. A may grant to B a legal <u>term of years</u> (usually 3000 years) with a <u>proviso</u> in the deed that if the principal loan, plus interest, is repaid on the agreed date, the term of years shall <u>cease</u>. A further agrees to repay the sum due plus interest on the date named.

Pacht(vertrag)
unbeschränkter Grundeigentümer

„zeitlich begrenztes Herrschaftsrecht" – Vorbehaltsklausel

weichen/erlöschen

b) Charges by way of legal mortgage

The charge by way of legal mortgage is created by a deed which <u>confers</u> on the mortgagee a <u>legal interest</u> not a <u>legal estate</u>. This legal interest entitles the mortgagee to the same rights as if the mortgage were by lease for a long term of years, as described above under *a)*.

verleihen – dingliche Berechtigung – Eigentumsrecht Grundeigentum)

3. Equitable mortgages

An equitable mortgage is one where the mortgagee receives only an equitable interest in the land.

billigkeitsrechtlich anerkanntes Anwartschaftsrecht –

It is made by way of assignment of the equitable interest concerned, with a proviso for reassignment upon payment by the mortgagor of principal and interest.

Übertragung/Abtretung – Rückübertragung
Hauptschuld und Zinsen

A deed is not required for the creation of an equitable mortgage but it must be made in writing.

Sometimes, a borrower needs a loan urgently and wishes to avoid the trouble and expense of drawing up a legal mortgage. In such a case, an agreement in writing to create a mortgage as an act of part performance of an oral agreement operates to create an equitable mortgage, which the courts will uphold. This is a consequence of the equity maxim *"equity looks upon that as done which ought to be done"*.

dringend

bestellen

Teilleistung/Teilerfüllung
verursachen/bewirken
aufrechterhalten/anerkennen
„Equity betrachtet das als getan, was getan werden muss" (s.o.)

4. The rights of the mortgagor

The main right of the mortgagor is the right to redeem the mortgaged property on payment of principal and interest. This amount falls due on the contractual date specified (usually six months later). This "equity of redemption", evolved by the jurisdiction of the Court of Chancery, applies the two equity maxims: *"Once a mortgage, always a mortgage"* and *"Equity looks at the intent rather than the form"*. The equity of redemption is inviolable. Thus, even after the date for redemption has passed, the mortgagor could get back the land when in a position to repay his debts plus interest.

wiedererlangen

verpfänden/hypothekarisch belasten – fällig werden – vertraglich bestimmter Zeitpunkt – Pfandauslösungsrecht

„Equity berücksichtigt den Zweck mehr als die Form" – unverletzlich

As long as an order of foreclosure has not been issued by a court, the equity of redemption exists. But there are conditions. The mortgagor, for example, must show proper conduct himself and must give to the mortgagee six months' notice of his desire to redeem, unless the contract states some shorter period. This period gives the mortgagee, who

Beschluss – Vollstreckung aus einem Grundpfandrecht

regards the mortgage transaction as an investment, time to reinvest the money in a suitable security elsewhere.

On the other hand, any term in a mortgage deed which greatly benefits the mortgagee at the expense of the mortgagor has always been viewed with suspicion.

beträchtlich – begünstigen – auf Kosten – betrachten – Verdacht/Vorbehalt

---

Example – Noakes v Rice (1902) –:

The tenant of a "free" public house, under a twenty-six-year lease, mortgaged the premises to a brewery company as security for a loan, and covenanted that during the remainder of the twenty-six years, he would not sell any beers except those provided by the brewery company (the mortgagees). The tenant paid off the mortgage three years later and sued for a declaration that he was free from the covenant.

Held: that the covenant was inconsistent with the express proviso for redemption (which entitled the tenant to demand a reconveyance of the premises upon repayment of the loan with the interest) and was a clog upon the equity. The tenant became entitled to trade as a "free" public house again.

Pächter – brauereiunabhängige Gaststätte

versprechen

unvermeidbar

Rückübertragung
billigkeitsrechtliche unzulässige Behinderung (des Pfandaus-lösungsrechts)

---

5. The rights of the mortgagee

Provided that the redemption date has passed, the mortgagee of a *legal* mortgage has the following rights: to take possession, to foreclose, to sell the land, to sue for the debt and to appoint a receiver.

vorausgesetzt, dass – Fällig-keits-/Verfalldatum

vollstrecken

a) To take possession

The mortgagee will normally only enter into possession of the property when he is not being paid the sum due and when he wishes to pay himself from the proceeds of the property. This is not a desirable remedy, however, because when the mortgagee takes possession, he is strictly accountable to the mortgagor, not only for what he has received but for what he might have received with the exercise of due diligence and proper management.

Veräußerungserlös

verantwortlich/haftbar

ordnungsgemäße Sorgfalt

Example – White v City of London Brewery Co. (1884) –:

The plaintiff had a lease of a public house in Canning Town and he mortgaged it to the defendants to secure a loan of £900 with interest. One year later, with no interest having been paid since the date of the mortgage, the defendants entered into possession of the public house. They later let the premises on a <u>tenancy</u>, <u>terminable</u> at three months' notice, under which the tenant was to take all his beer from the defendants. <u>Eventually</u>, the lease was sold by the defendants and the plaintiff asked the defendants to <u>account</u> and pay him what should be found due.

Held: that the defendants must account to the plaintiff for the increased rent they would have received if they had let the public house without the restrictive condition regarding the sale of the defendants' beer, since a "free house" would produce more rent than a "<u>tied house</u>".

> Pacht(verhältnis) – beendbar
>
> schließlich
>
> ausgleichen
>
> Brauereigaststätte

b) To foreclose

If the mortgagor fails to pay his debts for an unreasonable time, the mortgagee may obtain a <u>court order</u> <u>extinguishing</u> the mortgagor's equitable right of redemption and <u>vesting</u> the full legal estate in the mortgagee. The first order is a *foreclosure order nisi*, which <u>directs</u> that the money <u>due</u> must be repaid within a given time, e.g. six months. If not so paid, the court order is made absolute; the property then vests in the mortgagee free by the way of equity of redemption.

But even if the order is *absolute*, the court may <u>reopen</u> the foreclosure, giving the mortgagor a further opportunity to redeem the mortgage. Because of this, the right to foreclose is rarely excercised.

> Gerichtsbeschluss – auslöschen – übertragen
>
> vorläufiger Vollstreckungsbe- schluss – bestimmen – fällig
>
> endgültig – wieder eröffnen

c) To sell the land

This is the most <u>frequently</u> used right and is implied in all mortgages made by deed. This right gives – with exceptions

> häufig

– the mortgagee the statutory power to sell the whole of the mortgagor's interest in land as soon as the legal date for redemption has passed.

Mortgagees cannot purchase the land for themselves. The sale of the property is usually by <u>public auction</u>.

öffentliche Versteigerung

Out of the proceeds of the sale, the mortgagee may recover the principal sum due plus interest and any expenses <u>incurred</u> in the sale of the property, but he is not allowed to keep any <u>surplus</u> proceeds arising from the sale. Any surplus money belongs to the mortgagor.

entstehen bei
Überschuss

Example – Williams & Glyn's Bank v Boland (1980) –:

A husband and wife lived together in the matrimonial home which was owned by the husband and subject to a mortgage with the bank. The husband was registered as the owner for the purposes of the Land Registration Act 1925. It appeared that his wife had made a <u>substantial contribution</u> of money towards buying the house and that she had, accordingly, equitable rights in it. The husband failed to keep up the mortgage repayments and the bank asked the court for a possession order over the house with a view to selling it. The wife <u>raised an objection</u> to the possession order, claiming that her rights and actual occupation gave her an "overriding interest" in the home which overrode the bank's claim to possession under s70(1) of the Land Registration Act 1925. S70 includes, as an overriding interest: "The rights of every person in actual occupation...". The bank argued that the wife was not in actual occupation and also relied on s3 of the 1925 Act, which provides that equitable rights, such as the wife had, were not an overriding interest but a "minor interest" and it was admitted that these would not have defeated the bank's claim.

wesentlicher Beitrag

Widerspruch erheben

Held (by the House of Lords): that the wife's objection must be <u>sustained</u> and the bank's claim for an order for possession refused. The wife was in actual possession just as much as her husband and the fact that he was in <u>occupation</u> did not prejudice her right to be regarded as in

stattgeben

im Besitz

occupation also. If she had not been in occupation apparently, her equitable rights would have been a minor interest but, since she was also in occupation, this fact converted them into an overriding interest.

umwandeln

d) To sue for the debt

The repayment covenant is an ordinary contract. The amount due on the mortgagor's covenant to repay is the principal together with interest. Thus, the mortgagee may, at any time after the fixed date for redemption has passed, sue for the debt (i.e., sue for the recovery of the loan).

Rückzahlungsversprechen

e) To appoint a receiver

The *Law of Property Act 1925* s109 gives the mortgagee the right to appoint a receiver to receive the rents and profits on the mortgagee's behalf in order to pay the money due. The receiver is deemed to be the agent of the mortgagor, who is liable for the receiver's acts and defaults, unless otherwise provided by the mortgage terms. The mortgagee thus avoids the disadvantage of strict accountability to which he would be subject if he entered himself into possession, because it is the borrower, not the lender, who is responsible for the acts and defaults of the receiver.

mit dem Auftrag

gelten – Vertreter

Verantwortung/Haftung

Verleiher/Darlehensgeber

f) Equitable mortgages

Where the mortgage is equitable and created by deed, the mortgagee has practically the same rights as have been set out above for the legal mortgage. Unless, however, the power to do so is expressly reserved, the equitable mortgagee has no right to take possession. If the mortgage is created by a deposit of title deeds, the mortgagee must ask the court for an order to sell the property or for an order appointing a receiver.

darstellen

vorbehalten

Hinterlegung – Grundeigentumsurkunde (= Nachweis der Herrschaftsrechte am Grundstück)

Diagram 47

Mortgages of land

Legal mortgages

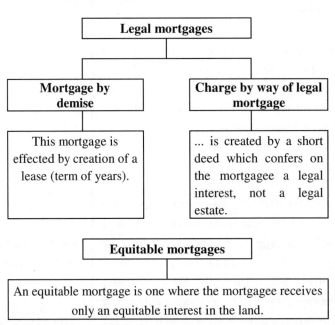

Mortgage by demise

This mortgage is effected by creation of a lease (term of years).

Charge by way of legal mortgage

... is created by a short deed which confers on the mortgagee a legal interest, not a legal estate.

Equitable mortgages

An equitable mortgage is one where the mortgagee receives only an equitable interest in the land.

The rights of mortgagor and mortgagee

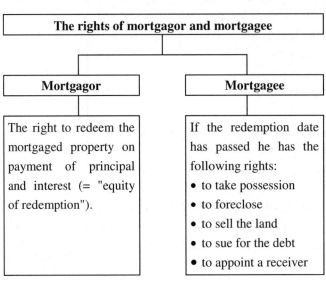

Mortgagor

The right to redeem the mortgaged property on payment of principal and interest (= "equity of redemption").

Mortgagee

If the redemption date has passed he has the following rights:

- to take possession
- to foreclose
- to sell the land
- to sue for the debt
- to appoint a receiver

VIII. Further reading[1]

Adams, Law for business students; *Barker & Padfield*, Law; *Bell*, Real property (Cracknell's law students' companion); *Boucher & Corns*, GCSE Law, Casebook; *Brown*, GCSE Law; *Chang & Welden*, Nutcases: Land Law; *Cheshire and Burn's*, Modern law of real property; *Geldart*, Introduction to English law; *Harris*, An Introduction to law; *James'* Introduction to English law; *Lawson and Kudden*, The Law of Property; *Lyall*, An Introduction to British law; *Megarry & Wade*, The Law of Real Property; *Scamell*, Butterworths property law handbook; *Smith & Keenan's* English law; *Stevens & Pearce*, Land law; *Templeman & Bell*, Land: The law of real property – Textbook – Casebook – Revision work book; *Templeman & Burr*, Conveyancing – Textbook – Casebook.

---

[1] Cf. p. 73.

Chapter Nine

The law of <u>trusts</u>

Treuhandverhältnis

I. Introduction and historical background

1. Introduction

Any good reader who has followed <u>attentively</u> what was said in the second chapter of vol. 1 (on. page 33 f.) must have already <u>appreciated</u> the nature of a trust, which is one of the most characteristic and <u>peculiar</u> institutions of English civil law. The <u>peculiarity</u> of the trust becomes obvious if you consider that there is no corresponding <u>legal institution</u> in German law nor in other continental legal systems, which fulfils all the <u>tasks</u> <u>inherent</u> in the trust in English law.

aufmerksam

schätzen/kennen lernen
auffällig
Auffälligkeit/das Besondere
Rechtsinstitut

Aufgabe – innewohnend/
immanent

If you were to look for the translation of the word *'trust'* in <u>legal (jargon) dictionaries</u>, you would probably find e.g.:

Rechtswörterbuch

„1. Treuhandverhältnis; Treuhandvermögen;
Ein trust *ist eine auf* equity *beruhende Rechtsbeziehung zwischen dem Treuhänder* (trustee) *und dem Begünstigten (beneficiary, früher:* cestui que trust[1]*) – auf beiden Seiten kann eine Mehrheit von Personen auftreten –, durch die das vom Besteller des* trust *(*settlor *oder* trustor*) auf den Treuhänder zugunsten des Begünstigten übertragene Vermögen von diesem verwaltet wird. Während der Begünstigte der* equitable owner *des Treuhandgutes ist, wird der Treuhänder der* legal owner *..." (cf. Dietl/Lorenz) where this "definition" is followed by 2 ½ pages of notions combined with "trust".*
Then follows "trust 2": under this heading „*Trust, Sonderform des Konzerns ...*" is mentioned as the second possible of translation. And in the dictionary by *Romain* we find for trust: „*Vertrauen, Treuhand, Treuhandverhältnis; ein auf Marktbeherrschung gerichteter Unternehmenszusammenschluss; Trust; Syndikat, Kartell, Konzern; Fideikommiss".*

---

[1] See below in this chapter.

The kind of trust we are concerned with in this chapter is the one dealt with in the former translation: „*Treuhandverhältnis*".

Before giving you a more detailed definition of the word "trust" in order to try and <u>illuminate</u> the darkness of its <u>incomprehensibility</u>, let us first consider its historical development.

erhellen

Unverständlichkeit

2. Historical background

Looking back at medieval England, you will note that <u>legal relationships</u>, which today are <u>denoted</u> as "trusts", were already known in the 12th and 13th centuries. If, for example a <u>knight</u> intended to participate in a <u>crusade</u>, he transferred his <u>feudal tenure</u> of land to a <u>person enjoying his confidence,</u> who had to administer the land <u>for the benefit of</u> the family of the absent knight. Instead of "for the benefit of", you can also say "<u>to the use of</u>".

Rechtsverhältnis – bezeichnen

Ritter – Kreuzzug
Lehen – Vertrauensperson
zugunsten

zum Nutzen von

This clarifies that legal relationships, which are today denoted as "trusts", were in the medieval times named *"uses"*.
The word "use" is said <u>to derive</u> from the Latin "<u>opus</u>".

A "use" arose in medieval times where a person conveyed property of any sort to another (the *feoffee to uses*), <u>upon the</u> <u>understanding that</u> the other was <u>to become seised</u> of it <u>on</u> <u>behalf of</u> himself (the <u>donor</u>) or on behalf of a third person (*cestui que use*).

In this relationship, the feoffee to uses was in a position of confidence which he could easily abuse. Therefore, the rights of the *cestui que use* <u>required protection</u>. The common law courts refused to recognize uses and failed to <u>afford</u> this protection because no "writ" existed which provided an action against the feoffee to uses.

So it was equity again which helped the donor in such a case. In the 15th century, the Court of Chancery <u>intervened</u> to force the feoffee to uses to administer the property for the benefit of the *cestui que use* according to the terms of the <u>grant</u>.

hier: Treuhand
entstammen/herrühren –
Werk/Hilfe/Nutzen

treuhänderischer Erwerber von Grundvermögen – unter der Bedingung, dass – zuständig werden – zugunsten von – Schenker/Treugeber – Begünstigter bei einer treuhänderischen Nutzungsüberlassung

Schutz verlangen
gewähren/bieten

eingreifen

Treuabrede

111

Over the course of time, the *cestui que use* came to have a special interest in the property <u>enforceable</u> only in the Court of Chancery.

einklagbar

Thus, this interest, protected by the Chancellor's equitable jurisdiction, became an *equitable interest*.

II. Definition of a trust

Many <u>attempts</u> have been made to define a trust but no definition is entirely <u>satisfactory</u>. The <u>varieties</u> of trusts lead to definitions which <u>omit</u> some of the types or are <u>vague</u> and unhelpful.

Versuch
zufrieden stellend – Verschiedenartigkeit
auslassen – vage

According to the <u>late</u> *Sir Arthur Underhill's*[1] definition, a trust is "an equitable obligation binding a person (who is called a <u>trustee</u>) to deal with property over which he has control (which is called trust property), for the benefit of persons (who are called beneficiaries or *cestuis que trust*), of whom he may himself be one, and anyone of whom may enforce the obligation."

verstorben

Treuhänder/Verwalter

Treugeber/Treuhandbegünstigter

This is certainly a good definition but it shows that it is impossible to give a <u>comprehensive</u> definition of all kinds of trusts, for *Underhill's* definition does not <u>cover</u> the so called "<u>charitable trusts</u>".

allumfassend

abdecken

wohltätige/gemeinnützige Stiftung

Instead of finding a definition of a trust, we should try to give <u>merely</u> an <u>explanation</u> of what a trust can be.

bloß – Erklärung

The main <u>characteristic</u> of the trust is the <u>duality of ownership</u> which can be acquired by <u>legal title</u> or <u>equitable title</u>. As a matter of fact, under trusts, the legal title will be <u>vested</u> in the trustees and the equitable title in the beneficiaries. This <u>might arise</u> where S (the <u>settlor</u>) transfers land to T1 and T2 (trustees) to hold the land on trust for the

Merkmal – Eigentumsspaltung – volles rechtliches Eigentum – vorläufiges (wirtschaftliches) Eigentum

fest erworben

kann vorkommen – Treugeber

---

[1] Whose definition, which he offered in *Underhill & Hayton*, Law of Trusts and Trustees, is cited in many textbooks, e.g. *James*, Introduction ..., p. 241 and *Parker & Mellows*, p. 9.

benefit of A, B and C (beneficiaries). The following diagram[1] may clarify this situation:

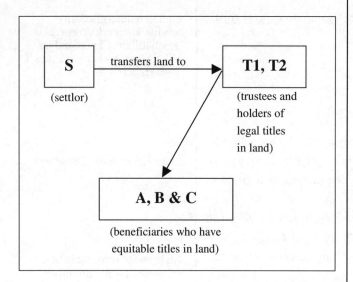

The trust does not <u>interfere with</u> the legal position of the title to the land; at law the title rests with T1 and T2, <u>since</u> it was tranferred to them by S.

beeinträchtigen

da

However, equity recognises that the title was not transferred to T1 and T2 for their own use, but for the benefit of A, B & C as the settlor S intended. The trustees are considered as having a "<u>bare</u> title" only and the benefits of the land will <u>accrue</u> to the beneficiaries. Through this <u>device</u>, the courts are able to <u>uphold</u> essential doctrines of common law and give effect to the true intention of the settlor.

nackt/bloß – zuwachsen / anfallen – Erfindung / Konstruktion – aufrecht-erhalten

III. Classification of trusts

Trusts may be classified into <u>private trusts</u> and charitable trusts. These must be considered separately, as there are important differences between them.

Trust zugunsten bestimmter Privatperson

---

[1] Borrowed from *Templeman/Halliwell*, p.1.

1. Private trusts

Private trusts can be <u>divided</u> once again into <u>express trusts</u>, <u>implied trusts</u> or <u>constructive trusts</u>.

einteilen/untergliedern – ausdrücklich erklärtes rechtsgeschäftliches Treuhandverhältnis (= T.) – konkludentes T. – gesetzliches T.

a) Express trusts

An express trust is a trust expressly created by the settlor by deed, by writing, sometimes orally <u>during life</u>, or by <u>will</u> for the benefit of one or more specified persons or a group of persons.

unter Lebenden – Testament

The essential elements of an express private trust were laid down in *Knight* v *Knight* (1840) by *Lord Langdale*, who declared that three "<u>certainties</u>" are necessary for the creation of a trust: <u>certainty of words</u>, <u>certainty of subject-matter</u> and <u>certainty of objects</u>.

Sicherheit/Gewissheit/Bestimmtheit – Bestimmtheit (= B.) der Worte – B. des Gegenstandes – B. des Objekts (= der Begünstigten)

Example – Knight v Knight (1840) –:

A man who died in 1824 left all his estates real and personal to his brother, Thomas Andrew Knight, and, <u>failing him</u>, to his nephew, Thomas Andrew Knight the younger. The will stated: "I do hereby <u>constitute</u> and appoint the person who shall <u>inherit</u> my <u>said estates</u> under this my will my sole <u>executor</u> and trustee, <u>to carry</u> the same and everything contained therein <u>duly into execution</u>; <u>confiding</u> in the approved honour and integrity of my family, to take no advantage of any technical <u>inaccuracies</u>, but to admit all the comparatively small <u>reservations</u> which <u>I make out of</u> so large a property ..."

The will stated that the <u>testator's</u> intention was that the estates should be <u>settled on</u> the next <u>descendant</u> in the <u>direct male line</u> of the testator's grandfather, Richard Knight of Downton. On the testator's death, Thomas Andrew Knight, the testator's brother, succeeded to the estates. In 1827, Thomas Andrew Knight the younger died childless, <u>intestate</u>, and the testator's brother immediately

falls er ausfällt

bestimmen
erben – bezeichnetes Vermögen
Testamentvollstrecker – pflichtgemäß ausführen – (an)vertrauen

Ungenauigkeiten
Vorbehalt – verbinden mit

Erblasser
vermachen – Abkömmling – gerade männliche Linie

testamentlos

114

settled the estates upon persons who were not the next descendants in the direct male line of Richard Knight of Downton. The question arose whether the testator had imposed a binding trust on his brother.

Held: that the words which the testator had used in his will were not sufficiently <u>imperative</u> to create a trust which was binding.

Lord Langdale MR:

zwingend

"As a general rule, it has been laid down, that when property is <u>given</u> absolutely to any person, and the same person is, by the <u>giver</u> who has power to <u>command</u>, <u>recommended</u> or <u>entreated</u>, or wished, to dispose of that property in favour of another, the recommendation, <u>entreaty</u>, or wish shall be held to create a trust.

schenken
Schenker – verfügen
empfehlen – ersuchen

Bitte

First, if the words were so used, that upon the whole, they ought to be <u>construed</u> as imperative;

auslegen

Secondly, if the subject of the recommendation or wish be certain; and

Thirdly, if the objects or persons intended to have the benefit of the recommendation or wish be also certain."

Thus, the "three certainties" mean first, that the words used must show a clear *intention* that a trust shall arise. Secondly, the certainty of subject-matter speaks for itself: if the subject-matter to be held on trust is <u>indeterminate</u>, the courts cannot <u>enforce</u> the trust. Thirdly, the certainty of objects means that the persons whom the trust is intended to benefit must be <u>ascertainable</u>.

unbestimmt
vollstrecken

bestimmbar

b) Implied trusts

An implied trust is based upon the <u>presumed</u> intention of the settlor. The most common type of an implied trust is the <u>resulting trust</u>.

This kind of trust arises as a <u>result</u> of the presumed intention of the settler, where he has failed to express his intention <u>adequately</u> or <u>at all</u>.

vermuten

gesetzlich vermuteter Trust
Ergebnis

angemessen – überhaupt

115

An implied or resulting trust would arise, e.g. if a settlor created a trust of £100,000 "for A for life". This does not indicate what is to happen to the money on A's death and, thus, equity helps in such a case by presuming that the settlor intended that the money should result to himself or his estate on A's death.

hier: zurückfallen an

Example – Abbot Fund Trusts, Re[1], Smith v Abbot (1900) –:

A fund was raised by subscription to support two distressed ladies and to enable them to live in lodgings in Cambridge. On their death, a surplus remained in the hands of the trustees.

Held: that it was not the intention of the subscribers that the money should become the absolute property of the ladies and it followed that the trustees held the balance on a resulting trust for the subscribers.

ein Sondervermögen einrichten
– als Spende – notleidend

Überschuss

Spender

das Guthaben behalten

---

c) Constructive trusts

Constructive trusts are imposed by equity regardless of the intention of the parties. The intentions of the parties are irrelevant to the imposition of a constructive trust because it arises by operation of law. A constructive trust, for example, will be imposed on a fiduciary who tries to make a secret profit from his fiduciary position; it is imposed whether or not he realises this.

auferlegen – ohne Rücksicht auf

Auferlegung

Treuhänder

Example – Keech v Sandford (1726) –:

A trustee held a lease of Romford Market on trust for an infant beneficiary. The trustee attempted to renew the lease for the benefit of the infant but the lessor refused to grant a renewal to the infant. The lessor agreed, however,

Pacht

Pächter

---

[1] "Re" means "in that matter" *(= in dieser Angelegenheit/in diesem Rechtsstreit); diese Zitierweise ist in Streitigkeiten üblich, in die mehr Personen als nur ein Kläger und Beklagter verwickelt sind.*

to renew the lease in favour of the trustee personally. The lease was accordingly made out to the trustee.

Held: that the trustee held the new lease on constructive trust for the infant.

Another more modern case which illustrates this is:

Example – AGIP (Africa Ltd) v *Jackson (1991) –:*

The plaintiffs <u>requested</u> the defendants not to arrange for the transfer of money in their possession to a third party, as it had been obtained by fraud by one of the plaintiff's employees. The defendants ignored the <u>request</u>.

Held: that the defendants were liable as constructive trustees.

ersuchen/verlangen

das Verlangen

2. <u>Charitable</u> (public) trusts

karitativ/gemeinnützig

There is no <u>comprehensive</u> definition of a legal "<u>charity</u>" provided either by the courts or by statute. However, the meaning is not the same as the popular meaning and it has to be determined <u>by reference to</u> the relevant case law. For a trust to be charitable, it must <u>satisfy</u> three <u>requirements</u>: a) it must be charitable in the legal sense, b) it must benefit the public as a whole or at least a section of it and c) it must be wholly and <u>exclusively</u> charitable.

verständlich – Wohltätigkeit/ gemeinnützige Stiftung

unter Bezugnahme auf Voraussetzungen erfüllen

ausschließlich

a) Charity in the legal sense

The classification of a charitable trust is given in nearly all textbooks regarding the law of trust, with reference to the words of *Lord Macnaghten* in the following leading case:

Example – Income Tax Special Purposes Commissioners v *Pemsel (1891) –:*	
Land was conveyed in 1813 to trustees on trust <u>to apply</u> a <u>proportion</u> of the <u>rents</u> and profits for missionary establishments commonly known as the Moravian Church, of which Pemsel was the <u>treasurer</u>. It was claimed that the gift was for 'charitable purposes' under the *Income Tax Act 1842* and, <u>hence</u>, exempt from income tax.	verwenden Anteil – Pachtzins Schatzmeister von nun an
Held: that since the trust <u>contemplated purposes</u> which had no relation to the <u>relief of poverty</u>, the purposes were not 'charitable' within the meaning of the 1842 Act and, thus, income tax was payable. *Lord Macnaghten* stated "How far then, it may be asked, does the popular meaning of the word 'charity' correspond with its legal meaning? 'Charity' in the legal sense comprises four principal divisions: (1) trusts for the relief of poverty; (2) trusts for the <u>advancement of education</u>; (3) trusts for the <u>advancement of religion</u>; and (4) trust for other purposes beneficial to the community, not falling under any of the preceding heads."	Zweck verfolgen Armenhilfe Förderung der Bildung Förderung der Religion

The fourth category includes such purposes as the <u>welfare</u> of animals, the provision of public works such as bridges and museums, the setting up of <u>fire brigades</u> and <u>distress</u> funds and the <u>promotion</u> of <u>efficiency</u> in the armed forces. Trusts for political purposes are not charitable and will therefore fail.

Wohlergehen

Feuerwehr – Not/Elend
Förderung – Leistungsfähigkeit

Examples:

South Place Ethical Society, Re, Barralet v Attorney-General (1980)	
The South Place <u>Ethical</u> Society, which was first established in 1824, had as its aims the study and <u>dissemination</u> of ethical principles and the cultivation of a <u>rational</u> religious sentiment. Ethics is concerned with the belief in the <u>excellence</u> of truth, love and beauty, but not a belief in	ethisch Verbreitung vernünftig Außergewöhnlichkeit

anything supernatural. It also regards the objective of human existence as being the discovery of truth by reason and not by <u>revelation</u>. The society held regular Sunday meetings which were open to the public and also had as one of its aims the study and dissemination of ethical principles. The society asked the court for a declaration as to whether its objects were charitable. It <u>contended</u> that its purposes were for the advancement of religion but alternatively contended it was for the advancement of education.

Held: that the society was not for the advancement of religion because religion is concerned with man's relations with God whereas ethics is concerned with man's relations with man. Further essential features of 'religion' were faith in a God and <u>worship</u> of that God. There could be no worship of ethical principles. However, the society could attain charitable status as being for the advancement of education and for the benefit of the community.

Offenbarung

vorbringen

Anbetung

Inland Revenue Commissioners v McMullen (1981)

The objective of a trust was the provision of <u>facilities</u> which would enable and encourage school and university students to play association football or other games or sports and thereby to assist in ensuring that due attention is given to the physical education and development of such pupils as well as to the development and occupation of their minds.

Held: that the trust was charitable as being for the advancement of education.

Einrichtungen

Koeppler's Will Trusts, Re v Slack (1985)

A testator <u>bequeathed</u> part of his estate to 'the institution known as Wilton Park ... as long as Wilton Park remains a British <u>contribution</u> to the formation of an informed public opinion and to the <u>promotion</u> of greater cooperation in Europe and the West in general'. 'Wilton Park' was, in fact, a series of private conferences, initiated by the testator, for

vermachen

Beitrag
Förderung

key people capable of influencing opinion in member states of the Organisation for Economic Cooperation and Development. The conferences were accommodated and manned by the Foreign Office and they were not intended to conform to any particular party political line.

Held: that the gift was valid, as it had created a charitable trust for the advancement of education, i.e. the furtherance of the work of the Wilton Park project. The words 'as long as Wilton Park remains ...' were a condition precedent which, on the facts, at the testator's death, had been satisfied.

Menschen in Schlüssel-positionen

begleiten
(mit Personal) besetzen

Geschenk/Zuwendung
Erweiterung

Vorbedingung

b) Benefit for the public

If the main intention of a trust is to benefit certain specified persons, no charitable trust arises. For example, a trust for the education of the lawful descendants of three named persons is not charitable.

ganz bestimmte

gesetzliche Erben/
Abkömmlinge

Example – Compton, Re, Powell v Compton (1945) –:

By her will, a testatrix left money on trust for the education of the children of C, P and M, who were under twenty-six years of age. There were twenty-eight descendants of these persons eligible.

Held: that a class of persons determined by reference to a personal relationship was not a sufficient section of the public so as to satisfy the requirement that to be charitable a trust must be for the public benefit. The trust was therefore not charitable.

Erblasserin

wählbar/geeignet

hier: Bereich

Employees of a company do not form a section of the public for this purpose. Thus, a trust to educate children of a company has been held to be not charitable.

hier: Abteilung
in diesem Sinne

Example – Oppenheim v *Tobacco Securities Trust Co. Ltd. (1951) –:*

The Tobacco Securities Trust Co. Ltd. held certain investments on trust to apply the income 'in providing for the ... education of children of employees or former employees' of British American Tobacco Co. Ltd.

Held: that a class of persons determined by applying a test of relationship with a given person or body is not a section of the public for the purpose of satisfying the requirement that for a gift to be charitable it must be for the 'public benefit'. The trust was thus not charitable.

Kapitalanlage – verwenden – Einkünfte

beschenkt

Trusts for the relief of poverty are, however, exempt from this public benefit requirement. Thus, in the case of relief of poverty, trusts in favour of poor relations of the donor, or of poor employees (even of a specified firm) are charitable.

ausgenommen/befreit

Verwandte

c) Whole and exclusive charity

The requirement that a charitable trust must be wholly and exclusively charitable is not satisfied if, under the terms of the trust, the property can be applied to non-charitable as well as to charitable purposes. Therefore, trusts for "charitable or benevolent purposes" have been held void.

hier: erfüllt
verwendet werden

d) The Charity Acts

Wohltätigkeitsgesetze

The difficulties in distinguishing whether the purpose of a trust is charitable or non-charitable were clarified, but not completely ironed out, by the *Charity Acts 1960, 1985* and *1992*. Among the major reforms of the 1992 Act, was a provision whereby the Secretary of State could order that charitable trustees would not be bound by the "half/half-rule" in s2(1) of the *Trustee Investments Act 1961*. This

beseitigen
unter

121

provision gives trustees a statutory power to invest up to one half of the trust fund in the ordinary shares of companies. The other half must be invested in safer items, such as National Savings certificates, government stocks and local authority loans.

Vorschrift – gesetzliche Ermächtigung – Trust-vermögen
Gegenstand

Spargelder (staatliche verzinste Wertpapiere) – Staatsobliga-tionen – Darlehen

Diagram 48

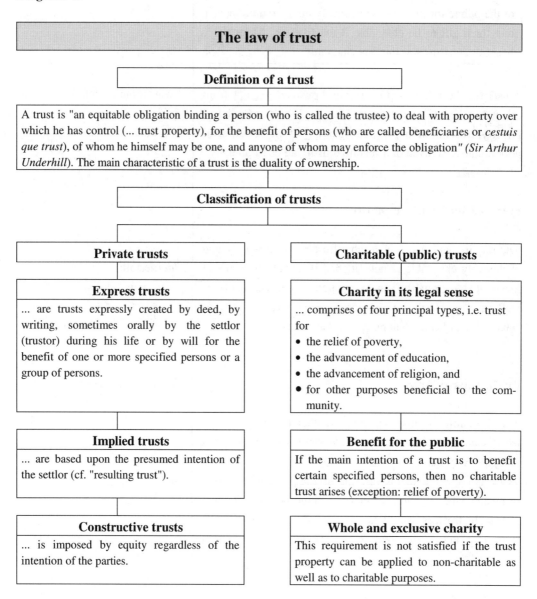

The law of trust

Definition of a trust

A trust is "an equitable obligation binding a person (who is called the trustee) to deal with property over which he has control (... trust property), for the benefit of persons (who are called beneficiaries or *cestuis que trust*), of whom he himself may be one, and anyone of whom may enforce the obligation" *(Sir Arthur Underhill)*. The main characteristic of a trust is the duality of ownership.

Classification of trusts

Private trusts	**Charitable (public) trusts**
Express trusts	**Charity in its legal sense**
... are trusts expressly created by deed, by writing, sometimes orally by the settlor (trustor) during his life or by will for the benefit of one or more specified persons or a group of persons.	... comprises of four principal types, i.e. trust for • the relief of poverty, • the advancement of education, • the advancement of religion, and • for other purposes beneficial to the community.
Implied trusts	**Benefit for the public**
... are based upon the presumed intention of the settlor (cf. "resulting trust").	If the main intention of a trust is to benefit certain specified persons, then no charitable trust arises (exception: relief of poverty).
Constructive trusts	**Whole and exclusive charity**
... is imposed by equity regardless of the intention of the parties.	This requirement is not satisfied if the trust property can be applied to non-charitable as well as to charitable purposes.

3. Differences between private and charitable trusts

a) Private trusts are created for the benefit of specified persons or groups of persons; charitable trusts are created to further a purpose that will benefit society as a whole at large or an appreciable part of it.

hier: fördern – als Ganzes
beträchtlich

b) Private trusts are governed by the rules against perpetuities[1]; charitable trusts enjoy, to a certain extent, exemptions from these rules.

unterliegen – „Verbot von Zuwendungen auf ewige Zeit"
Ausnahme

c) Charitable trusts are wholly or partly exempt from many taxes that affect private trusts, and they also enjoy reduced rates. The income of a charitable trust, used for charitable purposes is largely exempt from income tax.

befreit
beeinträchtigen
ermäßigt – Kommunalabgaben
Einkommensteuer

d) The requirement of the "three certainties" is more important for private trusts than for charitable trusts: if the persons who are to be beneficiaries under a private trust are not defined with sufficient certainty, the trust will fail. However, if the objects of a charitable trust are undoubtedly charitable, the trust will not fail merely because those purposes are vague; the court can order a scheme for the application of the property.

bestimmt – ausreichend
unzweifelhaft – bloß
Plan – Verwendung

e) As charitable trusts enjoy part exemption from the rules against perpetuities, the *cy-près*[2] doctrine is applied to them: Where the literal execution of a charitable trust is or becomes inexpedient or impractical, the court will apply the *cy-près* doctrine to the property, which means it will adapt it to some charitable purpose as near as possible to the original purpose named by the donor. This is done by means of a scheme for the application of the property by the Charity Commissioners or the court.

buchstäbliche Ausführung
unzweckmäßig – undurchführbar – verwenden
mittels
Stiftungsaufsichtsbehörde

f) Private trusts are enforced by the beneficiaries; charitable trusts are enforced by the Attorney-General on behalf of the Crown.

einklagen/vollstrecken

---

[1] See below under IV.
[2] Vgl. frz. "cy-près que possible" = *so nahe wie möglich.*

IV. The rules against perpetuities

The rules against perpetuities deal with the question for what period of time the <u>tying up of wealth</u> should be possible.

Vermögensbindung

Two rules have been developed to deal with this, both of which apply to private trusts:

1. The rule against <u>remoteness</u> of <u>vesting</u>

Ferne – Eigentumsübertragung

This rule provides that property must <u>vest</u> in the <u>recipient</u> within the period of a life or lives in being at the time when the gift is made and 21 years thereafter (with <u>allowance</u> being made where appropriate for any <u>period of gestation</u>).

übergehen – Empfänger

Gewährung/Erlaubnis
anrechnungsfähige
Schwangerschaftszeit

Under English law, the purpose of this rule is to <u>avoid</u> the legal title and the equitable title being separated for an unlimited period of time. This rule was laid down by the House of Lords in *Cadell* v *Palmer* (1833) and has now been <u>amended</u> by the *Perpetuities and Accumulation Act 1964*.

vermeiden

ändern – Fortdauer/
Dauerzustand – Anhäufung
(von Vermögen)
vollberechtigt

The effect now is that where property is held on trust, the beneficiaries must become <u>absolutely entitled</u> to the property, either within a period of a life in being at the time when the trust came into existence, plus 21 years after the end of this life, *or* within a period not <u>exceeding</u> 80 years specified in the trust <u>instrument</u>.

überschreiten
Urkunde

Charitable trusts are <u>generally</u> subject to this rule.

grundsätzlich

2. The rule against perpetual trusts

This rule <u>renders void</u> any disposition that attempts to <u>tie up</u> property for a period longer than a life in being plus 21 years.

nichtig machen – binden

The rule does not apply to charitable trusts, which can therefore continue <u>indefinitely</u>.

unendlich

On the meaning of *"life (or lives) in being"*, the case *Re Kelly* (1932) is very <u>instructive</u>.

lehrreich

In this case, the <u>testator</u> <u>disposed by will</u> that a gift was <u>to take effect</u> after the death of the last of the testator's dogs. It

Erblasser – letztwillig verfügen – anfallen/gültig werden

was held that the gift was void for remoteness. Judge *Meredith* said: "... 'lives' means human beings, not animals or trees in California"!

V. Trustees

Most of the law concerning trusts and <u>trusteeships</u> originally evolved from the decisions of the Court of Chancery but much of it is now contained in the *Trustee Act 1925*.

Treuhänderschaft

1. <u>Appointment</u> and <u>discharge</u>

Ernennung – Entlassung

a) Appointment

Trustees are usually appointed by the settlor in the instrument which creates the trust. It is one of the maxims of equity that a trust shall never fail <u>for want</u> of a trustee. Thus, if a testator creates a trust by will but does not name trustees, or if those who are named refuse to act, then the testator's personal representatives must act as trustees until others are appointed.

wegen Bedürfnisses

There is no general rule as to the number to be appointed, although it is unusual to appoint only one person as a <u>sole</u> trustee. Where, however, land is <u>settled</u>, or held upon trust for sale under s34 (2) of the *Trustee Act 1925*, there may not normally be more than four trustees. Under s14 of this Act, no less than two trustees are required to give a valid receipt to a purchaser of such land. This rule is, however, subject to a further exception, namely that a *trust corporation* acting as a sole trustee can give a valid <u>receipt</u>. A trust corporation is a <u>corporate body</u> empowered to act as a trustee. Because a corporation is not a human trustee, there is never any problem of the trustee dying or retiring. Common examples for trust corporations are the trustee departments of banks or <u>insurance companies</u>.

alleinig
übertragen/zuwenden

Quittung
körperschaftliche Rechtsfigur

Versicherungsgesellschaft

b) Discharge

A trustee can be discharged under an <u>express power</u> in the trust instrument, under the provisions of s36 of the *Trustee Act 1925* (which <u>determine</u> that a trustee may be replaced by a new trustee under certain circumstances, e.g., if he remains abroad for over a year) or, in extreme cases by the court. Moreover, the termination of trusteeship is possible by <u>retirement</u>.

    ausdrückliche Ermächtigung

    bestimmen

    Rücktritt/Pensionierung

2. <u>Rights and Duties</u>

    Rechte und Pflichten

a) Rights

(1) As already mentioned above, the *Trustee Investments Act 1961* gives trustees a statutory power to invest up to one half of the trust fund in the ordinary shares of companies, whereas the <u>remainder</u> must be invested in safer items.

    Rest

(2) A trustee can only get <u>remuneration</u> for his activities if this is authorized by the trust instrument, by all beneficiaries (if of <u>full age</u> and <u>capacity</u>) or by the court. Trustees are entitled to be <u>reimbursed</u> out of the trust fund for any <u>expenses</u> properly <u>incurred</u> in the performance of their duties.

    Entschädigung/Entlohnung

    Volljährigkeit – Geschäfts-fähigkeit – vergüten/entschä-digen
    Ausgaben – anfallen

b) Duties

Trustees have two main duties:
(1) They must administer the trust property <u>prudently</u>. That means a trustee must take the same <u>care</u> of trust property as an <u>ordinary business person</u> would take of his (or her) own property. Moreover, a professional trustee must exercise the special <u>skills</u> that he <u>professes to have</u>.

    umsichtig/klug/gewissenhaft
    Sorgfalt
    „ordentlicher Kaufmann"

    Geschicklichkeit – erklärter-maßen haben (muss)

Example – Bartlett v Barclays Bank Trust Co. Ltd (1980) –
:

The plaintiff beneficiaries claimed against the defendant trustee <u>alleging</u> breach of trust. As trustee, the defendant had a controlling interest in a private company, but it was not represented on the <u>board</u> or at its meetings and it had relied on information <u>dispensed</u> at annual general meetings. The board had <u>engaged</u> in two <u>hazardous</u> property speculations and, although one had been successful, there had resulted an <u>overall loss</u> to the trust fund.

Held: that the defendant was liable for the loss, as he had failed to <u>discharge</u> the higher duty of care owed by a professional corporate trustee or even to act as a reasonably prudent businessman would have acted in his own affairs. The defendant could not be excused under s61 of the *Trustee Act 1925*: although he had acted 'honestly' (in failing to exercise greater control), he had not acted 'reasonably' in all the circumstances. However, the defendant was protected by s26 of the *Limitation Act 1939* (see now s32 of the 1980 Act) in respect of part of the income lost on the invested money, as he had not been guilty of '<u>fraud</u>' and he could off-set the profit made on the one transaction against the loss made on the other.

	behaupten
	Gremium/Vorstand
	verbreiten
	unternehmen – gefährlich
	Gesamtverlust
	erfüllen/entlasten
	Betrug

(2) Trustees must strictly <u>comply with</u> all the terms of the trust. If a trustee is careless or fails to comply strictly with the terms of the trust, he may be personally liable for <u>losses</u>. Trustees will not, however, be liable for mere <u>accidental</u> losses or <u>errors of judgment</u>. A trustee must actively exercise all powers – equity does not <u>countenance</u> a sleeping trustee.

erfüllen

Verluste
zufällig – falsche Beurteilung/ Fehleinschätzung

unterstützen/begünstigen

As a general rule, trustees may not <u>delegate</u> their duties. Under s23 of the *Trustee Act 1925*, however, there is a list of exceptions to this rule. These exceptions include, for example, the right to employ a solicitor, a banker or a <u>stockbroker</u> to <u>effect</u> transactions in connection with

delegieren

Aktienmakler – bewirken

the trust property. The costs of these agents are paid out of the trust estate.

hier: Vermögen

3. Liabilities for breaches of trust

Haftung für Treuhandver-tragsverletzungen

Where a loss occurs to the trust fund from some improper act, (neglect, default or omission of the trustee), the following actions are available to the beneficiaries:

vorkommen – unsauber/un-zulässig – Nachlässigkeit – Fehler – Unterlassung

- an action against the trustee(s) to compensate the trust for the loss sustained;

entschädigen

- a criminal prosecution in certain cases (theft or fraud);

Diebstahl

- 'following' the trust property (tracing) (which is explained below).

Nachforschung

The third remedy "following the trust property (tracing)" is best understood by an example[1]:

Rechtsmittel

Suppose that T, a trustee, holds a valuable painting in trust for the beneficiary B. If T, in breach of trust, sells the painting to X, the question arises as to whether B can sue X for the return of the painting. B has a right of action against T. If X had no notice, actual or constructive, that the painting purchased was held on trust, the painting may be kept by him. X, in this case, falls within the category of a person who *bonafide* (i.e. in good faith) purchased trust property without notice that it was such and is therefore protected. B's only remedy is against T, the trustee for the sale price. If, instead of *selling* the painting to X, T had *given* it, the beneficiary may lawfully claim the painting from X, for the latter is not a *bona fide* purchaser. Therefore the beneficiary can follow (= trace) the trust property[2].

wertvolles Gemälde

(gesetzlich) unterstellt

gutgläubig

schenken

der Letztere
auf der Spur bleiben

---

[1] According to *Barker & Padfield*, p. 234; cf. also the diagram in vol. 1, chapter two, p. 34.

[2] As a German law student who knows the *BGB* fairly well, you hopefully thought of *§§ 932 ff.* and *§ 816*? According to German legal history 'tracing' means: „*Wo Du Deinen Glauben gelassen hast, dort musst Du ihn suchen*".

Example – Re Hallet's Estate Knatchbull v Hallett (1880) –:

By a <u>marriage settlement</u>, money was settled for the benefit of Hallett, his wife and his children. The trustees of the settlement allowed the money to come into the hands of Hallett, who <u>appropriated</u> it to his own use. As a solicitor, Hallett also received money belonging to a client, Mrs. C, and this too he credited to his own account. He subsequently <u>drew</u> money out of the account for his own purposes, but paid in other sums.

Held: that where trust money is mixed with a trustee's own money in one fund, the beneficiaries have the first <u>charge</u> on the whole fund for the trust money. If a trustee <u>draws on</u> the mixed fund for his own purposes, he is <u>deemed</u> to draw out first his own money.

	Ehevertrag
	verwenden
	entnehmen
	Belastung/*hier:* Zugriff belasten beurteilen/halten für

Example – Re Diplock, Diplock v Wintle (1948) –:

A testator <u>directed</u> his executors to apply <u>the residue</u> of his estate 'for such charitable or benevolent object or objects in England' as they should select. The executors distributed a large part of the residue among various charities before the <u>next-of-kin</u> of the testator <u>challenged</u> the validity of the <u>bequest</u>. The next-of-kin claimed the amounts paid to the charities by the executors and, with the approval of the court, these claims were <u>compromised</u>. The next-of-kin also claimed against the various institutions which had received money from the executors. The claims of the next-of-kin were of two main kinds: (a) claims <u>in personam</u> against the institutions which had received money; (b) claims <u>in rem</u> against the assets held by the institutions.

Held: that, as to the claims in personam: (1) An unpaid or underpaid creditor, <u>legatee</u> or next-of-kin had an equitable right which could be claimed against a <u>recipient</u> who had been paid more than he was entitled to receive or who was not entitled to any payment. (2) The claim by the next-of-kin was not <u>defeated</u> by the fact that the payment to the re-

	anweisen – Rest
	die nächsten Angehörigen – anfechten – Vermächtnis
	Streit beilegen
	persönlich sachlich
	Vermächtnisnehmer Empfänger
	vereiteln

cipient had been made under a mistake of law, rather than of fact. (3) The next-of-kin's primary claim was against the personal representatives, and the claim against the charities was limited to the amount <u>irrecoverable</u> from the personal representatives. (4) The amount for which the defendants were liable under this head was to be <u>reckoned</u> without <u>interest</u>.

uneinbringlich

berechnen

Zinsen

As to the claims in rem: (1) A person whose money had been mixed with that of another might <u>trace</u> his money into the mixed fund, <u>notwithstanding</u> that the fund were held, or the mixing had been done, by an <u>innocent volunteer</u>.

nachforschen

ungeachtet dessen/obwohl

unschuldiger/uneigennütziger Treuhänder

(2) Where the money had passed to an innocent volunteer, and there was no question of mixing, the innocent volunteer held the money on behalf of the true owner.

(3) Where the money had passed to an innocent volunteer, who had mixed it with money of his own, then the <u>claimant</u> and the innocent volunteer <u>ranked pari passu</u> with regard to the mixed fund. Where the money had been paid into an active bank account, *prima facie* the rule in *Clayton's Case* applied. Thus, where the money received by a charity had been mixed by the charity with money of its own, the next-of-kin were entitled to recover pari passu with the charity. But where the money received by the charity had been expended on the <u>alteration</u> or <u>improvement</u> of its assets, e.g. by the <u>erection</u> of new buildings on its land, or in <u>discharging</u> debts of the charity, then the equitable remedy of a <u>charge</u> would <u>work</u> an injustice; in such circumstances the money could no longer be traced, and the next-of-kin had no remedy 'in rem' against the money or assets of the charity.

Antragsteller – den gleichen Rang einnehmen

Änderung

Verbesserung – Errichtung

tilgen

Anklage – hervorbringen

VI. Beneficiaries

The principal right of a beneficiary is his right to the <u>enjoyment</u> of the interest in the trust property.

In the case of a private trust, they have a right to force the trustees, by action if necessary, to administer the property

Ausübung

according to the terms of the trust. As just mentioned under "liabilities" of *trustees* for a breach of trust, the possible actions that can be made by the beneficiaries are:

- they may bring a personal action against the trustee(s);
- they may be able to follow the trust property itself (tracing) or to claim anything into which it has been converted;

umwandeln

- they may be able to institute criminal proceedings against the trustees.

anstrengen/einleiten

Further details can be found in the literature which is mentioned under "Further reading" after the next diagram.

Diagram 49

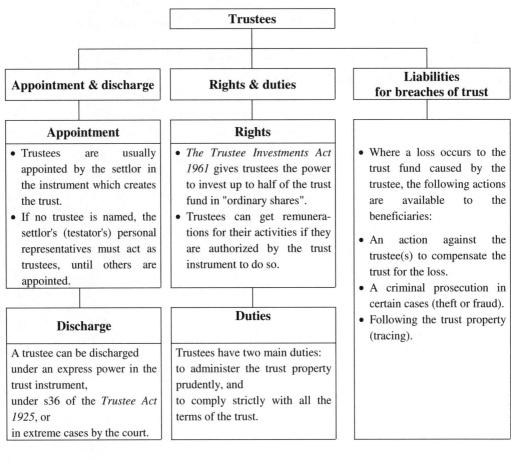

Trustees and beneficiaries

Trustees

Appointment & discharge

Appointment

- Trustees are usually appointed by the settlor in the instrument which creates the trust.
- If no trustee is named, the settlor's (testator's) personal representatives must act as trustees, until others are appointed.

Discharge

A trustee can be discharged under an express power in the trust instrument,
under s36 of the *Trustee Act 1925*, or
in extreme cases by the court.

Rights & duties

Rights

- *The Trustee Investments Act 1961* gives trustees the power to invest up to half of the trust fund in "ordinary shares".
- Trustees can get remunerations for their activities if they are authorized by the trust instrument to do so.

Duties

Trustees have two main duties:
to administer the trust property prudently, and
to comply strictly with all the terms of the trust.

Liabilities for breaches of trust

- Where a loss occurs to the trust fund caused by the trustee, the following actions are available to the beneficiaries:
- An action against the trustee(s) to compensate the trust for the loss.
- A criminal prosecution in certain cases (theft or fraud).
- Following the trust property (tracing).

Beneficiaries

Rights to the enjoyment of their interest in the trust property.

Private trusts: Right to force the trustees, by action if necessary, to administer the property according to the trust instrument.

In the case of breaches of trust by a trustee:
- action for compensation
- criminal prosecution, or
- tracing

VII. Further reading[1]

Barker & Padfield, Law; *Brown*, GCSE Law; *Chang & Welden*, Nutcases: Equity and Trust; *Cracknell*, Equity and Trust (*Cracknell's* law students' companion); *Edwards and Stockwell*, Trust and Equity; *Geldart*, Introduction to English law; *Hudson*, Equity & Trust; *James'* Introduction to English law; *Lyall*, An Introduction to British law; *Parker & Mellows*, The modern law of trusts; *Pearce & Stevens*, The law of trusts and equitable obligations; *Pettit*, Equity and the Law of Trust; *Riddall*, The law of trusts; *Smith & Keenan's* English law; *Sydenham*, Nutshells: Equity & Trust; *Templeman & Halliwell*, Equity and Trust, Textbook; *Templeman & Doherty*, Equity and Trust, Revision work book; *Templeman & Cutler*, Equity and Trust, Casebook.

---

[1] Cf. p. 73.

Chapter Ten

Family law

I. Historical background

Historically, there seems to be no doubt that the common law required nothing for the celebration of a marriage beyond the declared agreement of the parties, which might take the form either of a declaration of present intention or of a promise to marry followed by actual union. This was the general law in England and Western Europe in medieval times.

Ehe/Eheschließung – außer ausdrückliche Vereinbarung Willenserklärung tatsächlicher Zusammenschluss

The House of Lords, however, decided in an Irish case in the 19th century that the common law had always required the presence of an ordained priest.

geweihter Priester

The question for England has now become an academic one because several statutes, ranging from 1753 to 1994, have described the formalities necessary for a valid marriage.

von ... bis reichen

A marriage must be celebrated either in the presence of a clergyman of the Church of England or, since 1836, of a Registrar of Marriages or, since 1898, of an "authorised person", who is usually the minister of a nonconformist place of worship.

Geistlicher – seit
Standesbeamter
hier: Pfarrer – protestantische Freikirche

In the 19th century, family law was largely concerned with marriage and the consequences of a failed marriage. The principal remedy in the ecclesiastical courts was nullity.

gescheiterte Ehe
Kirchengericht – Nichtigkeit/ Ungültigkeit – Scheidung – erhalten mit großem Kostenaufwand

A divorce could only be obtained at great cost by a parliamentary Bill. Divorce law was mainly concerned with finding one of the spouses to have been at fault: having committed a "matrimonial offence".

Ehepartner, der sich fehlverhalten hat – schwere Ehrverletzung

The present divorce law was established through the *Divorce Reform Act 1969* which abolished the idea of fault in divorce proceedings.

Scheidungsrecht
abschaffen – Verschulden – Scheidungsprozess

Significant reforms to divorce law were made by the *Family Law Act 1996.*

As far as children were concerned, the law protected the overriding rights of the fathers with regard to their children. Children were regarded as the property of their parents, and, in particular, as the property of their father. The rights of the mother then became more important until the parents were largely recognised as equals.

soweit ... betroffen waren – schützen – vorrangige Rechte – unter Berücksichtigung

als Gleichberechtigte anerkennen

The law then moved on to recognise the rights of children, whose welfare is now the overriding consideration in proceedings concerning the upbringing of children.

deren – Wohlergehen – vorrangiger Gesichtspunkt – Erziehung

The *Children Act 1989* radically reformed the law in this area and is the most important statute on resolving disputes.

Streitigkeiten schlichten

II. Matrimonial law

Eherecht

Marriage had traditionally been defined in English law as "the voluntary union for life of one man to one woman to the exclusion of all others" [*Hyde* v *Hyde* (1866), cf. *Cretney/Masson*, Principals of Family Law, p.2].

This definition, which is based on a monogamous marriage, however, is nowadays inaccurate if you consider the steadily increasing number of divorces: marriage is indeed still a voluntary union, but cannot necessarily be regarded as lifelong!

monogam

heutzutage – ungenau/falsch – ständig – ansteigen

Before looking further into the institution of marriage, it is helpful to consider the legal consequences of the preliminaries that may lead to marriage, such as engagement and cohabitation.

hier: sich näher beschäftigen mit

Vorverhandlungen/vorbereitende Maßnahmen – Verlöbnis – Zusammenleben

1. Engagement

Since the *Law Reform (Miscellaneous Provisions) Act 1970*, an engagement is no longer a contract which needs consideration to be valid. Thus, there is now no right of action for "breach of promise". Before the Act of 1970 abolished this right, a party (usually the woman) could sue for damages for breach of contract if the other party refused to marry.

Gegenleistung

Engagements are usually formalised by the man giving the woman an "engagement ring". The ring remains the property of the woman should the engagement be broken, unless, at the time it was given, the man made clear that, in the event of the marriage not taking place, the ring was to be returned. Generally, engaged couples do not have the same rights as married couples.

Verlobungsring
es sei denn
im Fall, dass

Example – Mossop v Mossop (1988) –:

P and D became engaged and lived together in D's house. They then separated and P claimed a property transfer order under s24 of the *Matrimonial Causes Act 1973* by virtue of s2(1) *Law Reform (Miscellaneous Provisions) Act 1970.*

Held: that dismissing the application of s2(1) of the 1970 Act, did not put engaged couples on a par with married couples. The making of a property transfer order under s24 of the *Matrimonial Causes Act 1973* was conditional on there having been a decree for divorce, nullity or judicial separation, which could not arise in the case of an engaged couple who have never been married.

Gesetz betreffend Ehesachen – gemäß

gleichstellen

Urteil – Ungültigkeit
getrennt leben

---

2. Cohabitation without marriage

The legal statutes of an unmarried couple living together is very complex because the law does not recognise such an arrangement as a "marriage". Legislation, however, has recognised that, in certain matters, these partners have similar rights and duties as legally married partners and has provided the appropriate status. For example, a woman may claim against the estate of her deceased partner as a dependant and the *Supplementary Benefits Act 1976* treats the partners as if they were married.

Zusammenleben ohne Trauschein
unverheiratet

verheiratet

verstorben
Unterhaltsberechtigter – Sozialhilfegesetz

3. Formalities of <u>marriage</u>

hier: Eheschließung

We have already seen, when dealing with the historical background, that a marriage may be <u>solemnised</u> by a Church of England ceremony, by ceremonies of another religion or in a <u>Registrar's Office</u>.

feierlich schließen

Standesamt

Church of England marriages demand the presence of two <u>witnesses</u> and will only be valid if

Trauzeugen

(1) there has been either a <u>publication of banns</u>, or

Aufgebot

(2) a <u>common licence</u> has been issued by a bishop for the marriage to take place within the <u>parish</u> of one of the parties, or

allgemeine Erlaubnis
Pfarrbezirk

(3) a special licence has been issued by the <u>Archbishop</u> of Canterbury, which permits the parties to marry anywhere, or

Erzbischof

(4) the certificate of a <u>superintendent registrar</u> has been obtained.

„Oberstandesbeamter"

As it is in the public interest that people should know whether or not other people are married, civil marriages without a religious ceremony are normally celebrated either in a <u>registered building</u> or in the office of a superintendent registrar.

amtliches Gebäude

The *Marriage Act 1994*, however, permits that civil marriages may take place in "<u>approved premises</u>". Premises have to be approved by the <u>local authority</u> and must <u>provide</u> the opportunity for members of the public <u>to attend</u>. The marriage must have two witnesses, a superintendent registrar and a registrar of the <u>district</u> in which the premises are situated.

Ehegesetz
genehmigte Räumlichkeiten
örtliche Behörde – vorsehen
teilnehmen/anwesend sein

Bezirk

The aim of the 1994 Act is to <u>maintain</u> the <u>sanctity</u> of marriage.

aufrechterhalten –
Unantastbarkeit

The *Marriage Act 1983* <u>enables</u> people suffering from continuing illness and <u>detained persons</u> to be lawfully married upon a superintendent registrar's certificate in the place where they <u>reside</u>.

ermächtigt
inhaftierte Personen

wohnen

4. Requirements of a valid marriage

a) Minimum age

Both parties must be 16 years or older. If one of them is under 18, <u>consent</u> must be given by both parents. If the parents refuse to give their consent, the minor may <u>apply to</u> the magistrates' court where a decision will then be made based on what is considered to be in the best interests of the minor.

A marriage which is formally solemnised (as described above) without this consent will be valid.

Zustimmung
sich wenden an

b) <u>Prohibited degrees of relationship</u>

The prohibited degrees are <u>set out</u> in the *Marriage Act 1949*. Of course <u>close relations</u> are not allowed to marry, e.g., a man cannot <u>marry</u> his mother, daughter or grand-daughter and a woman cannot marry her father, son or grandson.

The *Marriage Act 1949*, as amended by the *Marriage (Enabling) Act 1960*, provides two complete lists of the prohibited degrees. One list shows the relations a woman may not marry and the other list shows the relations a man may not marry.

The <u>extent</u> of the prohibited degrees on these lists is surprising.

The reason for these <u>prohibitions</u> is, on the one hand, <u>public policy</u> and, on the other hand, the <u>genetic</u> risk which might produce <u>undesirable</u> <u>side-effects</u> in a child born of a marriage between <u>blood relatives</u>.

verbotene Verwandtschafts-grade
aufgelistet
enge Verwandte
heiraten

Ermächtigungsgesetz

Ausmaß

Verbote – öffentliches Interesse
genetisch
unerwünscht – Nebeneffekt
Blutsverwandte

c) Prohibition of <u>bigamous marriage</u>

Doppelehe

A person who marries for a second time during an existing marriage commits the crime of <u>bigamy</u> but the following defences may be <u>pleaded</u>:

Bigamie
vorbringen

- That, in <u>good faith</u> and on reasonable grounds, it was believed that the spouse was dead.

guter Glaube

- That, under the same preconditions, it was believed that the first marriage was <u>annulled</u> or <u>dissolved</u>.

annulliert – aufgelöst

- That the first spouse had been missing continuously for seven years, and that there was no reason for <u>supposing</u> that spouse to be alive.

vermuten

d) Partners of <u>different sexes</u>

verschiedenes Geschlecht

In English law, it is impossible for homosexual or lesbian couples to marry.

e) Formalities required by statute

A marriage ceremony must be performed and solemnised as described in the paragraph before, i.e. as stated in the *Marriage Acts 1949 and 1983*.

5. Void and voidable marriages

A void marriage means that no marriage has ever legally existed and that the parties are in a single status.

A voidable marriage is regarded as legally valid until a court <u>pronounces it a nullity</u>.

für nichtig erklären

a) Void marriages

Marriages will be void if:

(1) one of the parties is under 16,
(2) the parties are within the prohibited degrees of relationship,
(3) the parties have <u>intermarried</u> <u>in disregard</u> of certain required formalities (such as <u>wilful</u> <u>omission</u> to obtain a <u>marriage certificate</u>),

die Eheschließung vornehmen – unter Missachtung – vorsätzlich – Unterlassung Trauschein

(4) at the time of marriage either party was already legally married,

(5) the parties are not of different sexes (male and female).
This last ground for a void marriage has posed problems for
the courts concerning transsexual persons.

Example – Corbett v Corbett (1970) –:

H[1] and W (April Ashley) went through a ceremony of
marriage in 1963. H (a transvestite) knew that W had
been registered at birth as a male and had undergone a
"sex change" operation, and had since lived as a woman.
Three months later, H petitioned for a declaration that the
marriage was <u>null and void</u> because W was of the male
sex or, alternatively, for a <u>decree</u> of nullity on the ground
of either <u>incapacity</u> or <u>wilful refusal to consummate</u>. W
<u>requested</u> a decree of nullity on the ground of H's
incapacity or wilful refusal to consummate. "She" also
pleaded that H was <u>estopped</u> from alleging the marriage
was void.

Held: that (1) <u>Sexual condition</u> is <u>assessed</u> by four <u>criteria</u>
(chromosomal factors, <u>gonadal</u> factors, <u>genital</u> factors and
psychological factors). Doubt was expressed about the
value of a fifth <u>criterion</u> <u>viz</u>, hormonal factors, i.e.
<u>secondary</u> sexual characteristics. Where the first three tests
produce a congruent result, the law should (at least within
the context of marriage) determine sex accordingly and
ignore any operative intervention. This was because
marriage was essentially a relationship between a man and
a woman. In the <u>instant</u> case there was congruence of
chromosomes, gonads, and genitalia, and W was
accordingly of the male sex. "Her" <u>gender</u> was not deemed
relevant. The judge <u>conceded</u> "the real difficulties would
occur if the three primary criteria were not congruent".
<u>Obiter</u>, he expressed the view that greater weight would
then be given to "genital criteria" than the other primary
<u>determinants</u>. (2) Assuming the marriage was valid and W
was a woman, "she" was physically incapable of
<u>consummating</u> a marriage, as <u>sexual intercourse</u> using the

„null und nichtig"	
Urteil	
Unfähigkeit – vorsätzlich – Weigerung der Vollziehung der Ehe – bitten um	
hindern	
Geschlechtszustand – bewertet – Kriterien Geschlechts- – Fortpflanzungs-	
Kriterium – nämlich	
sekundär	
hier: vorliegend	
Geschlecht	
einräumen	
nebenbei	
Determinanten	
vollziehen – Geschlechtsverkehr	

---

[1] In cases involving family law, the abbreviations H for "husband",
W for "wife", F for "father" and M for "mother" are used.

completely artificial <u>cavity</u> constructed in "her" case could never be ordinary and complete intercourse. (3) A ceremony of marriage which was wholly ineffectual and void in law could not be rendered effectual between the actual parties by some species of <u>estoppel.</u>

Aushöhlung

unzulässige Rechtsausübung

Example – Cossey v United Kingdom (1991) –:

C was a British citizen who was born as a male and registered at birth as a male. Though physically a male, she was psychologically female. She dressed as a female and was known as a female. She had an operation to give her a female appearance. She was issued with a passport as a female. She became engaged to a Mr L but was told that she could not marry him because, in English law, she was classified as male. She asked the Registrar-General to give her a birth certificate showing her to be female. He refused. She then married a Mr X but the marriage was held to be void because the parties were not respectively male and female. C alleged <u>violations</u> of article 8 (right to family life) and article 12 (right to marry) of the European Convention for the Protection of Human Rights and Fundamental Freedoms.

Verletzung

Held: that the case was not materially distinguishable from *Rees v UK (1986)* which had found no violations. Though the court was not bound by its previous decisions, it normally followed them unless there were <u>cogent</u> reasons which could include changes in society. The refusal to alter the birth certificate did not violate article 8. There had to be a fair balance between the general interest of the community and the interests of the individual. The birth registration system was a public record which *Rees* decided should not be altered. A <u>departure</u> from *Rees* was not warranted to reflect present day conditions, though the law would be kept under <u>review</u>. Article 12's main concern was to protect marriage as the basis of the family. The legal <u>impediment</u>

zwingend

Abweichung

Überprüfung/Revision
Hindernis

in the UK on the marriage of persons who were not of the opposite biological sex did not <u>restrict</u> or <u>reduce</u> the right to marry in the traditional sense of marriage which was guaranteed by article 12. Though some contracting states did recognise the validity of persons in C's position, this was not evidence of any general <u>abandonment</u> of the traditional concept of marriage. It was not open to take a new <u>approach</u> to the interpretation of article 12.

einschränken – vermindern

Aufgabe/Verzicht

Annäherung

b) Voidable marriages

According to s.12 of the *Matrimonial Causes Act 1973*, a marriage is voidable for the following reasons:

Ehesachen

(1) it has not been <u>consummated</u> due to the incapacity of either party,

vollziehen/durchführen

(2) it has not been consummated due to the wilful refusal to consummate it by the <u>respondent</u>,

Antragsgegner/Beklagter

(3) either party did not consent to it, whether in consequence of <u>duress</u>, mistake, <u>unsoundness of mind</u> or otherwise,

Nötigung/Drohung – Geistes-schwäche

(4) at the time of the marriage, either party, though capable of giving a valid consent, was suffering (whether continuously or not) from a <u>mental disorder</u> within the meaning of the *Mental Health Act 1983*,

Geisteskrankheit
Gesetz betreffend Geistes-kranke

(5) at the time of the marriage one party was suffering from <u>venereal disease</u> in a <u>communicable</u> form,

Geschlechtskrankheit – ansteckend

(6) at the time of the marriage the man did not know that the woman was <u>pregnant</u> by another man.

schwanger

Of all these reasons, the third one seems to be particularly interesting, because it illustrates the contractual aspect of marriage. Like an ordinary contract, the basis of a marriage lies in <u>consent</u>. Consequently, an essential mistake, for example concerning identity, or <u>deceit</u>, which <u>sets aside</u> the consent, will make the marriage voidable.

hier: Übereinstimmung
Täuschung – aufheben

6. Effects of marriage

The legal consequence of marriage is that <u>reciprocal</u> <u>obligations</u> <u>fall upon</u> both parties. Some of the duties of husband and wife are laid down by statute, while others are provided by the common law. The main duties are the following:

a) Obligation to maintain

Every spouse has a duty <u>to maintain</u> his or her partner but the corresponding right to be maintained is lost if a partner commits <u>adultery</u> or <u>desertion.</u>

A husband has a common law duty to maintain his wife but a wife will have to maintain her husband if he is ill and not capable of earning an income.

Although the old rule by which a <u>deserted</u> wife was <u>entitled</u> to obtain credit against her husband's <u>account</u> as an "<u>agent of</u> <u>necessity</u>" was abolished in 1970, a wife who lives with her husband is entitled <u>to pledge the</u> husband's <u>credit</u> for buying necessary household goods. This <u>authority</u> is based on the <u>presumed consent</u> of the husband that she is his <u>agent</u>. This presumption may be <u>rebutted</u> by the husband informing the <u>trader</u> not to give credit to his wife, or by showing the court that the wife had a <u>sufficient supply</u> of the goods in question, or that she had a sufficient <u>allowance</u> to pay for them herself.

b) Custody of children

Mothers and fathers have equal <u>parental responsibility</u>.

Thus, both parents normally have custody of their children until they are 18, although it can be lost earlier if the children marry or leave home. Parents may lose the right of custody if the marriage ends in divorce or if the children are <u>taken into care</u> because they are considered to be in danger.

Ehewirkungen

wechselseitige Verpflichtungen
anfallen auf

Unterhaltspflicht

unterhalten

Ehebruch – Verlassen des Ehe-
partners

verlassen – berechtigt
Konto – Geschäftsführer ohne
Auftrag
mit (seinen = ihren) Schulden
belasten –
Berechtigung
vermutetes Einverständnis
Stellvertreterin – widerlegen
Händler/Kaufmann
ausreichender Vorrat
hier: Haushaltsgeld

Personensorge/Erziehungs-
gewalt

elterliche Fürsorgepflicht

in Obhut nehmen

c) Further duties

Both parents have duties, depending on the age of the children, to:

(1) financially support and maintain their children,

(2) educate their children, which usually means sending them to school,

(3) protect them from dangers in the home (for example <u>unguarded</u> fires),

unbewacht

(4) protect them from many other dangers which could <u>harm</u> their <u>health physically or mentally</u> (for example alcohol, drugs or prostitution).

beeinträchtigen – körperliche oder geistige Gesundheit

Diagram 50

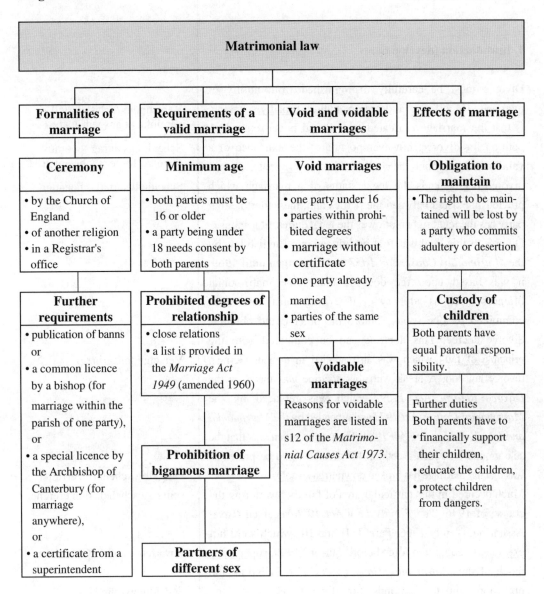

III. <u>The law of divorce</u>

Scheidungsrecht

1. Introduction (development)

Divorce must be carefully distinguished from nullity of marriage. The effect of a <u>decree</u> of nullity, <u>broadly speaking</u>, is that the marriage is treated as if it had never existed. A <u>petition for divorce</u>, however <u>postulates</u> the existence of a valid marriage, which the court is asked to <u>terminate</u>. Thus, a <u>divorce decree</u> <u>ends</u> the legal status of a marriage which previously existed between the parties and, thereafter, neither party has the legal rights, or owes the legal duties, of a spouse. Divorce of this kind was first introduced into English law by the *Matrimonial Causes Act 1857* and, from then until 1969, it was based upon the doctrine that some matrimonial offences (such as adultery or desertion) must have been committed by one spouse before the other could obtain a divorce decree. This doctrine can be compared with the <u>principle of fault</u> which was also applied in ancient German divorce law too. A break with this doctrine was made by the *Divorce Reform Act 1969*, which was replaced by the *Matrimonial Causes Act 1973* and amended by the *Matrimonial and Family Proceeding Act 1984*. The position then was that the sole ground on which a petition for divorce could be presented was that the marriage has <u>broken down irretrievably</u>.

Much <u>occured</u> in this particular area of family law during the course of 1996. The *Family Law Act 1996* received Royal Assent on 4th July 1996. Parts I, II and III, which were not <u>expected</u> to come into force before January 1999, <u>superseded</u> much of the *Matrimonial Causes Act 1973*, including the provisions on the <u>grounds for divorce</u>. However, the provisions of the Act of 1973 concerning divorce are still, in fact, in force at the time of writing.

This chapter, therefore, presents the law as it stood before the *Family Law Act 1996* and then introduces the new provisions at the end.

Verordnung/Erlass/Urteil – vereinfacht ausgedrückt

Scheidungsantrag – voraussetzen/erfordern – beenden

Scheidungsurteil – beenden

Verschuldensprinzip

endgültig scheitern/zerrüttet sein – geschehen/sich ereignen

erwarten – außer Kraft setzen

Scheidungsgründe

2. Grounds for divorce

The only reason for a petition for divorce is, as just mentioned, that "the marriage has broken down irretrievably". Such a petition may not, without the special leave of the court, be presented until one year has passed since the marriage.

Some connection with the doctrine of matrimonial offences has been retained by the further provision that the court may not decide that the marriage has broken down irretrievably unless the petitioner can establish one or more of the five following grounds. On the other hand, even if one or more of these grounds are established, the court will not grant a divorce if it remains unconvinced about the breakdown of the marriage. The five grounds, which can lead to a divorce, are:

Erlaubnis

Verbindung
zurückbehalten

wenn nicht – Antragsteller –
vorbringen

bleiben – nicht überzeugt –
Zusammenbruch

a) Adultery plus intolerability

Unzumutbarkeit/Unerträglichkeit

Adultery is voluntary sexual intercourse between two persons, one or both of whom are married, but not to each other.

freiwillig – Geschlechtsverkehr
miteinander

The petitioner must prove that the other spouse committed adultery and that he finds it intolerable to live with the respondent.

unzumutbar/unerträglich

However, an attempt at adultery is not sufficient.

Versuch

Example – Dennis v Dennis (1955) –:

This was a husband's cross petition on the grounds of the wife's adultery. There was evidence of an attempt to commit adultery but the court was satisfied that there had been no penetration.

Widerklage

Held: that, although to constitute an act of adultery the sexual intercourse need not have been complete, there had to be some degree of penetration, and an attempt at adultery without any penetration was insufficient.

Eindringen

Example – Preston-Jones v Preston-Jones (1951) –:

H was abroad on business from 17 August 1945 to 9 February 1946. His wife, W, gave birth to a normal child on 13 August 1946. There was no evidence of W having any suspicious relations with other men or that she was anything but a hard working and respectable woman. H petitioned for divorce on the grounds of W's adultery because he could not possibly be the father of the child.

Held: that the court would apply the standards of the existing state of medical science and belief, which stated that the husband could not be the father of the child. H's petition was be granted.

b) <u>Behaviour</u>

(ehewidriges) Verhalten

The petitioner must show that the respondent has behaved in such a way that the petitioner cannot reasonably be expected to live with the respondent. In such a case, the court would expect to see evidence of very unreasonable behaviour, such as <u>violence</u>, <u>drunkenness</u> or <u>obsessive jealousy</u>.

Gewalttätigkeit – Trunkenheit – übertriebene Eifersucht

Example – Bannister v Bannister (1980) –:

The husband had not taken his wife out for two years. He did not speak to her unless it was <u>unavoidable</u>. He stayed out at nights without telling her where he was going. He led an entirely independent life ignoring his wife. She petitioned for divorce on the grounds of his behaviour.

Held: that the basis of the *Matrimonial Causes Act 1973* s1(2)(b) is not "unreasonable behaviour" but behaving in such a way that the petitioner "cannot reasonably be expected to live with the respondent", a significantly different concept. In this case, the wife made out a clear case of behaviour such that she could not reasonably be expected to live with the husband and, therefore, she proved irretrievable breakdown of the marriage.

unvermeidbar

c) Desertion

Desertion requires that the respondent had deserted the petitioner for a continuous period of at least two years immediately preceding the presentation of the petition.

unmittelbar vorausgehen

Desertion should involve:

enthalten/umfassen

(1) the fact of separation,

Trennung

(2) an intention to desert by the respondent,

(3) a lack of consent by the petitioner, and

Mangel an Zustimmung

(4) that the separation was without just cause.

ohne ersichtlichen Grund

Example – Naylor v Naylor (1961) –:

In March 1960, during a quarrel with H, the wife cast off her wedding ring and thereafter the parties lived separate lives, but both remained in the matrimonial home. H used one small room for sleeping, W performed no wifely services for him and there was a complete absence of any communal or family life. W intended to leave H.
Held: that W had deserted H, even though the parties were still living under the same roof, because they were leading entirely separate lives and residing separately from each other.

Streit – wegwerfen

erbringen

---

d) Separation for two years and consent

The petitioner must show that the parties have lived apart for a continuous period of at least two years immediately preceding the presentation of the petition and the respondent consents to a decree of divorce.

getrennt leben

Example – Santos v Santos (1972) –:

W petitioned for divorce under s1(1) and (2)(d) of the *Matrimonial Causes Act 1973*. She had left H in late 1966 but on three subsequent occasions returned to H and occupied the same bed as H. These visits together did not exceed six months.

Held: that the phrase "living apart" imports something more than physical separation. "That state of affairs does not exist whilst both parties recognise the marriage as subsisting" (per *Sachs* LJ). The element that is required, in addition to physical separation, is one which is capable of being brought into existence unilaterally, in that it depends on the state of mind of one of the parties to the marriage. This state of mind must involve at least a recognition that the marriage is in truth at an end. It is not necessary that the existence of the additional element be communicated to the other party before it becomes operative in law. *Sachs* LJ also made observations on s2(6) and approved *Denning* LJ in *Hopes v Hopes (1948)*: "When two spouses are living in the same house, then, they are to be held to be living apart if not living in the same household."

getrennt leben
Sachlage

noch bestehen

Bemerkung

e) Separation for five years

It is sufficient under this heading to show that the parties have lived apart for a continuous period of at least five years immediately preceding the presentation of the petition.

Überschrift

f) Amendments by the *Family Law Act 1996*

The reform of English divorce law had the following objectives:

Ziele

(1) to support the institution of marriage,
(2) to include practical steps,
(3) to ensure that spouses understand the practical consequences of divorce before taking any irreversible decision,
(4) where divorce is unavoidable, to minimise the bitterness and hostility between the parties and to reduce the trauma for the children, and
(5) to keep to a minimum the costs to the parties and the taxpayer.

aufrechterhalten
geeignete Maßnahmen
sicherstellen
nicht rückgängig zu machen/ unumstößlich

Erbitterung
Feindschaft

Steuerzahler

The general principles of divorce are laid down in s1 of the *Family Law Act 1996*:

"The court and any person exercising functions under Parts II and III of the *Family Law Act 1996* must have regard to the following general principles:

(1) that the institution of marriage is to be supported;

(2) that the parties to a marriage which may have broken down are to be encouraged to take all practicable steps, whether by <u>marriage counselling</u> or otherwise, to save the marriage; — Eheberatung

(3) that a marriage which has <u>irretrievably</u> broken down and is being brought to an end should be brought to an end – — unwiederbringlich/endgültig

   (a) with minimum <u>distress</u> to the parties and to the children <u>affected</u>; — Leid/Not — betroffen

   (b) with questions dealt with in a manner <u>designed</u> to <u>promote</u> as good a continuing relationship between the parties and any children affected as is possible in the circumstances; and — gestalten — fördern

   (c) without costs being unreasonably <u>incurred</u> in connection with the procedures to be followed in bringing the marriage to an end; and — entstehen

(4) that any risk to one of the parties to a marriage, and to any children, of violence from the other party should, so far as reasonably practicable, be <u>removed</u> or <u>diminished</u>." — fernhalten — vermindern

3. <u>Legal consequences of divorce</u>

Scheidungsfolgen

Upon a decree of divorce, the court may make orders for the <u>residence</u>, <u>parental contact</u>, <u>maintenance</u>, property and education of the children, if the parents cannot agree on these matters, for <u>financial provision</u> to be made for the spouse, and for different <u>marriage settlements</u>. <u>Maintenance</u> cases are the most frequent consequences of a divorce.

Wohnsitz – elterliches Besuchsrecht – Unterhalt

Unterhaltszahlungen
Eheverträge – Unterhaltssachen

Maintenance is a financial payment or settlement made by a spouse (usually a husband) to maintain the other spouse (usually a wife) and family.

As it is still more common that the husband is ordered to compensate his wife than the <u>reverse</u>, the following text refers to wives claiming from husbands.

Two kinds of <u>maintenance claims</u> must be distinguished:

a) Maintenance claims made before or after divorce

(1) *Before* the divorce, the courts may <u>award periodical cash payments</u> to be paid by <u>the person liable to provide</u> maintenance. The amount payable is what the court considers reasonable under the special circumstances. Maintenance for children may also be claimed at this time.

(2) After the divorce, the courts may award in addition to periodical cash payments:
- a <u>lump sum</u> for the wife and the children, or
- a part of the husband's capital (usually not more than one third) to be secured for the benefit of the wife and the children, or
- a division of property belonging to the husband or which was owned <u>jointly</u>.

> *Example – Wachtel v Wachtel (1973) –:*
>
> H and W were married in 1954. There were two children. At first they lived in a flat, <u>pooling</u> their earnings to get a flat and furniture. In 1956, the matrimonial home was purchased in H's name for £5,000 with a 100 per cent mortgage. H paid the mortgage <u>instalments</u>. W worked until 1958. Thereafter, she looked after the children and helped H, who was a dentist, in his practice. The marriage broke down in March 1972. W left the matrimonial home but H continued to live there. In July 1972 both parties got decrees of divorce. The parties arranged that the son should stay with H, and the daughter with W. The matrimonial home was now worth £22,000 and £2,000 was owed on mortgage. H's earning capacity was £6,000 plus, and W had a potential earning capacity of £750. Both were

---

Marginal glosses:

- umgekehrt
- Unterhaltsklagen
- zusprechen – regelmäßige Barzahlungen – Unterhaltspflichtiger
- Pauschalbetrag/einmalige Bezahlung
- gemeinschaftlich
- zusammenlegen
- Raten

aged 46. W had contributed to the matrimonial home for 18 years by looking after the home and family and helping H, and she had been an excellent mother. W applied under the *Matrimonial Causes Act 1973* ss23 and 24 for periodical payments for herself and her daughter, <u>secured provision</u> and a lump sum, and a <u>settlement</u>, transfer of property or variation of <u>settlement order</u>. The judge, having found that responsibility for the breakdown of the marriage rested equally on H and W, determined that only <u>capital assets</u> (the home) should be divided approximately equally between the parties. He ordered H to pay periodical payments of £1,500 less tax to W and £500 less tax in respect of the daughter, and to pay a lump sum of £10,000 or half the value of the house to W. H appealed.

Held: that the appeal would be allowed and the order varied. The court did not interfere with the periodical payments to W, as £1,500 was one-third of the parties' joint earnings. It reduced the amount for the daughter's maintenance to £300. It held that the proper lump sum was £6,000, i.e., nearly one-third of the value of the matrimonial home. The court considered the principles which should be applied when granting <u>ancillary</u> relief <u>pursuant</u> to the powers <u>conferred</u> by the 1973 Act.

gesicherte Versorgung
Abfindung
Abfindungsbeschluss

Anlagevermögen

zusätzlich
übereinstimmend mit/gemäß – verleihen

It is at the court's <u>discretion</u> to choose the <u>award</u> applicable for the case in point. But if the court makes an award of a periodical payment order, the *Matrimonial and Family Proceeding Act 1984*, moreover, provides the courts have to <u>implement</u> the "<u>clean break</u>" principle.

Ermessen – Zuwendung

anwenden – endgültiger Abschluss (des nachehelichen Verfahrens)

Example – Ashley v Blackman (1988) –:
Following a divorce, the husband was ordered to pay maintenance to his wife. She was mentally ill and lived on state benefits. The husband remarried and had his second wife and two children to support. He earned a low income. He applied for the maintenance order to his ex-wife to be discharged pursuant to s31(7)(a) of the *Matrimonial Causes Act 1973*.

Held: that s31(7)(a) was intended <u>to leave scope</u> for those of limited means <u>to be spared</u> the burden of having to pay their former spouses a few pounds a week indefinitely. Any maintenance the husband paid would be <u>swallowed</u> up in the benefits his ex-wife received. The clean break provisions were there to <u>prevent</u> a divorced couple of <u>acutely</u> limited means remaining <u>manacled</u> together indefinitely and returning regularly to court to <u>thrash out at public expense</u> the precise figure one should pay the other, not for their benefit but for the relief of the tax paying section of the community to which neither had sufficient means to belong. A clean break was applied and the wife's maintenance terminated.

„Ermessensspielraum lassen"
verschont bleiben

verschlingen

vermeiden
scharf/sehr – behindern/fesseln
auf Kosten der Öffentlichkeit beziehen

The courts should <u>consider</u> whether it would be <u>appropriate</u> to either award a lump sum payment or to limit the duration of the periodical payments for a time considered sufficient to enable the <u>recipient</u> <u>to reach</u> the termination of <u>financial dependence</u> from the other party.

erwägen – angemessen/sinnvoll

Empfänger – erreichen – finanzielle Abhängigkeit

Further details the courts should consider are:

(1) the income and financial <u>resources</u> of both parties,
(2) the financial <u>needs</u> and obligations the parties have, or <u>are likely to have,</u>
(3) the standard of living enjoyed by the family before the breakdown of the marriage,
(4) the age of the parties, and the <u>duration</u> of the marriage,
(5) any <u>disability</u> of either of the parties, physical or mental,
(6) the contribution each party made to the <u>welfare of the family</u> (see next example below),
(7) the value of loss of some <u>benefit</u> (such as a pension) which cannot be <u>acquired</u> because of the termination of the marriage,
(8) the <u>special regard</u> of any child of the family under the age of 18.

Eigenmittel
Bedürfnisse
wahrscheinlich haben werden

Dauer
Behinderung
Familienfürsorge

hier: Versorgungsleistung
erhalten

besondere Berücksichtigung

Example – Gojkovic v Gojkovic (1990) –:

H and W <u>turned</u> a property into a hotel. W worked hard to make the hotel successful while H was involved in other business activities. When they divorced H, had £4 million in family assets and W had very little by way of <u>legal interest</u>. H offered that W received a maisonette worth £295,000 and a lump sum of £532,000 as a clean break order calculated <u>to meet</u> the reasonable needs of the former wife of a wealthy husband. W wanted a larger lump sum so that she could buy and run her own hotel. The judge found that W had made exceptional contributions which were equal to those of H and awarded her a £1 million lump sum. H appealed, arguing that the order was excessive, that the judge had been wrong in allowing W to buy a hotel and that all the court need to provide was <u>self-sufficiency</u> for W which is <u>what his offer aimed to do</u>.

Held: that dismissing the appeal, the court was concerned with an exceptional degree of contribution by W from a time when the parties were <u>virtually penniless</u> until the end of the marriage. There was nothing wrong in allowing W to continue as an active business woman by enabling her to buy and run a hotel within the context of s25 of the *Matrimonial Causes Act 1973*.

umwandeln

hier: gesicherte Rechtsposition

übereinstimmen mit

(wirtschaftliche) Unabhängigkeit – was er mit seinem Angebot beabsichtigte

fast ohne einen Pfennig Geld

The courts have the power to vary the awards <u>at the request</u> of either party. The amounts may be increased or reduced, moreover the <u>method of payment</u> may be changed or even stopped.

auf Antrag

Zahlungsweise

Example – Can v Can (1977) –:

A wife obtained a <u>matrimonial order</u> from the magistrates' court and a year later, in 1961, the spouses were divorced. In 1974, the wife successfully <u>applied for</u> a variation and the order was increased to £7 per week. Two years later, the former husband retired and applied for a reduction. His weekly income was £23 and the former wife's income was £13.

Beschluss in Ehesachen

beantragen

Held: that the "one third rule" was inappropriate in this case. The court reduced the order to £5 per week, with the result that both parties had weekly incomes of £18.

Example – Clutton v Clutton (1991) –:

After 20 years of marriage, H and W divorced. There was only one child, aged 16, living at home. She had left school and was working. The matrimonial home, which was in H's sole name, was transferred to W. W had a stable sexual relationship with a Mr D but did not intend to live with him or marry him. H appealed against the property order.

Held: that an order whereby the sale of the matrimonial home was postponed until the youngest child is aged 18 (or some other age) is known as a *Mesher* order [see *Mesher v Mesher (1973)*]. An order whereby the sale is postponed until the wife dies, remarries or cohabits with another man is usually known as a *Martin* order [see *Martin v Martin (1978)*]. In this case, the matrimonial home was the sole asset of the parties. H asked for a *Martin* order on terms that he have a one third share of the proceeds of sale. W was at first content with a *Mesher* order but later supported the clean break of a complete transfer of the house to her on the basis of the long marriage and her limited earning capacity as a part-time typist. H had a regular income as a bricklayer.

Held: that there was a danger in describing the clean break as a principle. Section 25A of the *Matrimonial Causes Act 1973* does not oblige courts to strive for a clean break regardless but to consider whether it would be appropriate. H was rightly not ordered to pay maintenance to W but the judge was wrong to refuse to make a *Martin* order. Such an order cannot be said to go against the clean break principle. Not to have made a *Martin* order deprived H of his share in the sole capital asset of the marriage, which was manifestly unfair. The judge should have ordered a charge in H's favour in the event of W's death or remarriage. A *Mesher* order was not suitable, since there were doubts

ständig

hier: Beschluss über die Vermögensverteilung
aufschieben/vertagen

einziges Vermögen

Verkaufserlös
hier: befürworten –
hier: klare Regelung

Halbtags-Schreibkraft
Maurer

bestrebt sein

verstoßen
berauben

offensichtlich – anordnen

about W's ability to <u>rehouse</u> herself if the house was sold when the youngest child became 18. *Mesher* orders could still be the best <u>solution</u> where the family assets are amply sufficient to provide both parties with a roof over their heads if the matrimonial home were sold, but the interests of the children required that they remain in the matrimonial home.

Wohnraum beschaffen für

Lösung

b) Maintenance claims made without <u>divorce proceedings</u>

Scheidungsprozess

A wife may apply to the courts for maintenance on the grounds that her husband has neglicted to pay maintenance for her and their children (if there are any).

Maintenance paid to <u>claimants</u> is a weekly sum and is based, as already mentioned, on one third of the <u>gross</u> total income of the parties. If, for instance a husband earned £180 and the wife had no income, she would receive £60 a week. However, if the husband earned £90 and the wife earned £90 per week, the wife would receive nothing because she earned more than one third of the total income.

Anspruchsteller
brutto

An important factor when <u>assessing</u> maintenance is the payment of <u>income support</u>. Anyone who receives income support will get these payments reduced by the amount of maintenance received.

festsetzen
Sozialhilfe

4. <u>Judicial Separation</u>

(gestattetes) Getrennt leben/ „Ehe ohne Trauschein"

English family law also considers other situations <u>wherein</u> a <u>married couple</u> do not wish to live together as husband and wife, but, at the same time, they do not want to obtain a divorce. The reasons for a judicial separation instead of divorce are usually religious or because children are involved.

in denen
Ehepaar

The petition may be made under the same preconditions as a petition for divorce, which means it must be based on one of the five grounds for divorce <u>outlined</u> above. The effect of a judicial separation is likely to be the same as the effect of a divorce.

darstellen

The main objective of a judicial separation is to release the parties from their obligation to cohabit.

Diagram 51

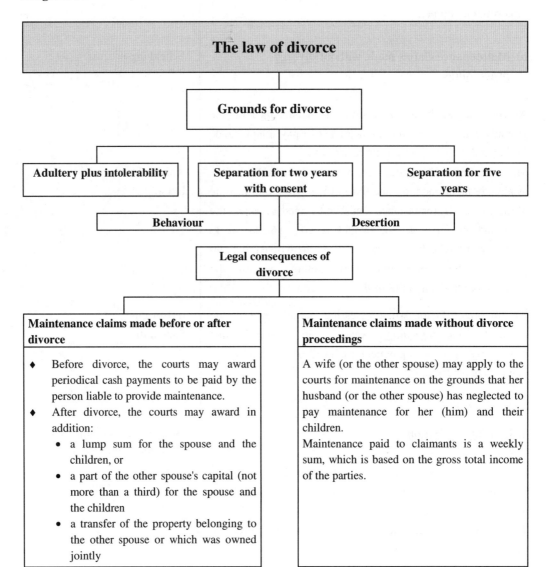

IV. Children and family law

1. Introduction

The *Children Act 1989* defines a child as "a person under the age of 18", who is generally called a "minor" or "infant".

We have already seen above (vol. 1, chapter five) the rights and duties that minors may have, as well as their capacity to contract (vol. 1, chapter six).

The subjects to be discussed now in this chapter are legitimacy, legitimation, adoption and the relevance of the *Children Act 1989*.

Legitimität (Ehelichkeit) – Ehelichkeitserklärung – Adoption – Bedeutung

2. Legitimacy

Legitimacy is mainly governed by the *Legitimacy Act 1926*.

geregelt

A child whose parents are lawfully married at the time when the child is conceived or born is legitimate.

erzeugt – ehelich

This presumption of legitimacy applies even if the marriage is dissolved (by divorce or nullity) after the child has been conceived but before the child is born, and it also applies if the father dies after the child has been conceived but before the child is born.

Ehelichkeitsvermutung

This presumption may be rebutted on the balance of probabilities. However, the courts have considered the status of a child to be a grave matter and, therefore, a very high probability must be shown to rebut the presumption.

widerlegt – „Wahrscheinlichkeitsrechnung"

schwerwiegende Angelegenheit

Example – W. v K.[1] (1988) –:

Two married couples, Mr and Mrs B and Mr and Mrs W, agreed to exchange partners for the purposes of sexual intercourse. Mrs B fell pregnant. At the material time, she

schwanger werden – maßgeblich

---

[1] For reasons of discretion in family proceedings, full names are often not quoted.

Diskretion

was having sexual intercourse with both her husband and Mr W. A child was born. She alleged that Mr W was the father.

He initially accepted <u>paternity</u> then <u>denied</u> it. Blood tests showed that the paternity index for him was 97.4 per cent, which showed that he was likely to be the father. There was also evidence that Mr B was <u>infertile</u>. Magistrates decided that the presumption of legitimacy had been rebutted applying s26 of the *Family Law Reform Act 1969* and that Mr W was the father. He appealed.

Held: that <u>dismissing</u> the appeal, the standard of proof in cases of paternity was a heavy one and <u>commensurate with</u> the gravity of the issue. The evidence established a strong probability amounting to <u>virtual certainty</u> that Mr W was the father.

Vaterschaft – leugnen

unfruchtbar

abweisen
entsprechend

hier: faktische Sicherheit

3. Legitimation

Every child which is not <u>born in lawful wedlock</u> is <u>initially illegitimate</u>.

Before the *Legitimacy Act 1926*, children so born could not be <u>legitimated</u> unless a special Act of Parliament was passed to make them so.

According to s2 of the 1926 Act, however, a child is legitimated by the subsequent marriage of his parents if his father was <u>domiciled</u> in England or Wales at the date of the marriage and even if, at the time of his birth, one or both parties were married to someone else.

The effect of legitimation is that the legitimated child is treated, in most respects, <u>as though</u> he had been born in lawful wedlock.

Formerly – as it was in German law too – an illegitimate child was subject to several disadvantages, in particular in regard to the <u>intestate succession</u> to his relatives. The *Family Law Reform Act 1987*, however, puts such a child in the same position as a legitimate one.

But some differences remain between legitimate and illegitimate persons. An illegitimate person cannot obtain a

ehelich geboren (wedlock = Ehestand) – zunächst – (unrechtmäßig)/nichtehelich

für ehelich erklären

seinen Wohnsitz haben

als ob

gesetzliche Erbfolge

title of honour and his or her entitlement to British citizenship is derived solely through his or her mother.

Ehrentitel – Berechtigung
Staatsbürgerschaft – herleiten

Although at common law neither parent was originally responsible for the maintenance of an illegitimate child, the rule came to be that this duty was cast upon the mother. But the mother could obtain an order for payment by the father.

zur Regel werden
zuweisen an
Beschluss

The position now, however, is that either the mother or the father may apply for an order under the *Children Act 1989* for financial relief in respect of maintenance of the child.

einen Beschluss beantragen
Entlastung

Finally, the unmarried father formerly had no rights or duties to an illegitimate child. Nowadays, however, under s4 of the *Family Law Reform Act 1987*, he can obtain a court order to give him all rights and duties (shared with the mother) that he would have had if the child had been born legitimate.

teilen

4. Adoption

Until 1926, English law did not recognize the institution of adoption. This was changed by the *Adoption of Children Act 1926* which was amended by the *Adoption of Children Act 1976*.

An adoption order gives parental responsibility for a child (under 18 years of age) born to another mother (and father) to the adopting parents. If a married couple are the adopting parents, they also have the same parental rights as against one another. They both have parental duties and rights, as if they were the child's natural father and mother.

Adoptionsbeschluss

Adoptiveltern

According to the 1976 Act, the adopting parents must fulfil one of the following requirements:

- If a married couple wants to adopt a child both must have attained the age of 21 and one of them, at least, must be domiciled in the United Kingdom.

erreicht

- If one person alone intends to adopt a child he or she must also be 21 years of age as well as be resident in the United Kingdom.

seinen Wohnsitz haben

No adoption order may be made unless the child's parents – if existing – or guardians give unconditional agreement to the adoption, or the child is regarded in law as "free for

Vormund – uneingeschränkt – Zustimmung

adoption" for a variety of reasons, for instance <u>abandonment</u>, <u>neglect</u> and <u>persistent ill-treatment.</u>

Aussetzen
Vernachlässigung – ständige Misshandlung

When a child has been legally adopted, it will be treated, in law, <u>in all respects</u> as though it were the natural child of the adopting parents.

in allen Belangen

Adoptions are arranged by adoption societies and by local authorities, which are bound by statute to work in cooperation with each other.

An adoption order is <u>final</u> and effects a permanent change in the status of the child and the adopting parents. If an adoption order has been <u>properly</u> made and <u>acted upon</u> and has not been appealed, it cannot be later <u>set aside</u>.

endgültig

ordnungsgemäß (sauber) – ausführen/vollziehen – aufheben

> *Example – Re B. (Adoption: Jurisdiction to set aside) (1995) –:*
>
> A boy was born to an English mother and an Arab father. He was adopted and <u>mistakenly</u> <u>brought up</u> by a Jewish couple. As an adult, he learned of his true background and wished to travel and work in the Middle East. He applied to have the adoption order set aside on the basis of the fundamental mistake about his background.
>
> *Held:* that his <u>application</u> must fail, because a <u>legal</u> adoption order is final.

falsch – auf-/großziehen

Ersuchen – rechtmäßig

5. The *Children Act 1989*

This Act tries to bring together all public and private law relating to children into one Act of Parliament and, therefore, is very <u>wide ranging</u> and detailed. There are over 100 sections and 15 <u>schedules</u>. As this book is not a fundamental textbook on family law, but only an introduction to some fields of civil law, I find it sufficient to cite *James'* "Introduction to English Law" in order to summarise the Act: *"<u>Broadly</u>, the Act <u>covers</u> orders with respect to children in family proceedings, local authority <u>support</u> for*

weit reichend
hier: Tabellen

grob umrissen – enthalten/ abdecken – Unterstützung

---

[1]   Cf. bibliography: *Shears & Stevenson.*

children and families, <u>care</u> and <u>supervision</u>, protection of children, <u>community homes</u>, <u>voluntary homes</u> and voluntary organisations, <u>registered children's homes</u>, private agreements for <u>fostering</u> children, child<u>minding</u> and day care for young children and the Secretary of State's <u>supervisory</u> responsibilities and functions.

The basic philosophy behind this Act is that a child should be brought up within his or her family and that local authority support should be provided when necessary to support and <u>facilitate</u> this."

I have not read the whole of the *Children Act 1989*, but I did read some more <u>summaries</u> of it. The above cited summary, in its <u>brevity</u>, was the best of them all.

Unfortunately, an individual's life must come to an end as <u>inevitably</u> as any book.

For human beings the end is death. We do not know exactly what will happen to us after death. The only thing we can be sure of is that: "<u>Death</u> brings <u>heirs</u>[1]."

The end of a book does not have to mean its death. Books may live endlessly. So this leads us almost to the end of this book on English civil law. But certainly before ending it, what else could be better than finishing it off with a chapter on the <u>law of succession</u>?

Fürsorge – Beaufsichtigung

Erziehungsheim – durch Spenden unterhaltenes Jugendheim – staatliches Kinderheim – In Pflege geben – Beaufsichtigung

Aufsichts-

erleichtern

Zusammenfassung
Kürze

unvermeidbar

Tod (juristisch) – Erben

Erbrecht

---

[1] German <u>law proverb</u>: *"Sterben bringt Erben".*

Rechtssprichwort

Diagram 52

Children and family law

Legitimacy	Legitimation
A child whose parents are lawfully married at the time when the child is conceived or born is legitimate: the *presumption of legitimacy*	Every child, who is not born in lawful wedlock, is illegitimate. According to the *Legitimacy Act 1926*, a child is legitimated by the subsequent marriage of its parents.

Adoption
An adoption order gives parental responsibility for a child (under 18), born to another mother (and father), to the adopting parents. If a married couple are the adopting parents, they have both parental rights and duties as if they were the child's natural parents. The detailed requirements for adoption are to be found in the *Adoption of Children Act 1976.*

V. Further reading[1]

Barker & Padfield, Law; *Brown*, GCSE Law; *Cretney & Masson*, Principles of family law; *Dodds*, Family Law (Cracknell's law students' companion); *Geldart* Introduction to English law; *James'* Introduction to English Law; *Lowe & Douglas* (Bromley's) Family Law; *Lyall*, An Introduction to British law; *Templeman & Dodds*, Family Law – Textbook – Casebook – Revision work book; *Wragg*, Nutshells: Familiy Law.

---

[1] Cf. p. 73.

Chapter Eleven

The law of succession

I. Introduction

Whenever one person transfers property to another, it may be said that the <u>transferee</u> "succeeds" to the rights of the <u>transferor</u>. In law, the word "<u>succession</u>" has a special meaning. The type of succession we are dealing with in this chapter is "<u>universal succession</u>". There are two basic possibilities of universal succession: succession on death and succession on bankruptcy. This chapter only deals with succession on death.

Erwerber

Veräußerer – Rechtsnach-folge

Gesamtrechtsnachfolge

<u>It goes without saying</u> that a person who is dead cannot own property or exercise rights over property. The legal consequence of this <u>inevitable</u> fact is that other persons will succeed to the property owned or possessed by the <u>deceased</u>.
This is common to all legal systems. And most legal systems provide two possibilities which govern succession following from a death. In the first case, we find <u>testamentary succession</u>, i.e. succession by will. In the second case, we find <u>intestate succession</u> (intestacy) wherein a person <u>leaves</u> no will at all and thus he (or she) is said to die <u>intestate</u>.

es ist selbstverständlich

unvermeidbar
Verstorbene(r)

gewillkürte Erbfolge

gesetzliche Erbfolge – hinter-lassen – testamentlos

Before 1926, in English law, <u>realty</u> and <u>personalty</u> were treated differently under the rules of intestate succession. The realty <u>vested in</u> the <u>heir</u> and the personalty in the <u>personal representatives</u> for the benefit of the next-of-kin.
Under the *Administration of Estates Act 1925*, no <u>distinction is drawn</u> between realty and personalty in the administration of the estate of an intestate person.

unbewegliches Vermögen/Immobilien – bewegliches Vermögen
zufallen – Erbe
Testamentsvollstrecker
Gesetz zur Regelung der gesetzlichen Erbfolge – einen Unterschied machen

II. Intestate succession (intestacy)

In addition to the *Administration of Estates Act 1925*, intestate succession is also governed now by the *Intestates' Estates Act 1952*, amended by the *Family Provision Act 1966*.

Vermögensverwaltungsgesetz
Gesetz zur Regelung der gesetzlichen Erbfolge/Pflichtteilsgesetz

Beerdigungskosten

After paying <u>funeral expenses</u>, <u>testamentary expenses</u> and <u>debts</u>, the personal representatives hold the estate on <u>trust for sale</u>, and then distribute the <u>proceeds</u> of sale according to the following rules.

Testamentvollstreckungskosten – Nachlassschulden – Verwertungs-/Veräußerungstreuhand – Ertrag/Erlös

Five main groups of people have to be considered:
- a <u>surviving</u> husband or wife,
- surviving children (<u>issue</u>),
- surviving parents,
- surviving brothers and sisters of the <u>whole blood</u>, and
- surviving relations of <u>remoter degree</u>.

überlebend
Abkömmlinge in gerader Linie

von denselben Eltern abstammend – entfernteren Grades

1. Rights of a surviving husband or wife

If there are no surviving issue, or parents, or brothers and sisters of the whole blood, the complete <u>estate</u> passes to the surviving husband or wife.

Vermögen

If there *is* issue, the surviving spouse takes

a) all the personal chattels (that is chattels such as furniture, cars, household articles or those for personal use, <u>jewellery</u>, and so on, but no chattels used for business purposes, and

Schmuck

b) up to £125,000 free of <u>inheritance tax</u>, and

Erbschaftssteuer

c) a <u>life interest</u> in half of the remaining estate, which may, at her or his option, be <u>redeemed</u> for a capital payment. The other half then goes to the issue on a "<u>statutory trust</u>" (which will be described below).

lebenslanges Nießbrauchsrecht
auslösen/einlösen
Nachlasstreuhand bei gesetzlicher Erbfolge

If there is *no* issue, the surviving spouse obtains

a) all the personal chattels (as above),
b) up to £200,000 free of inheritance tax, and
c) half the remaining estate absolutely. The other half goes to parents or, <u>as the case may be</u>, is held on a "statutory trust" for brothers and sisters of the whole blood.

je nach den Einzelfallumständen

The term "statutory trusts" <u>calls for</u> some explanation. The word "issue" includes not only children, but also the <u>children of the children</u>, who <u>have died before</u> the <u>intestate person</u>. Their <u>share</u> goes to the other (if any) surviving issue. If they have no issue, the property falls into the <u>common fund</u>. The <u>scheme</u> is that all "children" take an "<u>absolutely vested interest</u>" only on the <u>attainment</u> of the age of 18 or marriage. Until then, the estate is held on trust for them. Should a child die before obtaining an absolutely vested interest, his interest <u>passes on</u> to those next <u>entitled</u>, which means, other children, a parent, brothers and sisters of the whole blood, a surviving spouses or remoter relatives if there is no surviving spouse.

verlangt nach

Kindeskinder

vorverstorben sein – Erblasser (ohne Testament)
Anteil
gemeinsame Kasse

„absolutes wohlerworbenes Interesse/Anrecht" – Erreichung/ Vollendung

übergeben – Berechtigter

2. Rights of the surviving children

The term "children", in this context, calls for further explanation as well. It includes all children, whether legitimate, legitimated, adopted or (under the *Family Law Reform Act 1987*) illegitimate. Their rights may be <u>summarized</u> as follows:

zusammenfassen

a) If there *is* a surviving spouse, he or she is entitled as just mentioned above. The other half of the remaining estate (if any) will be held on a statutory trusts for the children. When the surviving spouse dies, the whole remaining estate will be held on a statutory trusts for the surviving child (or children).
b) If there is *no* surviving spouse, the remaining estate is held on a statutory trust for the child (or the children). All children are entitled to <u>equal shares</u> in it.

gleiche Anteile

3. Rights of surviving parents

Where there is no issue and no surviving spouse, the parents take the whole estate in equal shares. If only one parent is alive he or she gets all of it.

4. Rights of surviving brothers and sisters of the whole blood

Where there are surviving children, a surviving spouse or a surviving parent, the surviving brothers and sisters will receive nothing.

If spouse, children, and parents are all lacking, the estate is held on a statutory trust for brothers and sisters of the whole blood or *their* children, in the case that they are deceased.

Fehlen

5. Rights of surviving remoter relatives

entferntere Verwandte

If there exists anyone of the aforementioned nearer relatives or a spouse, the surviving remoter relatives will receive nothing. If none of these people are alive the remoter relatives will be heirs in the following order:

oben erwähnt

a) brothers and sisters of half blood,

halbbürtig (= ein gemeinsamer Elternteil)

b) grandparents,

c) uncles and aunts, who are brothers and sisters of the whole blood of a parent of the intestate,

Onkel und Tanten

d) uncles and aunts, who are brothers and sisters of the half blood of a parent of the intestate.

Persons mentioned under b) take the whole estate absolutely. In the cases of a), c) and d) the estate is held on a statutory trusts, as in the case of existing children.

This means, however, that just as grandchildren can take part of the inheritance, so can nephews and nieces and first cousins.

ebenso wie

Erbschaft – Neffen – Nichten – Vetter/Kusine ersten Grades

Diagram 53

Intestate succession (Intestacy)

Rights of a surviving spouse

- ♦ If there *is* issue the spouse takes:
  - all personal chattles, and
  - up to £125,000 free of inheritance tax, and
  - a life interest in half of the remaining estate.
- ♦ If there is *no* issue:
  - all personal chattles, and
  - up to £200,000 free of tax, and
  - half of the remaining estate absolutely.

Rights of surviving children

"Children" can be legitimate, legitimated, adopted and illegitimate.

- If there *is* a surviving spouse, the other half of the remaining estate will be held on a statutory trust for the children.
- If there is *no* spouse, the remaining estate is held on a statutory trust for them.

All children are entitled to equal shares.

Rights of surviving parents

If there is no issue and no surviving spouse, the parents take the whole estate in equal shares. If only one parent is alive, he or she gets all of it.

Rights of surviving brothers and sisters of the whole blood

- If there are surviving spouses, children or parents: nothing!
- If those are all lacking, the estate is held on a statutory trust for brothers and sisters or their children.

Rights of remoter surviving relations

- ♦ If there exists anyone of the above mentioned closer relatives or spouses: nothing!
- ♦ If none of these people are alive, they will be heirs in the following order:
  - brothers and sisters of half blood,
  - grand parents,
  - uncles and aunts of the whole blood of a parent of the intestate,
  - uncles and aunts of the half blood of a parent of the intestate.

III. Testate succession (wills)

1. Introduction

Testate succession (*testamentum* is Latin and means: <u>something attested</u>, i.e. the <u>last will</u>) arises where the deceased human being has expressed his (or her) wishes, during his lifetime, concerning the <u>devolution</u> of his property, in the form of a will.

gewillkürte Erbfolge
(Testament)

etwas bestätigen – letzter Wille

Übergang

The right of a person to make a will showing to whom his personal property should <u>pass to</u> was recognized in English law relatively early.

übergehen

In medieval times, a person had no right to dispose of <u>freehold land</u>, as the strict <u>feudal law</u> laid down that the land had <u>to devolve</u> to the <u>heir in law</u>.

Grundeigentum – Lehnsrecht
zufallen/übergehen – gesetzlicher Erbe

Later, the *Statute of <u>Military Tenures</u> 1660* permitted a <u>freeholder</u> <u>to devise</u> <u>lands</u> (i.e. leave by will) and the introduction of the "use" (cf. above chapter nine) provided a further <u>means</u> of making dispositions of freehold property on death. Just as birth and marriage, death has also always been of direct connection with the Church. In Norman and medieval times, the <u>ecclesiastical</u> courts had the jurisdiction on wills of property, including leaseholds.

Militärgrundbesitz
Grundeigentümer – letztwillig zuordnen – Grundbesitz

Mittel

geistlich/kirchlich

The *<u>Court of Probate Act</u> 1857* transferred this jurisdiction to the ordinary civil courts, where it has been <u>ever since</u>. Many of the rules applied today, however, are <u>derived</u> from the early Church courts, which applied <u>canon law</u>, not the common law.

Nachlassgerichtsgesetz
von da an/seitdem
herleiten
kanonisches Recht/Kirchenrecht

2. The <u>nature</u> of a will

Rechtsnatur

A will is a declaration made by a person in his lifetime of his wishes concerning the <u>disposition</u> of his property after death.

Übergang

<u>Unless</u> there is a clear intention to the contrary, a will takes effect from the time of death of the testator, not from the time it is <u>made</u>; it is said to be <u>ambulatory</u> until his death. Thus if A makes a <u>disposition of</u> "All my property to B", the successor B will be entitled to receive not only such property as A had at the time he made the will, but also any other property A may have acquired between that time and his death.

falls nicht

errichten – widerruflich
Verfügung

3. Testamentary capacity

Testierfähigkeit

The general rule is that any person (except a minor or a person of unsound mind) may make a valid will. If someone intends to show that a testator was not capable – through unsoundness of mind or for any other reason – of making a valid will, the fact of the testator's incapacity must be clearly proved.

hier: wegen (aus) Geistesschwäche

4. Formalities

Formvorschriften

A will is usually a formal declaration of intention. The formal requirements for making a will are governed by the *Wills Act 1837*, as amended by the *Administration of Justice Act 1982*. Its main provisions are as follows:

Willenserklärung

a) Writing

Schriftform

The will must be in writing and signed by the testator or by some other person in his presence and under his direction. It must clearly appear that the testator intended, by his signature, to give effect to the will. "In writing" in English law includes handwriting, print and typescript.

(An)weisung

Handschrift – Druck – Maschinenschrift

b) Signature and witnesses

The signature must be made, or acknowledged, by the testator in the presence of two or more witnesses, in the presence of each other. Acknowledgement will, for example, be necessary if the testator has signed before asking the witnesses to attend. Each witness must either attest and sign the will or acknowledge his signature in the presence of the testator.

anerkennen/bestätigen

bestätigen

The *Administration of Justice Act 1982* substituted a new section for section 9 of the *Wills Act 1837*, which relaxes the law governing the position of the testator's signature and the acknowledgement of this signature by an attesting witness. The result of this new section 9 is that the signature by, or on behalf of, the testator can be anywhere on the will, provided

an die Stelle setzen
erleichtern

im Namen von
vorausgesetzt

that the testator intended, by their signature, to give effect to the will.

> *Example – Wood* v *Smith (1993) –:*
>
> On 30th June 1978, the testator <u>duly</u> executed a will. Two days before his death, on 20th April 1986, he made another will: he wrote it in his own handwriting and it began 'My will by Percy Winterbone'. He did not sign his name <u>at the foot</u> of the will. Two attesting witnesses signed the will <u>at the bottom</u> and, when one of them pointed out that the testator had not signed it, he replied: 'Yes I have. I have signed it at the top. It can be signed anywhere.' Had this document satisfied the requirements of s9 of the *Wills Act 1837*?
>
> *Held:* that it had, since the writing of the document had been part of one operation; it did not matter that the testator had written his signature before writing the dispositive provisions. *Scott* LJ explained that the testator had indicated in clear terms that he regarded his name written by him as his signature and that established that he had <u>complied with</u> the terms of s9(a) of the 1837 Act. By writing 'My will by Percy Winterbone', it was also established that the testator had intended to give testamentary effect to the document and that satisfied the requirements of s9(b).

formgerecht

am Ende
unten

erfüllen/befolgen

5. Wills of soldiers

It was a rule of Roman law that soldiers "<u>in the field</u>" might make <u>informal</u> wills, for a soldier may often be in <u>imminent</u> fear of death and he may have no <u>legal advice</u> <u>near by</u>. This practical rule has passed into English law in the form of section 7 of the *Wills Act 1837*, which gives special privileges to soldiers who are in *actual military service*. They may make a will even though they are not of full age, provided that they have attained the age of 14 years. They may make informal wills. Even an oral declaration will be sufficient.

im Einsatz
formlos – unmittelbar/drohend
Rechtsbeistand – in der Nähe

The phrase "*actual military service*" requires that the soldier is engaged in hostilities or is about to proceed to a hostility, or is on embarkation leaving for a foreign station in connection with operations of war, which are imminent or taking place. Thus, a soldier in England in peace-time is not in "actual military service" in this sense.

im Kampfeinsatz – kurz vorm Kampfeinsatz stehen – Einschiffung – ausländisch – Kriegsverhandlungen

---

> *Example – Re Wingham, Andrews* v *Wingham (1949) –:*
>
> The deceased, a member of the Royal Air Force, was sent to Canada for training as an airman. He wrote out and signed a document, which he described as a will, but which was not attested. He was involved in an air accident during his training and died from the injuries he received. An informal will may be made by a soldier on actual military service (see s.11 of the *Wills Act 1837*); s5 of the *Wills (Soldiers and Sailors) Act 1918* extends this privilege to members of the Royal Air Force. Relying on these sections, the document was put forward as the deceased's will.
>
> *Held:* that it could be admitted to probate. *Bucknill* LJ said "the tests are (a) was the testator 'on military service'; (b) was such service 'active'? In my opinion, the adjective 'active' in this connection confines military service to such service as is directly concerned with operations in a war which is or has been in progress or is imminent". Applying these tests, he concluded that the deceased was so engaged, although he was not in the theatre of war.

Flieger/Pilot

Flugunfall

anerkannt

gerichtliche Anerkennung des Testaments – „zu prüfen ist"

gegenwärtig

Sailors may make informal wills when they are at sea or about to embark for a voyage, but not if they are on leave and do not have orders to join a ship.

Matrosen/Seeleute
beim Einschiffen – im Urlaub

6. Classes of testamentary dispositions

letztwillige Verfügung

Testamentary dispositions of real property (freehold land) are called *devises*. Dispositions of personal property (chattels), including leaseholds, are called *bequests* or *legacies*.

Erbeinsetzung

Vermächtnis/letztwillige Schenkung – Vermächtnis/ letztwillige Verfügung

a) Legacies

A legacy (or bequest) may be a <u>general legacy</u>, a <u>specific legacy</u>, a <u>demonstrative legacy</u> or a <u>residuary legacy</u>.

Gattungsvermächtnis – Einzel-
vermächtnis – beschränktes Gattungsvermächtnis – Restver-
mächtnis

aa) General legacy

This is a gift which does not refer to a specific or particular object. For example "I <u>leave</u> a car ..." or "... a horse ..." or "... a boat ...".

hinterlassen

bb) Specific legacy

This is a gift which is specifically described. For example "I leave my Rolls Royce ..." or "I give my horse 'Pilgrim' to Grace" or "I leave my boat 'Old Love No. I' to my darling Valentine ...".

cc) Demonstrative legacy

This is a gift of a sum of money to be paid out of a particular fund, for example "I leave £1,000 out of my 6.5 % <u>Federal Bond</u> ...".

Bundesanleihe

dd) Residuary legacy

This is a gift of the <u>residue</u> of the estate, or part of it, <u>left over</u> after all other gifts have been made and debts have been paid.

Rest – übrig bleiben

These distinctions are important because the nature of the gifts will determine whether they are liable to <u>ademption</u> or <u>abatement</u>.

Widerruf/Entziehung
Herabsetzung/Abschlag

ee) Ademption

If a specific thing to be given by will to a <u>legatee</u> is not in existence or no longer belongs to the testator at the time of the testator's death, the gift is <u>adeemed</u> and the legatee gets nothing.

Vermächtnisnehmer

widerrufen

ff) Abatement

Abatement occurs when there is not enough property to satisfy all beneficiaries after the creditors of the deceased have been paid. The consequence will be that some of the legacies will have to be reduced or even <u>repudiated</u> altogether. Residuary gifts <u>abate</u> first, then general legacies, and then specific legacies. A demonstrative legacy will not abate unless the fund out of which it is to be paid is itself <u>exhausted</u>. In that case the demonstrative legacy will be treated as general legacies and will abate with them.

zurückweisen
herabsetzen/mindern

erschöpft („pleite")

b) Devises

There are two types of devises. The essential nature of any devise is, as mentioned above, that it deals solely with the real property of the testator.

aa) Specific devise

A specific devise is a gift of real property under a will. The gift must be part of the testator's estate at his death and must be described in such a way as to <u>sever</u> or distinguish it from the rest of the estate. Thus "My house, No. 6 Downing Street, London" or "My cottage in Mullion, Cornwall" are specific devises. Such a devise passes all <u>benefits</u> and <u>burdens</u> which the testator had in the property.

trennen/teilen

Nutzen
Lasten

bb) General and residuary devises

A general devise, or <u>preferably</u> a residuary devise, is a gift of real property by description. Thus, gifts of "all my farms in the Lake District to A" or "all my real property to B" are residuary devises.

vorzugsweise/besser

Under s. 37 of the *Wills Act 1837*, a residuary devise includes any real estate over which the testator has a <u>power of appointment</u>, and such a devise shall <u>operate</u> as an execution of that power, unless there is a contrary intention expressed in the will.

Einsetzungs-/Verfügungsbefugnis
wirken

7. <u>Revocation</u>

Widerruf

A will may be <u>revoked</u> either expressly or <u>by implication</u> from the conduct of the testator.

widerrufen – stillschweigend

a) Express revocation

An express revocation has to be made in exactly the same way as the <u>making of a will</u>, which means: in writing, signed and witnessed.

Testamentserrichtung

b) Implied revocation

aa) By making a new will or <u>codicil</u>

Testamentsnachtrag

A will usually begins with a clause revoking all former wills. If such a clause is not <u>inserted</u>, the later will (or codicil) does not revoke the former will, except in so far as it is <u>inconsistent therewith</u>. Thus, if a testator in a first will leaves a specified named house to A, and, in a later will, leaves the same house to B, the house goes to B. If, however, the testator in his first will leaves £1,000 to A, and, in a later will (which does not contain a revocation clause), leaves £1,000 to B, both A and B will receive legacies of £1,000.

einfügen

widersprüchlich – damit

If a will is amended or varied by a codicil, it is necessary to have the codicil signed and witnessed.

Example – Re White, Barker v Gribble and Another (1991) –:

The testator's signature to the variation of this will was signed by witnesses in the proper manner. Unfortunately, the testator failed to sign again. The question arose whether the variation was valid, in accordance with the requirements of the *Wills Act 1837* ss9, 15, 21. The testator, who died on 26th February 1985, made his original will on 2nd January 1981. He attempted to alter the will on 14th December 1984 by, <u>inter alia</u>, <u>decreasing</u> the proportion of shares for X and Y and <u>increasing</u> the share

unter anderem – vermindern
erhöhen

for Z. In fact, however, the testator thereby created an intestacy under which X took a greater share. Z and another person witnessed the alterations and, in the presence of the testator and <u>at his request</u>, placed their signature near the original signature of the testator and beneath the words 'alterations to will dated 14.12.84 witnesses'. However, the testator did not sign the will again. X argued for <u>probate</u> of the amended will, claiming the alterations to be valid; Y and Z for probate of the original will (Z being aware of the possibility of the <u>forfeiture</u> of his entire share under s15 of the *Wills Act 1837* because he was both a witness and a beneficiary), claiming that the amendments were invalid.

Held: that the amendments were invalid because:

1. For alterations to be valid under s21 of the *Wills Act 1837*, they must be effected "in like manner as ... required for the execution of the will". However, the alterations in this case were not signed by the testator or by someone under his direction;

2. The question arises of whether what took place on 14th December 1984 <u>amounted</u> to the creation of a valid will. The answer here was that it did not because the formal requirements of s9(a)(b) and (d) were not complied with. In particular, regarding s9(a) the new will was not signed by the testator, as the signature already existed at the time of the alleged <u>re-execution</u>. As to s9(b) the testator did not by his existing signature, intend to give effect to the new will, and as to s9(d) there was no <u>conclusive evidence</u> that the witnesses were attesting the will as opposed to merely attesting the alteration.

auf sein Verlangen

gerichtliche Anerkennung

Verfall

hinauslaufen auf

Neuausfertigung

zwingender Beweis

bb) By <u>destroying</u> a will

A will is only revoked in this case if it is intentionally destroyed by the testator or by someone else in the testator's presence under his direction. It may be destroyed by burning, <u>tearing</u> or any other means, but it must be done with the clear intention to destroy the will. Thus, a will destroyed <u>accidentally</u> would still be valid. In such a case, the personal

zerstören

zerreißen

zufällig

representative would refer to other material, such as a copy of the will or oral evidence, to find the testator's intention.

Example – Re Adams (1990) –:
After her will had been returned to her by solicitors so that she could destroy it, the <u>testatrix</u> had heavily <u>scored</u> parts of the will with a <u>ballpoint pen</u>, including her signature and the witnesses' signatures, which were therefore almost impossible to read.
Held: that the will had been 'otherwise destroyed' within s20 of the *Wills Act 1837*. It had therefore been revoked and it could not be admitted to probate.

Erblasserin – durchstreichen
Kugelschreiber

cc) By *subsequent* divorce

A divorce or nullity of marriage revokes any gift to the former spouse, and revokes the appointment of the spouse as <u>executor</u> or <u>executrix</u>. If another person or other persons are also named as beneficiaries in the will, it would remain valid, and only the gift to the former spouse would be invalid. If the spouse was the only beneficiary, the dead person's estate would be distributed under the rules of intestacy (see above No. II of this chapter).

nachfolgend

Testamentsvollstrecker/in

dd) By subsequent marriage

A will of the deceased is revoked by a subsequent marriage but it will not be revoked if it is made <u>in contemplation of marriage</u>. Thus, it is not sufficient to state in the will that the testator intends to marry. The will would still be revoked by a subsequent marriage, unless the name of the intended spouse was also stated and the testator intended that the will would not be revoked by the marriage.

im Hinblick auf die bevorstehende Eheschließung

Diagram 54

Testate succession (wills)

The nature of a will
A will is a declaration made by a person in his lifetime of his wishes concerning the devolution of his property after his death.

Testamentary capacity
The general rule is that any person (except a minor or a person of unsound mind) may make a valid will.

Formalities
- The will must be in writing and signed by the testator or by some other person under his direction.
- The signature must be made or acknowledged by the testator in the presence of two or more witnesses.

Testamentary dispositions
- Types of legacies
  - General legacy
  - Specific legacy
  - Demonstrative legacy
  - Residuary legacy
  - Ademption
  - Abatement

- Types of devises
  - Specific devises
  - General and residuary devises

Revocation
- Express revocation

- Implied revocation
  - By making a new will or codicil
  - By destroying a will
  - By subsequent divorce
  - By subsequent marriage

IV. Family provision

1. Introduction

Until 1938 – unlike German law and other civil laws of the continent (and Scots law) – in English law, a testator could leave his property to <u>whomsoever</u> he wished and there were no requirements <u>to provide</u> for his family. The testator could give his entire estate to charity and leave his family <u>penniless</u>.

By the *Inheritance (Family Provision) Act 1938*, amended by the *Intestates' Estates Act 1952*, the court was given the power to <u>vary</u> a will <u>on the application</u> of certain persons.

gerichtlich festgesetzte Versorgung unterhaltsbedürftiger Familienangehöriger aus dem Nachlass (Pflichtteilsnachlass, Pflichtteil)

an wen auch immer
hier: (vor)sorgen

„ohne einen Pfennig"

Erbschaft

ändern – auf Antrag

Further and more extensive powers were given to the courts by the *Inheritance (Provision for Family and Dependants) Act 1975.*

weitere
Unterhaltsberechtigte

2. Persons entitled to apply to family provision

According to the 1975 Act, the court has a discretion to make an award out of the deceased person's estate to dependants who have not received "reasonable financial provision" from a will.

Ermessen – einen Betrag fest-setzen

angemessen

The following persons may apply to the court for family provsion:

sich wenden an/beantragen

a) the wife or husband of the dead person,
b) former spouses who have not remarried,
c) the children of the deceased, whether they be illegitimate, adopted, or treated as a child of the family.

wieder heiraten
„mögen sie auch ... sein"

There is no restriction as to age, incapacity, sex, or whether married or not.

Example – Re Callaghan (1984) –:

After his father's death, P and his mother lived in a house given to P's mother by P's grandfather. C moved into the house as a lodger and then lived with P's mother. They then married. C treated P as his own son. P married. The families remained close and P's children treated C as their grandfather. When C became seriously ill, he nominated P as next of kin and P and his wife cared for him. C died intestate. Under the rules of intestacy, C's estate (value £31,116), mainly the house given to P's mother (which she had transferred into the joint names of herself and C), passed to C's sisters. P applied for financial provision from the estate under s1(1)(d) of the *Inheritance (Provision for Family and Dependants) Act 1975* as a person 'treated by the deceased as a child of family'. C's sisters argued that a 'child of the family' could only be a minor or dependent child, which P was not when C met P's mother.

Zimmermieter

nächster Angehöriger
ohne Testament

finanzielle Unterstützung/Ver-sorgung

Held: that s1(1)(d) should not be <u>construed narrowly</u> and did include an 'adult child'. The word 'child' related to the relationship between the deceased and the <u>applicant</u> and the treatment referred to in s1(1)(d) was not limited to treatment of a minor or dependent child. After C had married P's mother, there was sufficient evidence that C had treated P as an adult child of the family. C had no obligations to his sisters whereas he was under a considerable obligation to P. C's estate originated from P's mother. P would be awarded a lump sum of £15,000.

> eng auslegen
>
> Antragsteller

d) Any other persons who, immediately before the death of the deceased, were being maintained by the deceased. To these persons may belong other relatives, such as brothers and sisters, mothers and fathers, also friends and a <u>cohabitee</u> who were receiving <u>substantial</u> financial support from the deceased before his death.

> Partner einer nicht ehelichen Lebensgemeinschaft – wesentlich/erheblich

3. Reasonable financial provision

The term "reasonable financial provision" is defined in s1(2)(a) of the 1975 Act. In the case of a surviving spouse, it means: "Such financial provision as it would be reasonable in all circumstances of the case for a husband or wife to receive, whether or not that provision is required for his or her <u>maintenance</u>."

> Lebensunterhalt

Other cases are ruled by s1(2)(b) of this Act: "Such financial provision as it would be reasonable in all circumstances of the case for the applicant to receive for his maintenance."

There is no specific definition of "maintenance" in the Act but there exist many definitions delivered by the courts themselves. According to *Templeman/Spedding*, to define maintenance one should refer to the statement found in *Re Borthwick* (1949), which is still relevant. In this case, it was said that: "Maintenance does not only mean the food the

<u>applicant</u> puts in her mouth, it means the clothes on her back, the house in which she lives, and the money which she has to have in her pocket, all of which vary according to the means of the deceased... Maintenance cannot mean <u>mere</u> <u>subsistence</u>."	Antragsteller
	bloß
	Verpflegungsgeld
<u>Applications</u> under this Act must be made within six months from the date on which <u>representation of the estate</u> is first <u>taken out</u>.	Antrag
	Vorstellung des Vermögens
	hier: vornehmen
The court can <u>make an order</u> for periodical payments or lump sum payments from the estate.	einen Beschluss erlassen
Moreover, the court may transfer certain property, such as the family house, or make <u>settlements</u> of other property.	Regelung
Before making a <u>provision order</u>, the court has to consider a number of circumstances: the value and the size of the estate and the provision already made for the applicant, the applicant's <u>resources</u> and the applicant's conduct towards the deceased. In the case of a spouse, consideration would be given to age, duration of marriage and the <u>contribution</u> made by the applicant to the family and its welfare. In the case of young children, <u>educational needs</u> would be considered and, in the case of older children the ability to reasonably maintain themselves. Moreover, the court would take into consideration statements (if any) by the deceased as to the reasons why certain provisions were made or not made.	Unterhaltszahlungsbeschluss
	Geldmittel
	Beitrag
	(Aus)bildungsbedarf

V. Personal representatives

It is a <u>feature</u> of English law that a deceased's property, whether personal or real, does not go directly to the persons to whom it had been left by will. It has, by law, to be distributed on an intestacy under the above stated rules.	Merkmal
The property <u>vests</u>, <u>in the first instance</u>, in the deceased's personal representatives, namely the <u>executor</u>(s) appointed by will, or where there is no will or no executor appointed under the will, the <u>administrator</u>(s) appointed by the court.	übergehen – im ersten Moment/ zunächst – Testamentvollstrecker
	Vermögensverwalter/Testament-vollstrecker

Before an executor may deal with the estate, it is necessary to apply to the court for a <u>grant of probate</u>.

Testamentsvollstreckerzeugnis

It is usually a <u>formal exercise</u> in presenting the will and giving details of the property and value of the deceased's estate. A beneficiary may be appointed executor, but frequently, more than one executor is named in the will. Often solicitors and banks act as executors. As soon as <u>probate</u> has been granted (which normally will happen in a relatively short period of time), the executor (or administrator), whose duties in many ways <u>resemble</u> those of a trustee, must, in the first instance, discharge the funeral expenses and the cost (including the payment of <u>inheritance tax</u>) of obtaining the grant of probate (or "<u>letters of administration</u>"). He then may collect and pay off debts and, finally, distribute the estate according to the terms of the will, or according to the rules of intestacy.

Formsache

hier: Testamentvollstreckung/ Nachlassverwaltung

ähneln

Erbschaftssteuer
Nachlassverwaltungszeugnis

In a book of such limited length, it is not possible to describe in detail all the <u>intricacies</u> of English civil law. Thus if anyone is interested to know more about any of the chapters dealt with in this book, they may refer to any of the other books mentioned at the end of each chapter under 'Further reading'.

Verwicklung/Verzweigtheit

VI. Further reading[1]

Barker & Padfield; *Borkowski*, Textbook on succession; *Brown,* GCSE Law; *Geldhart*, Introduction to English Law; *James*', Introduction to English Law; *Lyall*, An Introduction to British Law; *Parry & Clark*, The law of succession; *Templeman & Spedding*, Succession: The law of wills and estates – Textbook – Casebook – Revision workbook; *Ware*, Succession (Cracknell's law students companion).

---

[1] Cf. p. 73.

Index

– – –

Glossary
Civil Procedure Terms

Old Terms	New Terms 1998/99	German Terms
Anton Piller	Search order	Einstweilige Verfügung zur Urkundenbeweissicherung (auf dem Grundstück des Beklagten)
Discovery and inspection	Disclosure and inspection	Vorlagezwang zwecks Augenscheinseinnahme
Discovery	Disclosure	Offenlegung, Offenbarung
Ex parte	Without notice	auf einstweiligen Antrag (ohne Anhörung der Gegenseite)
Further and better particulars	Further information	weitere Einzelheiten
In camera	In private	unter Ausschluss der Öffentlichkeit (im Richterzimmer)
Interlocutory relief	Interim remedy	vorläufiger Rechtsschutz
Inter partes	With notice	im Innenverhältnis der Parteien
Interlocutory summons	Application notice	vorläufige Ladung (zum Gerichtstermin)
Leave of court	Permission of court	gerichtliche Erlaubnis
Mareva	Freezing injunction	einstweilige Vermögenssperre bei Gefährdung der vorläufigen Vollstreckbarkeit, dinglicher Arrest
Medical negligence	Clinical negligence	ärztliche Fahrlässigkeit
Minor/infant	Child	Minderjähriger, Kind
Next friend/guardian ad litem	Litigation friend	Prozesspfleger (Kläger in Prozessstandschaft für einen Minderjährigen)
Orders	Parts	Erlasse, Beschlüsse
Payment into court	Part 36 payment	Hinterlegung von Geld bei Gericht
Plaintiff	Claimant	Kläger
Pleading	Statement of Case	anwaltliche Prozessführung (Plädoyer)
Statement/particulars of claim	Particulars of claim	Einzelheiten, (Substantiierung) der Klagebegründung
Summons	Application notice	gerichtliche Ladung
Taxation	Detailed assessment	Schätzung
Third party proceedings/counterclaim	Part 20 claim	Streitverkündungsverfahren, Widerklage
Writ/default summons	Claim form	gerichtliche Anordnung, Beschluss, Mahnbescheid